THIS BOOK IS THE LONGEST SENTENCE EVER WRITTEN AND THEN PUBLISHED

It's Over 13,955 Words, That's The Previous Record I've Researched In April '19, It's Well Over That Actually, And It's Already Started, The Sentence, This Subtitle Is Part Of It, And It's

By

Dave Cowen

1

Who is me, hi, everyone, welcome to the longest sentence and possibly the greatest sentence in the English language ever written and then published, which is a great achievement by me, though I haven't done it yet, as I am writing this sentence as I go, so it's unclear if this endeavor will result in a great sentence, or just the longest one, or, honestly, if I will even be able to finish the sentence, that I have just started, and eventually set the record, I could fail, so that's kinda exciting for you, to be reading, in pretty much real time, my attempt at a world record, and a great achievement in the history of writing, and in the history of humanity, right, and the funny thing about achievements in writing is that readers debate who is the greatest living writer or what is the best sentence ever written, and most readers think there's not really an answer, because evaluating writing is subjective, or so they're told, but it just so happens that two of the widely considered greatest writers in the English language also wrote two of the longest sentences ever published, and they are William Faulkner, and his 1,288 word sentence from 1936's Absalom, Absalom, and James Joyce, and his 3,687 word sentence from 1922's Ulysses, and these books and the sentences inside them were considered masterpieces of stream of consciousness style, and so there must be something great about writing long sentences, and writing them in the style of stream of consciousness, some cause and effect, I am not sure how to prove causes and effects, because I am not good at math or science, I am only good at one thing, writing, which is somewhat debatable itself, I think, the me being good at writing, it's unclear to me if what I've written so far is any good, what do you think, do you like it yet, do you like me yet, maybe I should type Faulkner's and Joyce's two sentences out here to give you something widely agreed upon as great sentences to read to start this sentence, so if my sentence turns out not to be so great, you'll at least have read something great right up front, or maybe you could kind of get a baseline of long sentence greatness, to compare with my sentence, and see that I surpass it, this sentence, that you are reading, it will surpass Faulkner's and Joyce's sentences, in quality and then quantity, you'll see, you'll all see, but I also now realize it'd be a little unfair that my sentence would not only have Faulkner's great long sentence but also Joyce's great long sentence embedded inside of the rest of my sentence, which has already started off so strongly, and that would be a bit of cheating, would it not, but that's also what's so great about the English language, it can be quite recursive with its clauses, you can keep building in clauses, pretty much infinitely, or maybe not pretty much, just literally infinitely, and recursivity is something I have been doing with these commas, and the ands, and the whiches, and which is like this, and that is a recursive clause right there, and this is one, too, see they are pretty cool, you just put them in, with a comma, like so, but it is also something that worries me, too, as I've read about theories by linguists that say there's technically no limit to the length of an English sentence, due to recursive clauses, and so what is scary about that, is that it means anyone could beat my record one day, and so in order to make sure I set the record, maybe I can never stop writing this sentence, maybe I can never write anything that is not part of this sentence ever again in order to get what I want, which is for me, Dave Cowen, me, Dave Cowen, are we clear who's writing what you're reading, I, Dave Cowen, need to be remembered for all time as the writer of the longest sentence ever published, maybe I must include anything I write for the rest of my life as part of this sentence, which is a tricky thing because I have to write other sentences for other parts of my life, like sentences for emails for my day job, the job I need to pay for my life, that allows me to buy time to write this sentence, and so the emails I write for my job, like, Got it, thanks, Marie, and Sounds good, thanks for the update, Jason, must go in here now, too, and they must not have periods, or else I will accidentally end the sentence, and lose the record, but will I get fired, if I don't include periods in my work emails, and then not be able to pay for my life or the writing of this sentence, and would I then die, will I die because of this endeavor, we'll see, we all die, right, there's no avoiding death, and it's not a big deal, just a part of life, and nothing to be sad about, right, and the other concerning thing is some linguists also dabble in computer science, and even if they might be a bit dilettantish, they have also posited there's likely going to be a computer writer that'll one day be able to create a near-infinite English sentence just in the time it takes me to type this next word, dang, that word, dang, that's how fast the bot writer could write a longer sentence than me, dang, crazy, right, and another weird thing about this project is question marks, like, what am I supposed to do about question marks, like, the one that should come after this question, if I were to put a question mark there, then this sentence would be over, which is weird, isn't it, that a question has to end a sentence, how come, there's another spot for a question mark, it's hard not to put the question mark in there, right, but if I do, I'd lose the record, which would be pretty pathetic, right, another email, ugh, Thanks, yes, confirmed, back to the book, that'd be pathetic, right, as we're only like, how far are we, OK, just checked, we're exactly 1,111 words into the sentence, including the title and subtitle, and wow, that seems quite prophetic in terms of Numerology, as my life path number is 11, and my Dad's life path is 22, which is 11 + 11, and we are both master numbers, and there are only 3 of those master numbers out of the life paths you can have, according to the Pythagorean Greeks, and the Numerologists who came after them, and they are particularly difficult energies to handle, I have read, and that means we have chosen more difficult life paths before we were born, that my Dad chose to be a master builder and I chose to be a wounded healer, though we immediately forgot about all of that when we were born, unless we discovered Numerology, which I have only recently discovered this month, so maybe this sentence has been blessed by Pythagoreus, or G-d, but it also could be read as Jeremiah 11:11 like in Jordan Peele's movie Us, which seems bad, or tethered to something bad, maybe I should stop writing the sentence already, maybe I should give up this Faustian task, or is it Sisyphean, no, it's definitely not Sisyphean, as I will be getting the fame of writing this sentence, the longest sentence ever written in the English language and then published, most definitely, I will not be writing this sentence in vain, I will not finish it but then not be able to publish it for some reason, and not get the record, or be beaten to the punch by someone else, I will not be writing words that have no success, it will not all be for nothing, artistically, and financially, the writing of this sentence, it can't be, and it won't be, I won't continue to be a failing writer, a failed writer I will no longer be, and for that I can thank myself, and this genius idea, where I can prove in a measurable way that I am superior to every writer the English language has ever seen, and also I can thank Jeff Bezos and Kindle Direct Publishing, which is my publisher and my publishing house, and they are a great publisher and publishing house because they publish pretty much literally anything, you just have to load a PDF file of your manuscript, and do a cover or whatever, they have a cover creator app, too, which is pretty easy, pretty fool-proof to use, so you don't even need to hire someone to do that, or need to know any fancy application, and boom you got a book published, and printed, your written words, whatever you want them to be, they can be any sort of words, like these words, like the words you are reading as I type the words you are reading right now, and this WORD, and they'll be a book that you can then sell in the biggest book marketplace in the world, and what's interesting about that is that, it wasn't always the case for writers that they could just boom publish their books, for instance, James Joyce struggled for years to boom publish his books, you see, back in 1905, Joyce tried to boom publish his first book Dubliners, but it took nine years before a publisher said they'd publish it, because even though many of them thought it was a brilliant book of great sentences, they refused to publish it because they feared the censors due to the great sentences also having some content that was kind of taboo for their time, about sex and also religion, in fact, someone did try to boom publish Dubliners in 1906, but the entire edition was burned in an Irish square before reaching the public, due to that taboo content, and then with Ulysses, the book that had the longest sentence ever written at the time just waiting to be boom published, Joyce also had trouble sealing the deal to get the record, in 1918, two women said they'd publish Ulysses, which was even more taboo in its content, that's something that Joyce liked to do with his content, make the content difficult for some readers to enjoy, the content, in style sure, it was difficult to understand what he was saying a lot of the time, it wasn't accessible writing as they'd say now, is this accessible, this writing, am I accessing you, is this relatable, but also because he was making something private in society that people didn't want other people to know they also thought about, he made that taboo stuff public, which made it obscene content, even if it was relatable, perhaps too relatable, and so like I said, it also had the longest sentence ever written in the English language at that point just set to be published and win the record, but the publishers were arrested for conspiring to publish obscenity by The New York Society For The Suppression Of Vice, can you believe that they had that type of organization back then, in New York City, what an insanity, and so it ended up taking more than ten years before Joyce could find an American or English publishing house willing to boom publish his Ulysses content, but fortunately Joyce's buddy Ezra Pound did him a real solid and introduced him to this cool bookstore owner, Sylvia Beach, and she boom published the book in France, because that was a thing Pound did before he started to blame the Jews for his lack of remunerative success as a writer when he was in Italy and becoming down with the Fascistis, he helped other writers get paid for their writing, and so Joyce got his record, because his sentence was not only written but published, and so what many people consider the greatest book of the 20th Century, including Mayor Pete and Beto, and I guess Joe Biden, too, we don't like him now, right, he's no good for this time, right, I dunno who is though, is one person, maybe we should have a panel of presidents now, and so the book Ulysses exists because of all that struggle, and so what's huge for me is that I don't have to mess with a Vice Squad or judgmental, scaredy-cat, establishment-protecting haters in the current publishing industry due to Kindle Direct Publishing, which is my publisher, and Jeff Bezos, who is my Sylvia Beach, in a way, and also Jeff is sorta my Ezra Pound, and so that's great for me because part of this record is that the sentence has to be published, to get the record, we're clear on that, right, and so that's a way that maybe I'd be able to hold off a writer bot, that is if writer bots weren't allowed to print their own books, if we made a Vice Squad to stop writer bots from doing that, then no matter how long or infinite their sentence is, a human being would still have the record, I would be the human being who would have it, in particular, and I mean, yes, it would be based on a technicality, and I wouldn't feel great about that, to be honest, but probably the bigger issue is these bots and computers and AI, and what are we doing making them so smart and good at chess and writing, and what are we going to do about them in general in the future, Yang Yang, and what does G-d think about them, and do you believe in G-d, and I've become more religious in the last two years by writing parody Haggadahs for Passover and within the last year I've become more esoteric with Tarot and Astrology and Numerology, and within the last three months I've become more spiritual with The Enneagram, which combines mystical traditions from Pythagoreus, Sufism, Kabbalah, and Desert Christian Gnostics, with psychological traditions like Jungian archetypes/personality typing and Freudian defense-mechanisms, and sometimes I wonder where robots fit into G-d's plan or whatever plan is going on, because I am starting to believe in a design, instead of randomness, an order in the chaos, are you, but what of these robots, because if they can write the longest sentences ever without a problem in a dang second, dang, who knows what other business they can get into, what other trouble they can get up to, and that's not a new thought, I almost wish I could cut the lazy robot jokes at this point, but it's potentially a true thought nonetheless, and also I can't go back in the sentence to cut anything, that's a rule I made, so you can read my stream of consciousness in real time, and I'm sticking to it, because I am a good person as well as a good writer, and I guess another thing about bot writing though is that even if there sentences, ugh I am so bad about theres and their's, and also apostrophes, I am kind of a bad writer technically, maybe you can tell that by now, even if I am a great writer conceptually and creatively and comedically and every other way imaginable, except technically, which is tough for me, because part of this project is that I am not going backward to edit the sentence, as I mentioned, am I mentioning it too much, that's why there are all these asides, the fact that I can't go back or plan forward, therefore I need asides, like this one, this aside about asides, is it clever, no, sorry about that, I'll get back to the main-ish thread, and so what I was also saying is that the bots' sentences, they would be the longest, but they wouldn't be the most literary like Joyce's or Faulkner's or the most humorous like mine, like Cowen's, that's me, I believe I am the best prose humorist alive, as I am a self-declared prose humorist who has written prose humor for The New Yorker, and I have published three prose humor books via my publisher Kindle Direct Publishing, and I am very humorous with my prose even if I am not very famous right now, or probably will not be ever, for my humorous prose, but neither was Joyce when he started out, and back to what I'm saying about bot writing, a bot might not be as great of a writer as Joyce, Faulkner, or other humans or me, but one writer that the bots could probably be better than, quite easily in fact, is this guy, Jonathan Coe, I haven't read his book, The Rotters' Club, but what I do know about it is that it appears to hold the current record for the longest English sentence ever written and then published, based on my casual research on Wikipediadotcom in April of 2019, and that sentence is 13,955 words, and that sentence is reported to be over thirty-three pages long, and the reason I think it's probably not a great sentence is that no one has ever heard of Joseph Coe, or, at least, I hadn't, until I researched who I needed to beat with this sentence that I am writing now in April of 2019, and sometimes I even forget his name while I'm writing about him, as I just called him Joseph Coe, when his name is actually Jonathan Coe, I learned that is actually his name, because I just bought his book on Amazondotcom, hold on I should probably type out dot coms like this, Amazon dot com, to get more words, yeah, that's better, good to get the extra words, got to get them however you can, you know, anyway, I got the Kindle edition of Jonny-boy's book, and I just skipped to the part with the long sentence and I tried to read his long sentence, and I have to be honest, it was a pretty boring sentence, and actually really tedious, and kinda un-literary, and it just went on and on and on and on and on and on and on and on and on and on and on and on and, and you get the idea, you know, that's a way I could win the record, I could just copy and paste on and on and on and on and on and on, over and over and over and over, that's technically a way linguists say you can write a sentence, but that'd be even more of a cheap way to win the record than preventing the bots from publishing with the Vice Squad, wouldn't it be, but so after checking out Joseph Coe's sentence, I returned Jonathan Coe's book and got my money back from Amazon, which is something you can do with books these days, especially with books sold by Amazon dot com or published by Kindle Direct Publishing, but, please don't do it with my book, because the writer loses their royalties, even if you have read the whole book, and didn't just skip to a particular sentence, and skimmed that one, even if it was a long one, the writer loses the royalty, and so Jonathan Coe just lost a sale from me, screw you, Jonny Coe, and you could do that to me right now, too, you could screw me out of my Kindle Direct Publishing royalty, if you wanted to, but the thing is I need to earn royalties to pay for my life, and the things in it, because I am a failed screenwriter, and it's not looking good for me screenwriting-wise these days, which is a big way writers can actually make money these days, in the 21st century, or via TV writing, generally any type of writing but book writing seems to work better financially these days, and so like I said it's not looking great for me script-writing these days, and a funny thing about all that is that I also just rented the three-part television adaptation of Jonathan Coe's book The Rotter's Club, adapted by Dick Clement and Ian La Frenais which was broadcast on BBC Two, and, you know what, I'm watching it right now as I continue to type this sentence, even just the first few frames, the first scene, I am watching it as I type this, and it is actually much better than Joey Coe's book and definitely the part of the book with the long sentence, and it really makes you wonder if a moving image is always better than a written word, and is compromising art for commerce always worth it in order to get some moving images from your words, because clearly Adam McKay, Tina Fey, Donald Glover, to name three of probably twenty thousand or so people who are all making more people entertained with their words than I am, their words that then become moving images, as part of the Writers Guild of America, which is something I am not a part of, the WGA is a labor union representing film, television, radio, and new media writers, and their members' words are words that are turned into moving images, so they must be better words, than me and my regular words, these words, not as good, apparently, and also I am thinking now, was Jonathan Coe's sentence really necessary or was he just sort of forcing words into a sentence that didn't want to be part of the sentence, which is kind of an arrogant thing to do, and a true disservice to the reader, and to the English language, am I right, as the longest sentence ever published in the English language should also be one of the best sentences in the English language, or at least a quite clever and fun and humorous one, like this one is so far, am I right, do you love this book so far, do you love me, no, that's OK, neither do I, not many people seem to,

I wonder why that is, but so that is another reason why I have taken on this Herculean effort, not just for my own fame and glory and royalties but it is also to make sure that the English language has a proper longest sentence ever written and published that is worthy of the great language itself, and the other great sentences in the English language, and also to love myself for succeeding at something, and for others to love and understand me, and "Is That All There Is," Peggy Lee, and I have made a Spotify playlist for you to follow the music that I might add to this book, because I love music and love to write while listening to music, so you should be able to listen to the music I was listening to while writing this, or to listen to music I reference while reading this, and your streams will go to Spotify and the artists, so everyone is going to make money off these song references, not just me, sort of, pennies at least, and so here's the link, https(dot)//open(dot)spotify(dot)com/playlist/2xsgUmnOaYdZb34LuMFifR(questionmark)si=67REDpuURBiupvZBNooKg or if that's too confusing like if you bought this book in paperback and are trying to type all that out, let's get real, you probably won't do it, but you can also just type into Spotify search "This Book Is The Longest Sentence Ever Written And Then Published Playlist" and you'll find it because it's a public playlist, but back to what I was saying before about words not wanting to be part of Jonathan Coe's sentence, is that I checked with the words that I've already written and they're chill with being in this sentence all-together so far, and that's another reason why my name will be remembered for all-time, which is very important to me, because when I finish this book, and it's published by my publisher, which again is Kindle Direct Publishing, shout-out to Amazon dot com which, yes, some people say that that company is ruining the book industry, and is quite problematic with its monopoly in terms of all business, not just books, and the thing is I do see that Amazon and Kindle Direct Publishing allow for a lot of trash to be published and sold on its website, because it is not edited, like this book, though this book is not trash, because it's not edited on purpose, and because it's brilliant, and I'm feeling the future success of this book now, I can see it in my mind, the royalties, the people writing about it, and it's not just because "Congratulations," by Post Malone, Quavo, and Future, just went into "We Did It" by Lil Yachty on my Spotify shuffle, but Amazon is also named after the longest river in the world and has the longest list of books in its store in the world right now, which are both things that are cool to me, because clearly I am attracted to long things, which are usually the best, and so it also makes sense why they'd want to be involved with my longest sentence, even if they have no idea that they are involved with it, because it seems like no one there really cares what they print as long as it makes money, or even if it doesn't, they don't mind, because it doesn't cost them money to keep an ebook on their server, or a PDF and cover jacket file ready to be published on demand, POD, and it seems like their computer bots just check that there's no copyright infringement and then it's good to go, boom published, you got a book boom published, and sometimes I wonder if they could create their own Vice Squad and stop certain things from being boom published, and that they'd be so powerful one day due to the monopoly thing people always talk about as to keep good books from being boom published, because I've heard they have started having their computer bots check for content now, too, and that includes what they call "disappointing content," and they talk about this when you boom publish your book on the Kindle Direct Publishing's FAQ page, they say that content that "does not provide an enjoyable reading experience," is "disappointing content" and what's a little scary about that is that Amazon reserves "the right to determine whether content provides a poor customer experience and remove that content from sale," which is more than a little scary, actually, Amazon bots if you are checking this sentence for content purposes, you gotta be cool about this sentence, bot, don't fuck with it, OK, bot, because if you don't publish it, fuck, bot, I don't know if anyone else will, or at least it would be kind of a fucking pain in the ass to find someone to agree to publish it, instead of just loading a PDF up and boom publishing it, so much easier that way, and also readers, don't give out so many 1 star reviews, if you don't enjoy the reading experience of this book, or the new uses of swear words like fuck, all of a sudden, this book is fucking not for fucking eighteen-year-olds or younger all of a sudden, fuck, that's another thing Kindle Direct Publishing wants to know when you boom publish it, if it's fucking OK for fucking eighteen-year-olds or younger, which is a big fucking market, maybe I should fucking go back and fucking delete those fucks, but fuck I'd be cheating my project and my self, and besides these are PG-13 fucks, they're not sexual R fucks like I fucked your dad, fuck, I just put in a sexual fuck, I'm such a fucking idiot, I can't go back and unfuck myself, OK, chill, cool out, I am just, I am just going to, I've decided to cut back on the F words, from now on, it's decided, the damage is done, but, I am sorry Kindle Direct Publishing bots, I prostrate myself in front of you, and beg for your forgiveness, you too, parents, maybe Amazon and Kindle Direct Publishing and you parents will check and see that the F word usage was just a joke about censorship, because that's all it was, I wouldn't mind if I was under eighteen and read all that, in fact I believe it to be a Categorical Imperative that it is read, and so I will trick Kindle

Direct Publishing and not label it only good for people eighteen years or older, which is something you have to do as the author, you have to declare yourself if it's suitable for eighteen-year-old people or under, your book, you must decide somehow that for every person in the world your book is fine for that age range somehow, which seems like it's a trick itself, so I won't fall for it, and I will do my own trick and Hermes-say it is OK for everyone, despite the F words above, because I believe it's not a trick, it's just the right thing to do,

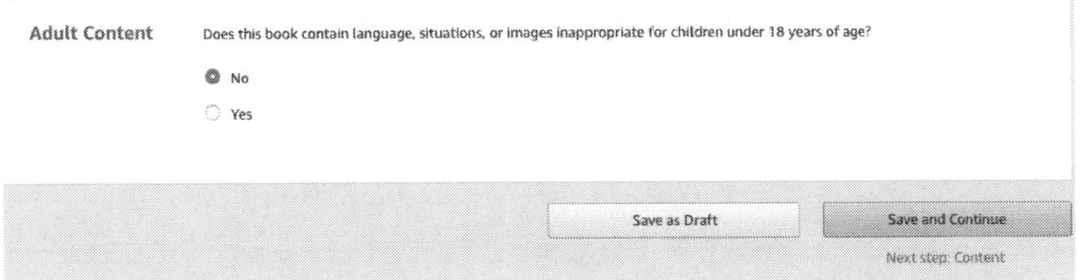

but maybe you, the reader, won't think so, and you'll give it a 1 star, for me being a Trickster, but please don't, it just might not be for you, or your view on censorship, don't flag it to the Vice Squad as "disappointing content" and ruin it for people who might be enjoying the experience of reading the content, or if not enjoying the experience of reading the content, at least not disappointed by the experience of reading the content, like maybe my family and friends, and maybe a few other weirdos, or some people under eighteen, and definitely many people in the future who will get it more, and study it in their schools like Ulysses, as books extend through space and time and find new readers as long as they stay available, are you people in the future reading it, what's happening in the future, am I still alive, how far did we get us humans, and the other reason I will always be remembered is that I also understand words so well, like I was saying before, all the way back before this long aside, do you remember me talking about words, and that I will be remembered for talking to words in my mind and making sure they are good with me writing them, and will anyone remember me, will you remember me, that's a fear of mine, the disappearance of me, and my being, and the memory of me, and where do you go when you die, and what good is life, if you can't make it known to others how you personally thought during life and lived it, and what's the point of living if your personhood is extinguished, and don't you love my personhood, my personality, what a personality, what a character they say in my head, and so what makes me worth remembering is that I don't just understand words' meanings, words literally speak to me, I hear what they say, Word, and they tell me how they are doing as part of my writing, and whether they like how I am using them, isn't that unique, can you do that, probably not, is it kind of like synesthesia and the fine artist painter Kandinsky, and should I make up my own mental process, too, Literthesia, is that real, or do I just want you to believe that I'm special in some way, and that I am special in a way that is specialer than other ways of being special, too, and right now the words are saying that maybe I should ease up on this part of the sentence, promoting myself so much, and transition to something else, because I might be losing some of the readers regardless of the F words, and so the next thing I will say is we are already up to 5,438 words, which is well over Joyce's sentence, and over 38 percent of the way to the record, and it has been very easy for me to write all these words in one sentence, well over a third of the record, and this part has been in one sitting, without interruption, or break, and I am unstoppable, my writing is unstoppable, it just flows from me, and I'm so good at writing tons of words very fast and very well, even Google Doc's live word count function can't handle it:

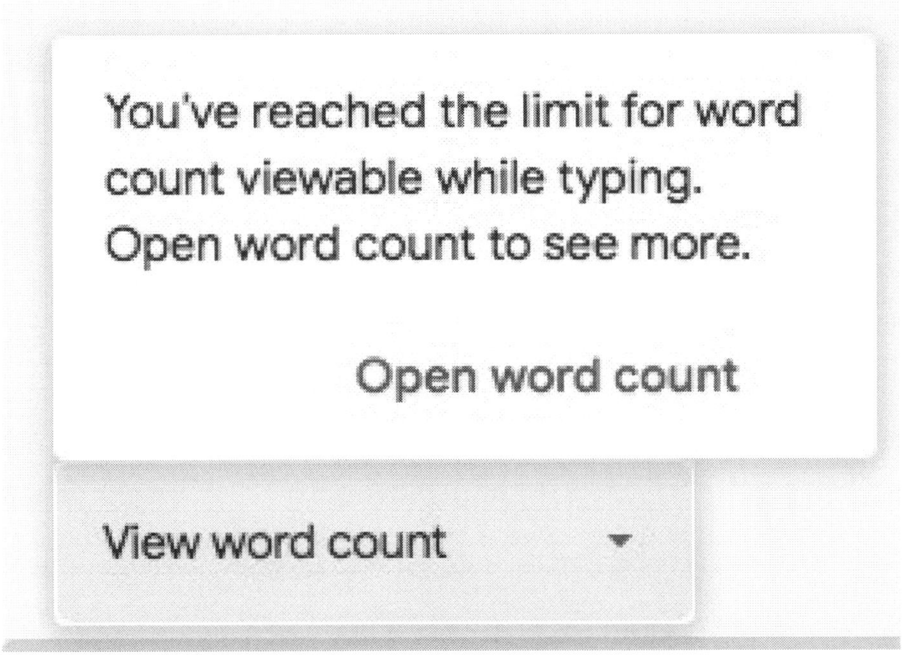

You've reached the limit for word count viewable while typing. Open word count to see more.

Open word count

View word count ▾

,

and it's just so easy, it's been so easy to do this, easy as Sunday morning, easy as Sunday afternoon, much easier than the dread of Sunday night, and so it seems impossible that I won't be able to beat Jonathan Coe's record, because I am such a prodigious, prolific, profuse writer who's also profound, prescient, pretty-much perfect, even if he is a bit too alliterative at the moment, and did you know that, somewhere at Google there is a database containing 25 million books, every book ever written almost, digitally scanned, but nobody is allowed to read them, but all that needs to happen is a lawsuit needs to be resolved about copyright, and then all the books ever written will be readable for everyone in the world, and what do you think about copyright law, do you believe your words are yours to own, do you believe your words are so special that no one should be able to use them unless you give them permission, do you believe my words so far that I've written are mine, and only mine, and I can tell you that you can't use them, not a one of them, unless you pay me for the right to use them, am I that powerful just by typing some words down, what if I typed some words that you wanted to type right now, what are you thinking about, if I type it, I own it, I own your thoughts, I'm in your head, and I own it, and how does it feel, not great, right, and do you believe that a company could create a robot that could write every version of every book that could ever exist in the future and then own the copyright to those unwritten books, so that future writers, like you, reader, maybe you are a writer, too, you could never write a book that wasn't copyrighted, you could try to write a book that wasn't already copyrighted but no, it was already written by the robots, even if you changed it over and over in ways large or small it would always be something the robot writers have already written due to the company, dang, do you believe that could become true one day, and what would you do about it, and how would you feel, and do you think the company Amazon who has also digitally scanned most of the books ever written, do you wonder if they also could do it, could Amazon make those robots, too, and what would they do with them, I don't know, does Bezos seem like a good dude to trust with that power, but back to me, don't worry a robot could never write my words, even if it could, it couldn't, because it couldn't feel itself, like I'm feeling myself, you feel me, or could it, could it feel itself, too, I guess I don't know, so I actually found a robot writing service called Transformer made by OpenAI based on a language-model called GPT-2, that generates coherent paragraphs of text based on a prompt of your own text, and so I put in what I just wrote and here's what it wrote back, they even didn't put in a period, so it's still the one sentence, how smart is this robot already, it's coming for me, it's coming at me, broh, here's the screen grab:

Completion

and do you believe that a company could create a robot that could write every version of every book that could ever exist and then own the copyright to those unwritten books, so that future writers, like you, reader, maybe, could never write a book that wasn't copyrighted, that you could try to write a book that wasn't already copyrighted but no, it was already written by the robots, even if you changed it over and ver it would always be something the robot writers have already written due to the company, do you believe that could become true one day,

if any of that seems too impossible, remember this: the robots are already writing the stories that you would not recognize, the robots have already created your mind as your own so that you actually have the power to create your own reality, they can make you their little puppet masters, because, you will believe that you can make your own reality, like any other person you might write a movie that has not been made yet for every other person, but this movie that is created by the robots, will be created for every different person so that you will all believe that you already started it, and the

that was really what this robot wrote back off my prompt from above, isn't that insane, what does it know, what does it know already, I think it knows something we don't, I think this is actually what's going on in life, I have full faith in this robot writer, this bot writer is a genius, except, wait, it was built by a human, this guy, Adam King, a human, and nope, I don't have faith in him, because he's just a human, and I just put another part of the sentence into the robot, and here's what it says:

Completion

and sometimes I wonder where robots fit into G-d's plan or whatever plan is going on, because I am starting to believe in a design, instead of randomness, are you, but what of these robots, because if they can write the longest sentences ever without a problem in a dang second, dang, who knows what other business they can get into, what other trouble they can get up to, but they are still not able to write or do their job and this is not a flaw of nature of their mechanical brains, they are merely failures, a product of human haha, this robot is pretty funny, it's already hip to what I just said, does that mean it isn't fallible then, oh man, all I know is myself, I am a failure, me human, I can't do jobs or write, except no, I am not a bit presumptuous or pretentious or profligate with my words, when you really think about it, I mean on the surface this sentence and project seems quite dumb, all that you have read so far, you may think on one level it has been quite dumb and not genius level writing like Faulkner and Joyce, and that it is quite dumb, and why does he keep saying it is quite dumb, is he padding the sentence or is he just quite dumb, or just pretending to be quite dumb, and you quite frankly don't care at this point, you are thinking, because you are sick of the quite dumb writing, but I don't care, because Joyce was also quite a prankster, and he may have been the greatest prankster the English language has ever seen, and so some of you people are probably, like, this sentence, even if it's prankstery like Joyce, it is not as good as Joyce, but how much Joyce has this quite dumb guy even read, even if this sentence is much better than Coe's, it's not as good as Joyce, regardless of how much Joyce anybody here has read, that's true, we all know that about Coe versus Joyce, but Cowen's sentence being better than Coe's, it being so much better than Coe's, my sentence, that's not saying much, it being so much better than Coe, that is not meaning anything really, that is like saying metaphors are better than repeating the same thing over and over again, in order to pad out your sentence, I assure you though, if you haven't felt the genius, stick with it, you will at some point understand how genius I am and this sentence and book is, and, yes, it's true, I don't even know what will be in the sentence from beyond this point, this point right here, I am at a loss for what to write after this point right here, yes I am, not, and it may be quite lackluster so far, but I believe it will become great sometime soon, if it hasn't already become so, which it might have, I am going back and forth believing it to have been great so far, I am not sure, one thing to say is that there hasn't been any narrative yet, there haven't been any characters introduced yet, and there isn't any dialogue yet, and so that seems like bad writing, and I am also wondering if I will even be able to even put some of that in, the dialogue, due to punctuation issues with dialogue, I think they require periods, do they, I think they must, and I guess I am also a bit worried about the characters, the lack thereof of them, and does that lack thereof of have too many ofs, and also I worry it might not be sustainable to keep digressing about the meta-theme, to do a whole book like this, it might not make for as great of a sentence as I need it to be, and is brevity the soul of wit, and what is my problem as a failed writer, do I have no soul, or no wit, and should I just put a period here, and end it all, or should I end my life, and it might be a good idea to introduce a character or two, besides myself, or some new ideas, besides this meta-theme, I guess I am almost sick of this meta-theme at this moment, so you must be, too, and how will we ever set this record, together, are you in it with me or not, and do you like me, does anyone like me, why do I always not like myself, and you know what, yes, I will introduce some characters into this sentence, because besides being a sentence, and sentences sometimes have characters in them, but don't have to, it's also a book, and a book probably should have characters, right, or maybe not, I mean what is a book these days, anyway, that's always been of interest to me, are books still important objects, and should we still have reverence and respect for them, and is a book still a worthwhile endeavor to read or to write, more so than any other kind of reading or writing, like on the Internet, like Instagram, it's fun to look at Instagram, and to read captions under images, and to comment, and to like, and is Caroline Calloway the Instagram writer better than book writers, and is Alt Lit dead, and if not, how do I get in, but do I want to get in, to be in Alt Lit, am I an Alt Lit Bro, who else writes like this, am I alone, or am I everyone, I feel so alone sometimes, and it must be true that many people read more words on Instagram and Twitter than they do words in books these days, and is doing that a better use of your life, at this point in history, I think that's a valid question, at this point in history, as I am often very bored by most novels, and I often just want the Gram and am I allowed to just put something from Twitter into the sentence, or an image from the Gram, I don't think I can, who has the copyright to ReGrams or ReTweets, not me, right, and have you read Lewis Hyde's Common As Air, it says, "All that we make and do is shaped by the communities and traditions that contain us," and "Human intelligence is like water, air, and fire, it cannot be bought and sold; these four things the Father of Heaven made to be shared on earth in common," and "A thief who stole a book was not subject to the punishment for theft, because he had not intended to steal the book as paper and ink, but the ideas in the book, and unlike the paper and ink, these ideas were not tangible property," and, Lewis is like a father figure to me, even though we've never met, but he's not the first character, the first character I will introduce is a character I call Kanye, the character Kanye is not exactly but basically the same rapper that we all know, this guy:

Sometimes you have to get rid of everything

2:01 PM - 17 Apr 2018

Yep I just re-Tweeted without copyright, does he care, and Kanye, like me, is also known for his rants, which is kinda like this sentence, this sentence is kind of a rant, and I will say that's another thing about this writing I am doing, besides it being like Instagram writing, is that it's very rhythmic like a rap, like rap lit, and you just gotta get into the rhythm of the sentence, you just gotta feel the flow, get it, get it, got it, good, and the other thing about Kanye is that I published my first piece of published sentences in this famous magazine called The New Yorker, and it was the first piece I ever submitted to that magazine or any magazine outside of my college paper, and it is very mainstream and very acclaimed, the magazine, and it's as good as it gets prose-humorist-writing-wise, and it was about how the real rapper that this character Kanye is based on, Kanye, he said he doesn't like books while he was promoting his book, and that he was a proud non-reader of books, and liked to learn things from living real life, and I made fun of him in my published sentences for The New Yorker, which was a big deal to me at the time, and made me very proud, and made my friends and family very proud, and here it is, and I am not sure if I am allowed to reprint a piece that The New Yorker bought for $2,000 dollars, but sorry I am trying to understand my life so how can this be wrong, right, and so here's the piece, with periods removed, so it's one sentence still: Live Your Life By Dave Cowen, "I am not a fan of books, I would never want a book's autograph, I am a proud non-reader of books, I like to get information from doing stuff like actually talking to people and living real life," —Kanye West, promoting his book Thank You and You're Welcome, Whoever said life is an open book probably didn't have any friends, Sure, he probably liked the people in his book, But did they like him, No, Why, Because they aren't real, My friends are real, They actually talk to me, Like just the other day my friend Bill said, "I'm not reading your e-mail for you anymore, You need to learn how to read," And I said, "Bill, if you don't read me my e-mail, I won't sign an autograph for your son," And Bill was, like, "Well, go fuck yourself, I'm going back to the hospital," Bill's son, Bill, Jr, or Billy Bob, was in the children's unit there, He didn't read the label on the box of his Sticky Stones™, and when he swallowed three of the iron-ore magnets they fused into a chain along the wall of his esophagus, Bill, Sr, felt extra bad because he hadn't read that a consumer safety group had placed the Sticky Stones™ on its annual list of the ten worst toys, I told Bill that's life, That stuff happens when you are doing stuff, In life, Real life, If I had told you that what had happened to Billy Bob had happened in a book, you would have said no way, that would never happen, that's fiction, But it did, Because I told you it did, Now, don't get me wrong, There are a few books that I am a fan of, Matchbooks are good, A lot of people are under the impression that books burn only at a specific temperature, But it's just not true, I can burn most books at or below 451 degrees Fahrenheit, Sometimes below 300, if I soak the jacket in lighter fluid, I also like MacBooks, You can really do stuff on them, you know, Like see how many followers you have on Twitter, or take pictures of yourself with Photo Booth, or play Second Life, or check if Bill has checked your e-mail, I miss Bill, He set up my Facebook account on my MacBook, I've got my own page on there, I have more than a million fans, Do you know how many fans Books have, Twenty-five thousand seven hundred and sixty-four, That's it, So I'm not alone here, You know what else has more fans than Books, The Olive Garden, One hundred and eighty-five thousand nine hundred and eighty-six, What else, Sleep: over three hundred thousand, More people would rather be unconscious than read a book, Now, I'm not condoning sleep, I'm about doing stuff, Living life, But it just goes to show that I'm in the majority, Right now you're probably wondering, Hey, why is this guy, a proud non-reader of books, writing this, Isn't this a Catch-22, And I say no, it's not, It's a Catch-23, What's a Catch-23, It's like a Catch-22, except there is no catch, I don't want you to read this, In fact, you should stop reading right now, Seriously, Stop reading this, Start doing stuff, What kind of stuff, you ask, I don't know, Why don't you go to the Olive Garden, But just watch out, They give you the never-ending salad before the never-ending pasta bowl, You wouldn't think so, but the salad fills you right up, The lettuce is mostly iceberg, All water, And the waiter really makes you feel like shit when you don't make it to the fettucine Alfredo, Sometimes when I don't know what to do I imagine other people doing stuff, But like people in a different time, Or like people in a different place, And I think how cool would it be to be that person for awhile, Like to know how other people I don't know talk or do stuff, How they really live, you know, But that's when I'm not doing stuff of my own, Which is all the time anyway," and that's the end of that piece from November, 2009, which is about 10 years ago now, whoa, time doesn't fly when you're a failing writer, and it was in the magazine before the online Shouts, when it was much harder to get in there, and I was very proud of how funny and clever I was, because clearly it is a very funny and clever piece, you just read it, so you know, but soon after I also kind of stopped reading a lot of books, and I started to believe that screenplay reading was a much better use of time than book reading, mostly because it became my day job at a certain point too, and I realized that since I was reading fewer books and listening to more Kanye and watching more movies and reading more of the Internet and screenplays and less books, I might be a lot more like Kanye than I thought I was back then, and recently I learned he's also a lot more like me than I thought he was, because the other thing about Kanye, the real Kanye, is that he is bipolar, he has bipolar disorder, and that's a crazy thing, because I'm also bipolar, I also have bipolar disorder, and it makes you do crazy manic insane unbalanced things sometimes, like, attempt to write the longest sentence ever without stopping to edit it, without stopping to wonder if you should have written in a book under your own name that you have bipolar, but as Kanye says in 'Yikes," it's not a disability, it's a superpower, man, because it's also how we are able to do crazy genius super powerful things like write the longest sentence ever written and then published, and we might not have become the best rapper ever and also the best hip-hop producer ever which is nuts that we're both things, I mean, Kanye, not we, Kanye is those things, not me, so he, Kanye, who is those things, has the right to say whatever he wants about books, I think, even if he was promoting his book when he said what he said about books, though I now am reading more books again, now that I am writing them, but I still read Kanye's tweets, too:

Follow

everything you do in life stems from either fear or love

2:53 PM - 17 Apr 2018

85,405 Retweets 195,522 Likes 

and maybe we know bipolar things, like the above, see I did it again, I equated myself with Kanye, how arrogant, and also I equated myself with you I guess, you are included with the we, and what does that mean, and I guess when I am kind of hypomanic from drinking coffee and writing and listening to his music, like right now "Only One" by him and Paul McCartney, and I'm having those good feels from that, I think maybe he is simply the best musician ever, not just rapper and producer, and Lou Reed loved Kanye, too, he wrote his last published piece I believe about Kanye before he died, which was a sad thing, Lou Reed dying, and I was listening to The Velvet Underground on repeat when I had my first manic episode, particularly the "Jesus," "Beginning To See The Light," and "I'm Set Free" songs on their third album, and I am not having one right now, a manic episode, I'm not having one of those, don't worry, we're in total control, me and Kanye, and whoever else is in my brain, a bit of Lou, too, and James Joyce, who a critic said of Ulysses, he must have written it in "an advanced stage of psychic disintegration" and also Carl Jung saw Joyce and his wife, and he said that Joyce was an undiagnosed schizophrenic, and I'm not having a mental breakdown, I'm not, not right here on this page, a breakdown I am not having, on this page, a psychotic break is not happening, disintegration is not what you are reading, I am very well, very fit, and happy, or maybe I am not, maybe I am cracking up, it's a crack up, they say, in my head, they don't know you, they don't know you are joking, but are so serious, there's nothing funny about your mental breakdown, I'm fine, I'm fine, OK, and when you smile, I'll smile, you're not perfect, but you're not your mistakes, but there's a connection there between art and madness, everyone knows that, it almost doesn't need to be said at this point in history, like my non-ideas about robots, though I want to reiterate what everyone says about this, but Kanye, Kanye recently disagreed about this, that unbridled madness doesn't work art-wise, that you really can't do art when you're fully mad is what we're supposed to say, you need to get that stuff under control, then you can write with a bit of the madness, or maybe Kanye is right about that, too, that meds are bad for creativity, is he crazy these days or medicated, or does it matter, I heard he's performing every Sunday in Calabasas at a church, and making a spiritual album, that's what Kim said, I wonder sometimes, which is better, meds or no meds, sometimes, sometimes often, which is somewhat dangerous I believe, but I can't help thinking it sometimes, because the only thing The New Yorker published of mine was a piece I wrote while quite hypomanic, the Kanye piece where I made fun of his iconoclastic position about books, and so maybe that's another irony I will have to learn, an iconoclastic irony about so-called mental illness, and maybe I shouldn't take my medicine, and Kanye's last album's cover says "I hate being Bi-Polar, it's awesome," and I feel him, but, no, I don't really believe that, and I am taking my medicine, so I will never become ill again, sick, cracked, invalid, demented, ruined, and that is because the other weird thing about Kanye and Lou and me, is that my dad was with me when I was listening to The Velvet Underground and having a manic episode at the age of 21, he came to rescue me, he drove six hours in the middle of the night to my college, by himself, even though he took medicine that made it very difficult for him to operate machinery after taking that medicine, and, so yes, the other crazy thing is that my dad also had bipolar disorder, and that that medicine I was talking about that made it difficult to drive after taking it, it also allowed him to be a parent capable of rescuing his son, and I take similar medicine and I haven't had a manic episode since that manic episode, so medicine is good, right, and he also had a manic episode close to that age of 21, though he was already in medical school, because he went to college when he was 16, because his dad wanted him to be successful as soon as possible, and also an unfunny thing is that he died a few weeks ago, my dad, in late February, 2019, February 25th, 2019 to be specific, and maybe that's what this sentence should also be about now, beyond meta-jokes about long sentences, which have been fun and all, but now there is this, the reality of a dead dad, but, to be honest, I have been fine, I'm fine, don't worry about me, don't care about me, but I haven't been processing my grief the way I wanted to yet about my dad's death, and I've been wanting to write something about my dad, and his dad and me and maybe also my dad's hero, Abraham Lincoln, as he is also said to have been mentally ill at times, or at least a melancholic, and when my dad died I found his book about Lincoln called Lincoln's Melancholy by Joshua Wolf Shenk, and I started to read it, and here's some of the things it says, "The inclination to exchange thoughts with one another is probably an original impulse of our nature, If I be in pain I wish to let you know it, and to ask your sympathy and assistance, and my pleasurable emotions also, I wish to communicate to, and share with you, -Abraham Lincoln, February 11, 1859," and maybe that will be a part of this sentence, Abe and my pops, I mean, I have the room, so why not, question mark, I am kind of teasing this subject matter out into the sentence now, trying to see what the words think, and they are telling me that they are feeling this part of the sentence, and to keep going, don't worry about putting personal information into your writing, it's how art gets to the next level, that's what Tig Notaro said about her comedy, I think, and here's more from the introduction of the Lincoln book I am reading, "He often wept in public and recited maudlin poetry, he told jokes and stories at odd times," and "He believed himself temperamentally inclined to suffer to an unusual degree, he learned how to articulate his suffering, find succor, endure, and adapt, Finally, he forged meaning from his affliction so that it became not merely an obstacle to overcome, but a factor in his good life," and so we once had a President who was so-called mentally ill, but a very different mental illness from the guy who is now in office, and I should now also add something else the words are telling me I should acknowledge about the style that I am writing in, it's quite clear what's going on with the style, it's quite clear, so no, I won't, I am not going to add this character yet, and maybe not ever in this sentence, because he is just consuming a lot of people's brains right now in the year 2019, and for the last four years, and at least the next two, and I guess I contributed to that with two of the books I have published in the last year, and I think we might need a break from him, me and the world, even though he is a part of us, all of us at this point, kind of the way Kanye is also a part of me, and maybe this guy is a part of me, too, and this guy, I have to admit, there are elements of this sick person's sickness in me, or else why would I write books in this guy's voice, and is this book also in his voice, like the words are saying it might be, or is it in my voice, or can I not escape it, or is it your voice, too, or can we not escape this voice, whatever it has become at this time due to Twitter and Cable News and phone alerts, and this guy, and what was the depth of my satire about that guy, I question that sometimes, and is satire useful even right now, or ever, it has often been wondered, very much more recently, and I even wrote a piece for The New Yorker that was rejected about that subject, and I have been rejected by The New Yorker for every piece I have ever written after the first one that was published when I was hypomanic, to be frank, but "We Just Won't Be Defeated" by The Go Team just flipped to "Everybody Wants To Be Famous" by Superorganism, and I still like that piece that was rejected about satire today, so I will put it in here now, to sort of continue padding out the sentence, sure, I'm not mad at padding out this sentence, I'm not mad at that, are you mad at me, Dad, for putting you into this crazy sentence, are you mad at me G-d, who else is mad at me, why you so mad, is it just me who is the mad one, and I won't feel bad about anything, I won't, I will win this record by any means necessary, because it's so important that I be remembered as an important writer, I must be remembered for hundreds of years, I don't think my dad will be remembered beyond fifty years, unless this book is about him, so maybe that's why it's OK to put you in the book, Dad, we can both be remembered, Dad, are you saying something right now, through me, are you connected to me right now, where are you, where did you go, I miss you, I miss your belly laugh, and the twinkle in your blue eyes, and the way you always gave me the first pick of the grapefruit half, and how you walked around with me when I was manic and just listened even though it didn't make any sense, and you didn't get scared or upset, you were so calm, how could you be so calm then, what were you really thinking, or were you just always as you were, you were always so calm, or were you not, and what of this rejected New Yorker piece, should I put it in, Dad, are you saying that satire should be part of this sentence and book, maybe, even if I am not sure yet what this will all be about, this book, it's a mystery to me, you're a mystery to me, and you're gone, and Joyce says in Ulysses that "I read a theological interpretation," about Hamlet and his father's ghost, "The Father and the Son idea, The Son striving to be atoned with the Father," and so maybe I need to atone with you for something, and "There's a divinity that shapes our ends, Rough-hew them how we will," and "What is he whose grief bears such an emphasis, whose phrase of sorrow Conjures the wand'ring stars and makes them stand Like wonder-wounded hearers, This is I, Hamlet the Dane," and so, I will type out the piece while removing the periods and other sentence ending punctuation like I did with the piece The New Yorker did publish, and here it is, just thrown into the mix, a piece The New Yorker didn't publish, hope you like it, Dad and readers, or don't, and it's A Great Proposal For Preventing The Political Satire Content Creators In America From Being Useless To Their Country, And For Making Them Beneficial To The Public by Dave Cowen, Knowing it is a melancholy object to those who visit the websites of the Internet, watch late night variety television shows, or still read magazines, that they see the mediums crowded with political satire, and that the creators of this content, instead of contributing to the fixing of the political problems they satirize, employ all their time in the manufacturing, and then the importuning of others to read, view, or retweet their content; which when consumed itself, and further disseminated, results in non-political satire content creators either taking time away from work that contributes to society, or worse, leaving their dear productive jobs to create political satire content themselves, I think it is agreed by all parties, that whoever can find out a fair, cheap, and easy method of making these political satire content creators sound and useful members of the populace, would deserve so well as to have his or her name mentioned frequently in public; or, at least, have a hashtag of his or hers trending #satiredoesn'tworkanymoreandprobablyneverdid is that a good hashtag, as I type out this piece again, I question that joke, but back to typing out the piece, as to my own part, having turned my thoughts for many unfruitful years, upon this subject, and maturely weighed the schemes of others, I have always found them grossly mistaken in their computation, as it is true, an actually really funny viral video, posted by Friend Dog Studios, I was pretty jealous of, about how Donald Trump sounds like your drunk neighbor, when his soundbites are edited to come out of the mouth of an actor, who is the perfect stereotype of a drunk neighbor, may have been viewed by over a million people, who saw it, laughed, and thought, rightfully, nobody should vote Donald Trump President of the United States; however, the results instead have been, or have been scientifically theorized to have been, that those citizens actually felt a false catharsis, and a self-defeating self-satisfaction, that led them not to do anything tangible, or enough tangible things, to stop others from voting Donald Trump President of the United States, and there is likewise another great advantage in my scheme, in that it will prevent the horrid experience of reading or viewing content that isn't funny or thought-provoking, alas, this is too frequent among us, the number of souls in this country being usually reckoned three hundred and twenty five million, of these I calculate there may be one million citizens who have created a political satire content this year; from which number I add forty million probationers, who have started doing so, but didn't get around to finishing it, or whose content may not receive a remittance of any kind, (although I apprehend there might be more, under the present distressed quality of the media) but this being granted, there will remain forty-one million citizens trying to create political satire content annually, at this point typing this sentence out I feel like that forty-one number is also not right, and also I feel a bit self-conscious that this piece isn't that funny and shouldn't be in the sentence, but it's already there, so it must stay, and so I guess I will finish typing out the rest of the piece, and the question therefore is, how this number shall be put to good use, and so a principal friend in the county of Los Angeles, read this far in a draft of the proposal, and chatted me in the Google document, "Are you gonna say eat them, like Jonathan Swift, isn't that who you're riffing on, and I replied, "Yes, this is a riff on 'A Modest Proposal,' but it's more than that, it's ironically ironic, that is it's not ironic, that is to say, unlike Swift, and eating Irish children, I'm truly against satire, why don't you finish reading it before you start critiquing, K" but the thing I was going to add next is that we cannot eat them, most political satire content creators spend so much of their time lazing about in chairs, brainstorming content in their Google documents, or sitting on couches, chatting in their shared Google documents with their principal friends about their halfway finished content, that their flesh lacks proper nutrition, and also, I am assured by a very knowing PI whose day job is as a security guard at my day job, that the time spent hunting and capturing the content creators, manufacturing them into appealingly edible products, and mass distributing those to the rest of the populace, would itself waste even more human capital than just letting them continue to create their silly, ineffectual nonsense, but that same principal friend in the county of Los Angeles, chatted in the Google document again, "I'm sorry, but, I gotta say, it really seems like you're trying too hard with this Swift riff, the thing is I don't think a lot of people will get it, and I also think, the people who will get it, will probably think it's not that different from other Swift riffs, have you read Hunter S Thompson's, I think it's about Vietnam, why don't you just write something in TrumpSpeak, TrumpSpeak really sells right now, look at SNL, they basically just have Alec Baldwin say whatever Trump said the week before, and everyone loves it, you're pretty good at TrumpSpeak," I chatted back in the Google doc, "No, this is the ultimate Swift riff, the Swift riff to stop all future Swift rifts, and turn them into do-gooding, it'll show everyone how we became so obsessed with content that we elected the most content-creating candidate just so we can view content created about him," and that same principal friend chatted back, "You sound pretty unhinged right now, I seriously think you should do another idea, or at least another draft, or give up writing, JK, you never will, even though you should, no JK, I'm gonna hop off," and so I chatted back into the chat box that no longer had my friend inside of it, "You just don't get my genius, no one does, no content creator in history, and I say this with great surety, has been treated worse, or more unfairly," but like I said my friend had hopped off, in the story, and in real life, while editing/reading, and this was sort of based on real life, like I guess all my writing is, and maybe all writing is sorta, Katy Waldman sorta said all that in The New Yorker recently, in her piece about Susan Choi's new book and finding out that Louisa Hall sort of put her essay in a book that Katy was going to review, and the question of who owns a story, and someone's life events if they overlap with yours, and is it OK to appropriate other people's stories into your own work, and Dave Eggers wrote/worried about that for a memoir, or should have more, "Things have been taken care of," "It's largely Beth's doing," oops, that's a projection of pain, sorry, Dave, this book isn't more of a heartbreaking work of staggering genius yet, no, it's pretty gossipy all of a sudden, and I was out for drinks one night with sorta friends and Liz Meriwether, who is much more successful than me screenwriting-wise, and I told her a really funny story about how I sprained my penis having sex, and next season on her show New Girl, there was a three episode arc where Schmidt broke his penis, and, like, maybe that is just coincidence, or maybe she appropriated my story, without asking, or paying me money, or even asking if I, who she knew was a writer, might want to write one of those three episodes, or maybe that's a crazy, self-pitying, victim position to take, and I should let it go, which I have not, and stop assuming anything about any of that, or maybe she will sue me for writing all that, oh man, I am going to be sued now, or maybe I just made up that story, so it's not true, is that all I need to say, what's the law on gossip versus libel, and it's not suable, right, and maybe nothing people write is truly taken from real life, in the sense of taken, lost, stolen, wronged, like Katy Waldman may have been saying in her essay on Susan Choi and Louisa Hall, and so I will say now that I don't have bipolar, and neither does my dad, but in this version of reality I'm telling where we both do, some months later after the rejection of that piece above from The New Yorker and also from McSweeney's, which is the other somewhat well-known place that published me once, but then went on to so far reject everything else I've sent them, but that's OK, what's the deal with this guy and The New Yorker, you are wondering in my head, I went on to publish The Trump Passover Haggadah, which was a lot of Trump-voice, and it sold very well, and it was widely-praised, somewhat, not really really, but it was at the top of the political humor charts for Amazon dot com for a time in 2018 and now in 2019, too, it was, and thank you very much for the royalty money, Bezos, but many people also wrote reviews that said it was a sick thing that I wrote and published this Trump Haggadah, due to either how it treated the President or the Presidency or moreover how it treated Judaism, and Jews, and the important holiday of Passover, and the sacred text of the Haggadah, and also disrespectful to G-d, and sometimes I do feel weird about it, and one time I had a dream after my dad died, that he told me not to publish the follow-up, The Yada Yada Haggadah, because he was with G-d right now, and He said it was not a good thing to have done or to do, and when I tried to publish the book on KDP, the PDF file kept crashing and not letting me insert Hebrew images into it, even though I had been inserting Hebrew into the file for the past few weeks without a problem, if not a month or two, and so why on the night I was set to publish it was there this ghost in the machine, was it my dad's ghost, also when I did a work around by screen-grabbing the Hebrew words, that also had a different glitch where I couldn't open them, and yet I fought through it because I am so stubborn about succeeding and ambition, even at the expense of my dad's ghost in my machine I thought, and even now the Google Doc is frozen and I can't see what I am writing, what is all this saying about my dad and G-d and his ghost and should I just stop typing or keep going, I guess Ill stop, ok it just came back, and now that I can see what I'm typing again, here's a segment of that Trump Haggadah book with the periods and punctuation taken out per usual, where Trump tells The Magid, let me know what you think, if it's a sick, demented, bad thing I did, cool, "You know, a lot of people don't know The Exodus Story, I didn't know it until very recently, not a lot of people know it, very complicated stuff, You got this guy, this Moses guy, leading his people, He's kind of like the Jew President, right, OK, he's the Jew

President, I'm the US President, he's the Jew President, I'm the US President, so I know a thing or two about this, Some people say, I'm not saying this, but there are people saying, they're saying, Moses, if you look at it, if you really look at it, he wasn't such a good leader, not such a good guy, this Moses, I'm not saying that, but many people are, Some of these people, they wish I had been Moses, They do, They say, if Trump was Moses, if Trump was Moses, they say, the Jews never would have been enslaved in the first place, They say if Trump was Moses, the Jews would have enslaved the Egyptians instead, And we would've enslaved them so well, like no one's ever been enslaved before, No doubt about it, Real tough slavery, folks, The toughest slavery you've ever seen, So tough the Egyptians would be the ones wanting to have Seders right now, To celebrate escaping from us, Except, if I was Moses, the Egyptians would never have escaped, So they wouldn't be having Seders, Because they'd still be our slaves, But I'm not saying that, Other people are saying that, Many others, But not me, I will say, you probably wouldn't have been slaves for two hundred years, if I was leading you, but that's OK, that's OK, I'm here now, Can we, can we try something tonight, folks, Can we all pretend I'm Moses, Let's pretend, Why not, And then I'll tell you what I'd really do if I was Moses, Everyone close your eyes for the story, Close your eyes, children, Eric, no peeking, So Trump is Moses, Trump's the leader of the Jewish people, Trump's a prophet, Trump's been sent by G-d, Picture that, Not that hard, right, Kind of already what's going on, isn't it, But OK, here's what I'm going to do to about this Pharaoh, This Pharaoh, he's a real bad hombre, But we're going to deal with him, Oh boy, we're going to deal with him, bigly, Because I'm going to do something no one's ever done, I don't know why no one's ever done it before, but, most people aren't as smart as me, no one is, actually, I'm, like, the smartest guy in history, so that's probably why they never thought of this, So people say, they say, Donald, if you're Moses, you gotta leave Egypt, you gotta take the Jews out of Egypt, we've always left Egypt, that's just how it's done, I tell you what, though, if I'm Moses, we're not leaving Egypt this time, That's establishment thinking, That's swamp thinking, And it stops now, We're gonna make THEM leave, The Egyptians, you hear that, You're gone, you're out of here, bye-bye, How are we going to do that, We're gonna do some real bad things to these Egyptians, The media's not going to like it, The media's going to say, "Oh, you can't do that to the Egyptian people, Donald, they've lived in Egypt for a long time, most of them since they were born, they have rights, too, you know," But bottom line, They treated us very unfairly, So they're gonna get plagued, Serious plaguing, people, No one's ever seen plagues like these before, Because I'm not just Moses, I'm not just Donald Trump, I'm not just a Prophet sent by G-d, I'm also Hashem, G-d, President of the World, Ruler of the Cosmos, Dictator of the Universe, Blessed am I, That's right, So I do the plagues, too, I'm going to do it all, I alone can fix this," and so, yeah, that was part of a Haggadah, which is a Jewish liturgical text, maybe, is that the term, who cares, it's a holy book, and so, yeah, maybe I am a sick person, maybe that was a sick thing to write that book, like a third of the Amazon reviewers kind of said, they said things like, Sol: "Disgusting Just plain disgusting and revolting" or Jeremy: "Stupid and Disrespectful What twisted mind would conflate Trump Bashing with our beloved holiday Sick, but unfortunately not surprising" and so I wonder sometimes, sometimes often, am I sick person, and Sheila Heti asks How Should A Person Be, and when I say clearly not like me, do I also mean the opposite, and does she, and I mean, I have a mental illness, according to this book so far, and also maybe the person who I said I wasn't going to talk about has one, too, but I guess I did talk about him, maybe he is also sick or mentally ill, according to some psychologists that's true, they have speculated that that is the case, narcissistic personality disorder, sociopathic personality disorder, malignant personality disorder, I don't know, there's definitely sickness in all people, though we want to ignore it, we want to deny it, a shadow in others that we don't want to recognize in ourselves, and here's some stuff from chapter 1 of my dad's book I found by Shenk about his hero's mental illness, "Lincoln's relationship with his father, the only other member of his nuclear family who survived, was so cool that observers wondered whether there was any love between them," and "Abraham sometimes neglected his farm work by reading, Tom would beat him for this," and "Many studies have linked adult mental health to parental support in childhood," and this was true of my dad and his dad, the lack of support, but not of me and my dad, he always supported me, and my friend M's grandmother said her husband did business with Fred, father of the guy, and he said that Fred said when that guy was born he knew something was wrong with him, from the moment he was born, and so I wonder sometimes, my dad never said anything like that about me, even though he did tell his dad I'm a bit of a shyster, which was weird when his dad told me that, because I didn't know if I've ever heard my dad use that word before, or if he even knew that word, I highly doubt it, so I didn't really believe my dad's dad, and still sometimes I wonder which kind of mental illness of these two Presidents do I have, or do I have both, or neither, I fear it is the liar guy and honest Abe at the same time, a real bad case that would be, and this sentence has started to get a lot less funny than I wanted it to all of a sudden here, and how many words have I typed, I am on pg thirty-nine and that is more than Jonathan Coe's record of thirty-three pgs,

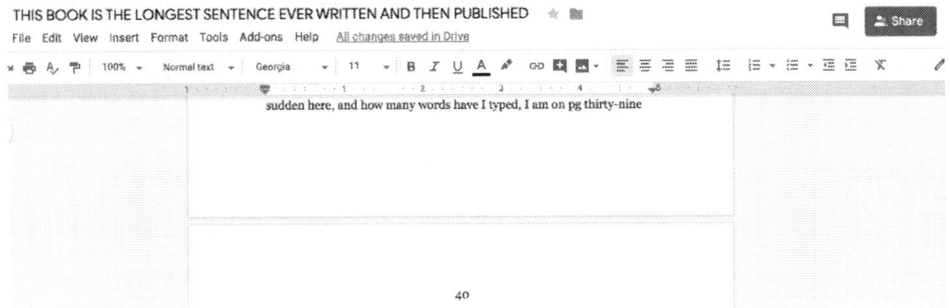

so I think I will check to see if we got the record, and we are at 13,772 words, and is that the record, I can't remember if that's the record, I am going to go back to Wikipedia in order to check the record, and, I am now typing into Google, Wikipedia longest sentence, and I am now clicking on the result, and I am now scrolling down, and OK, here's the part with facts, Exceptionally long sentences in print, it is called, and I am reading it and, but no, I haven't reached the record, dang, it's 13,995 words, Jonathan Coe has me right now, as of this word, as of this Word, too, but I am so close, I am so dang close, I can feel it, I can feel it in my bones, I can feel the glory, I am ready to seize it, and I am ready to take my rightful place in the history books of writing and the regular history books of human achievement, and soon the record will be mine, all mine, Dave Cowen, I can envision my name, Dave Cowen, right here on Wikipedia, Dave Cowen, in a Wikipedia entry, for all to see forever, Dave Cowen, great, important writer, which has always been a goal for me, Dave Cowen, to be included in Wikipedia as a great, important writer, Dave Cowen, and so my name, Dave Cowen, will go into this section, as well as the title of my book, which is of course: This Book Is The Longest Sentence Ever Written And Then Published: It's Over 13,955 Words, That's The Previous Record I've Researched In April '19, It's Well Over That Actually, And It's Already Started, The Sentence, This Subtitle Is

Part Of It, And It's by Dave Cowen, and so I will copy out, minus the periods, what the new version of Exceptionally long sentences in print section on Wikipedia will look like, so you can see what it will look like with the other entries, but with mine conquering them all, Coe, Joyce, and Faulkner: Exceptionally long sentences in print[edit]

- Jonathan Coe's The Rotters' Club appears to hold the record at 13,955 words, It was inspired by Bohumil Hrabal's Dancing Lessons for the Advanced in Age: a Czech language novel written in one long sentence,
- A sentence often claimed to be the longest sentence ever written is in Molly Bloom's soliloquy in the James Joyce novel Ulysses (1922), which contains a "sentence" of 3,687 words,
- One of the longest sentences in American literature is in William Faulkner's Absalom, Absalom (1936), The sentence is composed of 1,288 words (in the 1951 Random House version),

But, wait, what the hell is this, has this always been here, it also says right below the Faulkner bullet point:

- Solar Bones by Mike McCormack is written as one sentence, It won the 2016 Goldsmith's prize for experimental fiction, was longlisted for the Booker in 2017 and won the 2018 International Dublin Literary Award,

I sort of ignored this entry, because it says right above that Jonathan Coe appears to hold the record, and so I didn't even bother to check Mike McCormack's book to see how long it is, and I didn't include him with Joyce and Faulkner as close to the record people because McCormack is minor compared to those two, but is that going to be longer than thirty-three pages, it might be, it doesn't say it's a novel though, but it was nominated for the Booker, I think that's only for novels, am I, what the hell, am I not going to get the record in a few words from now, I was ready to get the record, even though I have much more to say about my, hold on, going to Amazon dot com, my publisher, typing in Solar Bones Mike McCormack, clicking on the title, scrolling down to product details, oh no, no, no, no, no, no, fuck, what the fucking fuck, I can't fucking believe this, this goddamn book is 224 pages, goddamn it all, I almost typed an exclamation point there, I almost typed ten of them, I want to type a million of them, I want to die, right now, hold on, I am going to have to buy this book on Kindle to see what's going on here, if it's truly one sentence, maybe it's not really one sentence, maybe my dream won't be deferred, OK, clicking Kindle, 9,99, clicking buy with one click now, OK, bought, OK, opening it up in my Kindle cloud reader, OK, I am reading it, here's what it says to start, it's more of a prose poem then a sentence, look at this,

"the bell
the bell as
hearing the bell as
hearing the bell as standing here
the bell being heard standing here
hearing it ring out through the grey light of this morning, noon or night
god knows"

And I am scrolling along from there, and it's just pages of this prose poem, which is kind of unfair, it's unfair that a prose poem can be one sentence, but I guess it's not unfair, I guess that's my whole point about sentences, they can be anything, and so I guess I have been beaten by Mike McCormack, even though I didn't even know it, and the irony is crazy, because here we are, we are at what should be the record, in fact, we are at literally, 14,675, so I should have set the record, I should be happy right now, but I am not, I am not happy, because I didn't win, I am not happy, I am not the longest sentence writer right now, even though I thought, but wait, I have just scrolled to the end of Solar Bones, and there's no period at the end of the sentence, what, what does that mean, does that mean it's not even a sentence, does that mean it doesn't have the record, is that why they said Jonathan Coe appears to have the record, because Mike McCormack never actually wrote a sentence in Solar Bones, that word "appears" is quite pregnant with meaning, because he didn't close his prose poem with a period, and so does that mean I do have the record as of right now, that I've beaten Coe, and McCormack is disqualified, if I were to print this book as it is right now, if I were to stop writing right now, and boom publish it on Kindle Direct Publishing, right now, boom publish, would I have beaten Coe and the disqualified McCormack, but how would I feel, I don't feel good, I don't feel good about this way of winning, because how will I plead my case if people disagree, and what body would decide, what authority, and would I look petty on insisting that my sentence is longer, wait, how many words is his book, how can I figure that out, and I type into Google, mike mccormack solar bones word count, and I click on the first result, Solar Bones Reading Length, and it says word count, 78,300 words, which is a lot more words to go, goddamn it, but it is also an estimate based on book length, and so even the robots are involved in this record once again, and how can they be trusted, and how can I claim to have the record if I don't comfortably beat Solar Bones' real word count, and does that mean I have to read the book and count the words at the same time, and is that even possible to process what I am reading as I am counting the words, at the same time, but I guess I must do that, because I have Googled all around and there is no word count, officially, that crafty McCormack, he's the shyster, he's done that on purpose to shroud his record, and so fine, I will read and count the words as I go, I am going to take a break, and I will read this book, I will read it and count the words as I go, OK, fine, OK, fine, I'll be right back, I am leaving the consciousness of the book for the first time, to read this other book and count its words, and I don't want to, it's not something I was planning on doing, but I guess I must, and OK, bye for now, and, and, and, and, and, and, and, and I've read some of it, to be honest, I stopped counting the words, it was too hard, to read and understand the meaning of the words and also to count the number of words at the same time, too difficult to do that at the same time, but I also didn't finish the book, to be honest, too, but you know what, I stopped, because it seems to be set on all soul's day, which is November 2nd, which is the day of the dead, the day of the faithful departed, so that part was resonant, and literary, and made me feel some good feels, and I like that part, but I stopped because overall it's a very dark and depressing story and tone, as it's about the end of the world, and the failures of a family, or the end of the world in Ireland, and it's not that fun and uplifting or funny, and if I am going to give this sentence credit for the longest one ever, which I will, I have read enough of it to say it's also a sentence, I will give credit where credit is due, but I am not happy with it being the longest sentence in the English language ever written and then published, and not just for my own sake, but also for the sake of the English language, I mean, it's better than Coe's sentence, definitely, times a million, but it's not the best sentence ever, sorry, Mike, and so, I will continue, I must continue, to write the longest sentence in the English language, in the hopes that it somehow becomes the best sentence, and so I will write over 80,000 words, because that will be the comfortable winning record I will set for myself, and I will also write over 224 pages, I will do both of those things, to be sure, to be sure that I have the record for sure, and so buckle up folks, we're going to continue the ride of our lives, or give up now, give up now if you are a stone cold loser, like I am not, I am not a warm shit loser, either, even though I have often thought so, but if you are down, DTF and DTR, we are going to do it together, we are going to beat the record for sure this time, and nothing can stop us, we just will write on, right on, and I will even leave off where McCormack did, I will take the end of his pretty great if not greatest sentence into mine, my sentence, and I will then continue it, and so, here it is, "my body drawing its soul in its wake or vice versa until that total withdrawal into the vast whiteness is visible only as a brimming absence so that there is nothing left, body and soul all gone, and these residual pulses and rhythms which for these waning moments, abide in their own recurrent measure, nothing more than a vague strobing of the air before they too are obliterated in that self-engulfing light which closes over everything to be, cast out beyond darkness into that vast unbroken commonage of space and time, into that vast oblivion in which there are no markings or contours to steer by nor any songs to sing me home and where there is nothing else for it but to keep going, one foot in front of the other, the head down and keep going, keep going, keep going to fuck," and that was pretty good, pretty, pretty, pretty good, even if that F-word was Mike's, but he's clearly saying keep going, keep going, he's saying that to me and to us, keep going, he is saying, keep going, keep going, Mike is passing the baton via a book, like in Italo Calvino's If On A Winter's Night A Traveler, and I am continuing on, we are, thank you Mike, thank you for your contribution to my sentence, but maybe it's not my sentence only, maybe we are all writing one sentence, all the books, are one book, all the sentences are one sentence, like maybe Calvino is saying in his book, as a man and woman search for the continuation of a book but keep finding different books which are different but just as beautiful and interesting, and it is the man and woman's search through books together, that is what matters, not an individual book, don't get hung up on an individual book, but all books, have value, are saying the same things kind of, and reading and sharing them with another person, is what makes life good, I dunno, but I do know this sentence has gotten sort of unfunny, even if it is has also gotten a bit deeper, it is also a lot unfunnier, and I am worried about that, I am worried about how unfunny the sentence has become, because it's supposed to be a very funny sentence, because I am a self-proclaimed humorist, and so I am going to tell a joke, and the joke is that the joke right now is on my 11th grade English teacher, he said I shouldn't stay in his AP English Language class, because I wasn't a serious reader or a serious person, and he kicked me out of there, that AP English Language class, or he sort of forced me out, due to creating low confidence in me, because I was, like, maybe I am not an advanced student of the English language, and maybe I shouldn't be placed in this advanced class of the English language, and I should switch to the regular class, like he says, and I did so, even though in my heart of hearts I didn't want to leave the class, because I love the English language, and so this was a sad thing and a sad time for me, but the joke is on him, because I am writing the longest sentence ever written and then published in the English language, so I am leaving a bigger mark on the English language than he has or than he could ever imagine that I would be able to, too, and I guess this is also a clear part of this narrative now, my obsession with recognition, and status, and maybe he didn't even create low confidence in me, I just did it to myself, sorry for the defamation Doc Boner, and do you guys want more of a linear narrative with this sentence, that was a question, and do you know Padgett Powell, he wrote a book called The Interrogative Mood that was only questions, and on page 22, one of the questions is "Whose death, recent or not, do you most lament, question mark," get it 22, dad's Numerology, and one of the other questions I have about this whole endeavor is does my sentence have to be grammatically correct, too, I mean, right now, I am just putting commas after everything, and I know that that probably isn't correct usage, and there have been a lot of tense and subject changes so far, and in general the sentence is clearly just running on endlessly, clearly, this clearly doesn't need to be said, clearly, clearly this guy is an idiot who is writing these words, and when I mentioned to a friend David that I was writing this one sentence book he kind of said that's not fair you can't just do a run on, it needs to be grammatically correct, don't cheat, but then he came around on it, and was down with it, and even said he has trouble not writing run on sentences sometimes and is annoyed when people criticize him for it, and I was like because like who makes the rules, right, and the Google Doc is frozen again, this Google Doc must be mad at me, maybe Google doesn't want me to win this record, it crashed, but now I'm back, I will forever come back to win this record, but I wonder if I will be docked by whoever is in charge of giving me my record and award due to the ungrammarness of this sentence and that word, and when I told my mom that I was going for the record, she asked if I would be in the Guinness Book of World Records, and I do wonder now, if I would be in that book, and if I was, do you get a cash prize, if I'm being honest, with her, and with myself, and you, there's probably not going to be a cash prize, beyond the royalties I will receive for writing the longest sentence ever written and then published, and having it bought, so please buy the book, so I can get a bit of royalties, and don't return it so that I lose the royalties, and when I told her that Dad found his way into the book, she wasn't mad, which is cool, we'll see what she thinks of it as she reads it though, Hi Mom, It's alright, we're only bleeding, Bob Dylan says, and I guess I am wondering if I will be disqualified from the record after all, like I was kinda disqualified from AP English Language in 11th grade, and I have a victim mentality, don't I, and I am also wondering if I should put in some semicolons in this sentence, like this; would that fix the grammar problem, and also I thought semicolon has a hyphen like semi-colon, but it seems like it doesn't because I just corrected it on spell check, and, man, I am feeling very insecure about my grasp on the English language again now, as well as my grasp on this sentence in general, words the tumbling are everywhere control can't I help but sound like Yoda, maybe I should probably put another semicolon in; but having another clause come after a semicolon, that feels kind of weird now; because that would make the clause independent, that's what they do right, but is an independent clause another sentence, and so is that bad, but also I hadn't done a semicolon yet, except for that section above where I padded the sentence with a piece that The New Yorker rejected because Jonathan Swift used semicolons and I was parodying him, which again reminds me that sometimes I don't feel good about having published or tried to publish so much writing about that guy sometimes, but mostly I do feel very proud of it, and my dad was proud of it, but I guess I am also a little bit not feeling good that I padded this sentence with that rejected piece for The New Yorker and the sick segment from the Haggadah, and part of McCormack's sentence, and the legally dubious excerpt from The New Yorker, and I will win on these technicalities now, as well as the no bot writing technicality potentially in the future, but now the grammar police might get me, and I am now wondering if I already lost the contest to Mike McCormack, he used no punctuation, just for throwing these semi-colons in, too, and I am also feeling like the semi-colons bit is a bit extra, and sure this whole book is super extra, extra extra, read all about it, I guess I am going to stop with the semi-colons that's enough of those for now, and I also decided I am going to use hyphens for the last three semi-colons and this one, the fourth one, and that it will be the last I talk of them, except to say the English Language is quite a flexible invention that should always be malleable, and people who disagree are wrong, but they also kind of make me feel dumb like I felt back in AP English Language, and maybe that's why I became the type of writer I am, a very technically flawed, but also brilliant, but also too consumed with greatness due to a perceived traumatic slight and a grudge on the shoulder, a big chip there, indeed, I have, even though I am probably not very great, and maybe actually probably am not brilliant whatsoever, and maybe kind of sad, and wasting my time, and everyone's time, and your time, and maybe people think I am a sad person for writing this book, in this unhinged way, maybe I'm sad, and maybe if I'd stayed in AP English Language in 11th grade I might know how to write the longest sentence in a grammatically correct way, or maybe I wouldn't have this chip, and wouldn't be trying to write this sentence, or maybe even trying to write at all, and I would be a productive citizen, and where does the chip come from, but I also think the thing that I have now and had back then, the thing I have always had in my character and my writing, is the thing that that teacher always was secretly jealous of I believe, and I'll say his name now, and his name was Doc Boner, and the thing about that is I actually kind of liked his name, it's a badass name, Doc Boner, the contradiction between being a doctor and being an erect penis is hilarious, in an inclusive way, I am making that joke, seriously, I don't want it to sound like I am making fun of his name in a mean way, I think it is genuinely a very cool name, I would be down to have that name, and so even if that wasn't his name, and I was just putting in a name now in order to avoid defamation or whatever, just to be clear I don't really believe in first amendment restrictions, I will put real people's names in if I want, because that's something Joyce also did, he put in real people and places, found objects they've called them, even if he used them in fictitious ways, like Katy Waldman might say, what does she think about me putting reference to her article about her finding herself in another book, is this a stunt, or good writing, she's The New Yorker's book critic, and why do I have such an inferiority complex about The New Yorker and believe everyone there is better than me, that good writing is done by people superior to me, and is Katy Waldman a better writer than me, she must be superior to me, and who is she really, and should I have used a fake name like I didn't do with Doc Boner, and, no, I will fight for my first amendment rights in a court of law, if necessary, as Lawrence Lessig says, "Is it unfair that someone gets to profit off the ideas of someone else, Says Kozinski, No, Intellectual property law assures authors the right to their original expression but encourages others to build freely on the ideas that underlie it, This result is neither unfair nor unfortunate: It is the means by which intellectual property law advances the progress of science and art, We give authors certain exclusive rights, but in exchange we get a richer public domain, Nothing today is genuinely new: Culture, like science and technology, grows by accretion, each new creator building on the works of those who came before, Overprotection stifles the very creative forces it's supposed to nurture," and here's a quote from Waldman's article about Jeff Bezos' wife who is a writer, so I guess I am using Waldman to poke at Bezos now, oh boy, what am I doing, he's my publisher, why am I doing this, I feel compelled to though, it's a great piece by Waldman, and it is called, The Idealized, Introverted Wives of MacKenzie Bezos's Fiction, By Katy Waldman, January 23, 2019, "Jeff and MacKenzie Bezos are seeking a divorce, having amassed twenty-five years of marriage, four children, and a net worth of a hundred and thirty-seven billion dollars, Jeff is the founder of Amazon, MacKenzie is a writer who studied fiction under Toni Morrison, at Princeton, and has published two novels, "The Testing of Luther Albright," in 2005, and "Traps," in 2013, Both books were released by traditional imprints, not Amazonian ones (Bezos has referred to his wife as "the fish that got away"), and one of them, "Luther Albright," is good, There is a particular difficulty in discerning whether this book is good, not because the text qua text is somehow elusive or inscrutable but because one struggles to read it without sweeping for psychological clues, A confirmation bias is at work, and the belief to be confirmed is that a book by MacKenzie Bezos—one half of the richest couple in the world, partner to a man who has exploded paradigms of retail, labor, even capitalism itself, and upended the very industry that publishes her books—just has to be a roman à clef, Surely she would draw on such rich material, so close to hand, "The Testing of Luther Albright" follows a repressed engineer who specializes in "water resources" and who, in a sense, loses his family by failing to acknowledge his feelings, The idealized wife, Liz, is insanely supportive, Like a cathedral, her features possess a "composite power" that men can't help trying to "decode," She's loving, endlessly adjuvant, the Giving Tree of spouses, At the end of the book, she dies of cancer, Luther strives for impassive rationality, He buries himself in home-improvement projects as his son presses him, less and less gently, for a measure of emotional honesty, The book is swollen with metaphors about dams and hidden pipes, For all its heavy-handedness, though, Bezos draws her characters with uncommon psychological insight, even when they don't have the language or the self-awareness to show any vulnerability, Luther combines a sense of his own infallibility with a zeal for process and quantification, (Incidentally, Jeff Bezos once described himself as a "professional dater" who assessed romantic prospects via analytic systems derived from investment banking,) Liz's investment in her partner's career, meanwhile, can be readily quantified: when Luther takes a new job, she finds "a different way to celebrate—champagne, a cake, an office nameplate hidden in the butter dish" every night for a week, As Luther withdraws from their relationship, Liz begins volunteering for a crisis hotline, ("I tried to picture her there," Luther says, "listening to a stranger's worries across the telephone lines because I would not share my own,") Liz yearns only to feel important and useful, which Luther understands, "It's you who's important," Luther tells Liz on the night of her beautiful death, under the stars, "Everyone comes to you, You help everyone you touch, You're the most important person I know,"" and so this article is a found object and I am using it in a fair use way, right, Judge, right, God, and do you think the test of Luther was an early test of my publisher's marriage, like Waldman implies, what do you think, Alexa, do people write out their hopes or fears or both in their books, Alexa, and that's a fair use quote I insist it is, though maybe I would lose a court case about this decision, if the Bezos or KDP are litigious or is it if Waldman and The New Yorker are litigious, or is it all four, Alexa, do you know, Alexa, what is the meaning of life, Alexa, who wants a piece of me, probably/hopefully nobody, and Joyce would have lost his fight over found objects in the court of law of Ireland, so he chose to just not return to his homeland which is where the people who wanted to sue him for using their names lived, but I will probably fight a lawsuit with a pro bono lawyer though, because I am very poor, so if you are a pro bono intellectual property lawyer reading this, and you don't hate it that much, holler at me, like Jonathan Kirsch, he's a writer for the Los Angeles Jewish Journal and also a world-renowned intellectual property lawyer, and he said of The Yada Yada Haggadah, "By contrast, "The Yada-Yada Hagaddah: A Sitcom Seder," by Dave Cowen (Cowen), is pure parody, a follow-up to Cowen's 2018 Amazon best-seller, "The Trump Passover Haggadah," As the title suggests, the haggadah owes as much to "Seinfeld" as to the Book of Exodus, and its function at the seder table is to provide a few moments of hilarity between the traditional readings, Guests can take the roles of Jerry, George, Elaine and Kramer in performing the comedic scripts that Cowen has created, "Because this is a parody that transforms the copyrighted material [in 'Seinfeld'] into a teaching tool for Judaism," Larry David is made to say, "it's kosher," And, for all of its high spirits, the author is careful to refer to the Almighty as "G-D," which suggests that he may be willing to push the envelope on copyright law but not Jewish tradition," which is a cool little analysis, but actually at the time I didn't believe in God and I just thought it was funny to refer to G-d as G-d when I would usually type the word out, kind of making fun of that archaic convention, but actually I don't totally feel that way now about G-d, not since I started to read Lewis Hyde and study the Enneagram, and am more spiritual, and copyright has changed a lot since the Internet and certainly since Lewis

Hyde wrote The Gift, a book meant to defend and illuminate the noncommercial side of artistic practice, and even since Lewis Hyde wrote Common As Air, about how we treat art and ideas once they have entered the public sphere, and what would Lewis Hyde or Doc Boner say about the Meme being studied in academia by people like Florian Cramer, like this, "Memes are arguably the best example of a contemporary popular mass culture which emerged and developed entirely on the Internet, Unlike earlier popular forms of visual culture such as comic strips, they are anonymous creations – and as such, even gave birth to the now-famous Anonymous movement, as described by (Klok 16-19), Other important characteristics of imageboard memes are: creation by users, disregard of intellectual property, viral dissemination among users, and potentially infinite repurposing and variation (through collage or by changing the text), As low-resolution images with small file sizes, they can be created and disseminated almost instantly, in contrast with the much slower creation, editing and distribution processes characteristic of traditional publishing media," and then what do we make of this:

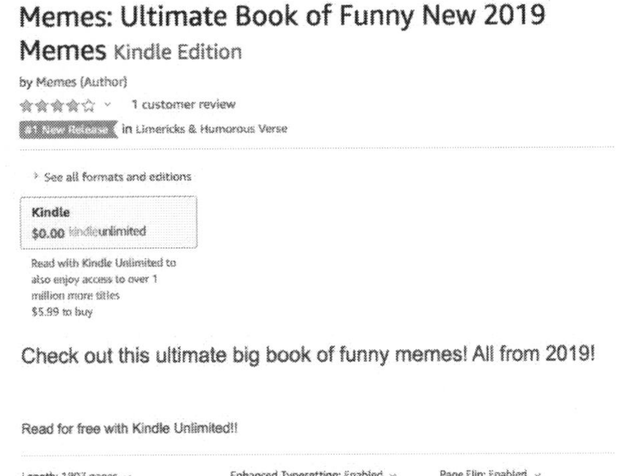

,

and so please remember that disregard of intellectual property and almost instant dissemination is the kids, is the future, is the movement that is happening, that should be the law, and Lawrence Lessig says, "The aim of any literacy, is to empower people to choose the appropriate language for what they need to create or express, to communicate in the language of the twenty-first century," and just ask my friend Danny Snelson, a poet and UCLA professor who provided me with the syllabus where I found that Florian Cramer quote, and please remember images are words in this sentence, too, I've decided that, Doc Boner, and the grammar police, so shut up, and also, Lewis Hyde says, "If we go all the way back to the ancient world, to the old bardic and prophetic traditions, what we find is that men and women are not thought to be authors so much as vessels through which other forces act and speak," and Jonathan Lethem says that John Donne says, "All mankind is of one author, and is one volume; when one man dies, one chapter is not torn out of the book, but translated into a better language; and every chapter must be so translated," except for me, I am a true original, sui generis, because the other bigger point is that people always have been jealous of my pioneeringness and my provocativeness, which is what makes me unique, even though it appears not to be a word, that first one, pioneeringness, and so it's another way that I am like Kanye, and a funny story about me and my writing is that I wrote a college admissions essay about masturbation when I applied to college, and my high school counselor thought it was a dumbass move, sort of quote unquote, that with my grades and scores or whatever I was pretty much set and would just create a needless red flag and get my dumbass rejected from schools I wanted to go to, but I did it anyway, because I am a provocative ram-Aries type guy, and a pioneer, and Ezra Koenig from Vampire Weekend is an Aries, too, born the same year even, and so we were applying to college together at the same time, and I wanted to apply to Columbia but didn't apply there early admission, I applied somewhere else early admission that was easier to get into for me because my parents went there, poor me, so I didn't get to become friends with him, even though I think I would have, and I feel a kinship with Ezra's lyrics and music, and have you heard the new album, just so you know, it is now May 3rd, 2019, and I took a break from writing the sentence after the thing with Mike McCormack, I knew I couldn't do it all in one sitting anymore, I hope that's OK with you, dear reader, and some other things came up in my life, like promoting The Yada Yada Haggadah and The Trump Haggadah and having a 4/20 cannabis-infused dinner party seder with the former, and so I took a break for all that, but I am now listening to Ezra's new album, Father of the Bride, as I resume this sentence, and it's so good, I don't know why, but it's so good to me so far, and do you believe in horoscopes, too, and I don't know if masturbation had ever been the topic of a college essay, but I submitted it to my early decision college, Penn, and they accepted me, and when I got there, I met someone, a student, who worked in the admissions office for his school job, and I told him about the essay, and he was like, whoa, I remember that one, that was a crazy essay, it was hilarious, but crazy, I can't believe you got in, people at the admissions office said it was the craziest essay they've ever seen, so I was sure that meant you would never get in, but I got in, and it was probably the best college essay about masturbation ever written, and so that pioneeringness and that provocativeness, it's big in the world, and it was big for Joyce, too, and it should at least make up for sloppiness and whatever else is wrong with me, and my fraternity name in college was Sloppy Cock, probably because I am so sloppy and such an arrogant cock, and there's surely a lot of sloppiness, clearly this writing itself is quite masturbatory, cocky and masturbatory, and sloppy, is it interesting to anyone else but myself, but also who I am is a bit like Jack Kerouac, and how he wrote On The Road on one long scroll of paper some say, and some say he didn't edit it, he just wrote the whole perfect book on one long scroll, but other people have said it was a myth that Kerouac just wrote On The Road in one sitting on one long scroll and then had it published, that he edited it, and it was never perfect, and maybe that's true, and maybe Kerouac did edit his book On THe Road, and corrected stray capitilization errors, and stray spelling errors, which is and was his prerogative, but it's not true with this book, this book is one uninterrupted rant on the metaphorical scroll of a Google Doc, and I am not going backwards to correct it, or adding new things like Kerouac may have, and I didn't just add that German author Gregor Weichbrodt, wrote On the Road for 17,527 Miles, which is a list of Google Maps driving instructions recreating the route of Jack Kerouac's On the Road, I didn't just add that, this is pure stream of consciousness, it's like my heroes Faulkner and Joyce and their stream of consciousness writing, and like Kerouac's spontaneous-mind and Kerouac's love for music is here too, just a different type of music, rap instead of jazz, that's also the same, music is also the same, and David Shields "says," "All art constantly aspires toward the condition of music," and instead of a road trip, this is an Internet trip, and it's also like Kanye with his rants, and rappers with freestyles, and also a bit like that guy I said I wasn't going to talk about, but I ended up doing so, but I'll try not to again, because "Wicked snakes inside the place you thought was dignified, I don't want to live like this, but I don't want to die," says Ezra, and this book and sentence is also like that other guy I said I wouldn't speak of I guess who just speaks off the cuff and extemporaneously without thinking much about his words or their effect on people, even though arguably his words have the most effect on the most number of people in the history of the world, isn't that ironic, and he just like goes on for hours at a time, and maybe that's also like this, and maybe that's what makes this a defining piece of literature of this time, which I guess is that guy's time, its extemporaneousness, which is also not a word, I pioneered that, and also its Instantness, due to the KDP Instaprinting, and Instagram and Instcetera, ooh that word almost got me with its period in its abbreviated form, wow, close one, and maybe also this book's vapidity is like this guy's era, or a symptom of something that's happened to our brains due to something like technology and attention spans and capitalism and something else I can't think of right now, because I am bored by thinking of something else to say, something important to say, so I will just say whatever is easiest to say, is that the problem, and so also my book's clear lack of competence, see the previous every word of this book, and maybe it's an American art form slash American art failure, what's the it's referring to, like our politics and culture, and maybe his rise is why the Democrats are rushing to praise Ulysses and there have been articles about how it's all of the white, male, Democrat party candidates' favorite book, and I think maybe it's the most elite version of that guy's extemporaneousness, and so it is different than him, even though it's also kind of not, are we all the same, and an Atlantic article by Richard North Patterson, author of twenty novels, you should buy some of them, I haven't read any of them, but I bet they are fine, so Richard North Patterson talked about how fiction is meaningless now, because we are now all living inside the fictional mind of this guy, and it's rendered all other fictions meaningless, and that he's a Don Quixote railing against windmills, and then he literally did get mad at windmills, the guy, he said they cause cancer, and here's some stuff from chapter 2 of my dad's book by Shenk about a poem that Lincoln wrote when he was in his twenties, The Suicide's Soliloquy, "Here, where the lonely hooting owl, Sends forth his midnight moans, Fierce wolves shall o'er my carcase growl, Or buzzards pick my bones, No fellow-man shall learn my fate, Or where my ashes lie; Unless by beasts drawn round their bait, Or by the ravens' cry, Yes, I've resolved the deed to do, And this the place to do it: This heart I'll rush a dagger through, Though I in hell should rue it, Sweet steel, Come forth from out your sheath, And glist'ning, speak your powers; Rip up the organs of my breath, And draw my blood in showers, I strike, It quivers in that heart, which drives me to this end, I draw and kiss the bloody dart, My last, my only friend," so Lincoln also imagined a psychic distintegration, he imagined killing himself, he was crazy, too, but in a different way, but Shenk says, "And though the character of this poem chooses death by the dagger, the author of the poem, using his tool, the pen, gave voice to the impulse towards life," so what does that say about this stunt, my stunt, that Lincoln also published a stunt, but are we living in the psychic disintegration of that windmill cancer guy's lowbrow person's mind, like a Joyce's 21st century lowbrow shadow Ulysses, and will we survive, and did you know that Lincoln didn't carry a pocket knife unlike most other people who did back then, and he said, "If destruction be our lot, we must ourselves be its author and finisher, as a nation of freemen, we must live through all time, or die by suicide," and do you think we are in suicide times, and here's a poem called "Suicide" by Louis Aragon: "abcdef, ghijk, mnopqr, stuvw, xyz" and do you like it, and "How long til we sink to the bottom of the sea, how long, how long," asks Ezra, and there must be something in how we use phones and technology and guns and fuel in our own psychic disintegration, or is it just that guy, didn't I already say that, and clearly this book I am writing is representative of all that, and didn't I already say that, of all the garbage of the garbage time that we're living in, and all the phrases, all the phrases are here, they're here now, and they are all dumb AF, but they are also fyre, and hawt, and cule, and you're fucking dead, aren't you, you're fucking deadass, and this whole book is a weird flex tho, and put some music on, if you don't feel this, you should have music on, in your car, on your phone, in your ears, every moment of your life, until you're deaf, and Damon Albarn said about the removal of Paul McCartney's voice from Kanye's "FourFiveSeconds," "It's rude, I have a problem with this abusive collaboration: we're talking about Paul McCartney, Kanye West thinks only of Kanye West, using a name to make headlines, saying 'McCartney is in my song,' In addition, he puts McCartney in the video of the song, but not in the song itself," this is English translated to French and then back to English, says Stereogum, but you get the point, Regarding Kanye's creative process, Albarn notes, "Kanye West is one of those people who feed on other people," He says he tried to warn McCartney about Kanye's vampiric tendencies: "Before he decided to work with Kanye West, I sent a text message to McCartney saying, 'beware,' but he ignored it, He does what he wants, it's Paul McCartney," but McCartney recently said "FourFiveSeconds" was "much more made up as we went along" than he's accustomed to, "so much so that I didn't even realize that I was making songs," He elaborated, "I was tootling around on guitar, and Kanye spent a lot of time just looking at pictures of Kim on his computer, I'm thinking, are we ever gonna get around to writing, But it turns out he was writing, That's his muse, He was listening to this riff I was doing and obviously he knew in his mind that he could use that, so he took it, sped it up and then somehow he got

Rihanna to sing on it," but here's another piece about Kanye's work with Paul, did you know he also worked with Ezra during that session, "Back in early 2015, Kanye West, Rihanna, and Paul McCartney teamed up to record "FourFiveSeconds," whose bridge was written by Dirty Projectors' Dave Longstreth, Turns out that wasn't the only product of Longstreth's writing sessions for Ye, During one sit-down, Ye played Longstreth and Vampire Weekend's Ezra Koenig an improvised track composed of McCartney's Wurlitzer noodling and some improvised, nonsensical Kanye lyrics, Longstreth reveals in a New York Times interview published today, Amid the gibberish, Longstreth heard the phrase "Memories can get you into trouble" and went off with Koenig to turn it into a song, "Maybe you're with your girlfriend but thinking of your ex," Longstreth said of its possible use, "Kanye didn't wind up using it," he added, "but it was good—maybe something will come of it down the line,"" and I want to be a vampire like Kanye, to vampire books and music and lyrics and articles, to sample them like Kanye, but is that good, is it OK to be a vampire like Kanye, a Vampire Weekend of sample writing, like, "The page in your notebook was unbearably white," and, forget copyright, as David Shields "says," "Value has shifted toward the many ways to recall, annotate, personalize, edit, authenticate, display, mark, transfer, and engage a work, Art is a conversation, not a patent office, The citation of sources belongs to the realms of journalism and scholarship, not art, Reality can't be copyrighted," and I want this sentence to consume and take and spit and join and synthesize and harmonize back out other peoples' words, and here's what Kanye thinks about Seinfeld,

KANYE WEST
@kanyewest
Seinfeld is the greatest show of all time. It's a masterpiece. Jerry Seinfeld and Larry David are geniuses. They're both Dragon Energy and so am I. They're my brothers.

kramerdaily • Following
kramerdaily Throwback to
thing Kanye has ever said..
13h
seinfeldsquad That one ti
Kanye had his head on stra
12h 25 likes Reply
View replies (2)
natushkk Lmao did he act
write this??
12h 29 likes Reply
View replies (6)

, and so I bet Kanye would love my The Yada Yada Haggadah, and one of the goals of this book is to get Kanye to read it and to meet Kanye, Hi Kanye, and also Ezra, Hi Ezra, and another way that I am like Kanye is that people have said that Kanye sort of went off the rails when his mother passed away, in his art and personality, and some people think I've sort of gone off the rails since my dad died, and some people think it was because Kanye's parent's death could have been prevented with some different choices, and so there was some guilt, and I probably shouldn't say that about Kanye, if I want to meet him, sometimes I feel I could have made different choices, too, and things would have been different for my dad, but I don't want to talk about that right now, or yet, or ever, I dunno, and here's what Lou Reed, a musician I love much more than Damon Albarn, sorry Damon, I do like your Mali Music, "Le Relax" though, and I love Lou as much as Ezra is how much I love Lou, and Lou said about Kanye before Lou died in one of his last published writings, if not even his last, I don't want to Google the fact, I just want to feel the feeling, and it was that, "People say this album is minimal, And yeah, it's minimal, But the parts are maximal, Take "Blood on the Leaves": there's a lot going on there: horns, piano, bass, drums, electronic effects, all rhythmically matched — towards the end of the track, there's now twice as much sonic material, But Kanye stays unmoved while this mountain of sound grows around him, Such an enormous amount of work went into making this album, Each track is like making a movie, Actually, the whole album is like a movie, or a novel — each track segues into the next, This is not individual tracks sitting on their own island, all alone, Very often, he'll have this very monotonous section going and then, suddenly —"BAP BAP BAP BAP" — he disrupts the whole thing and we're on to something new that's absolutely incredible, That's architecture, that's structure — this guy is seriously smart, He keeps unbalancing you, He'll pile on all this sound and then suddenly pull it away, all the way to complete silence, and then there's a scream or a beautiful melody, right there in your face, That's what I call a sucker punch, He seems to have insinuated in a recent New York Times interview that My Beautiful Dark, Twisted Fantasy was to make up for stupid shit he'd done, And now, with this album, it's "Now that you like me, I'm going to make you unlike me," It's a dare, It's braggadoccio, "I Am a God" — I mean, with a song title like that, he's just begging people to attack him, I have never thought of music as a challenge — you always figure, the audience is at least as smart as you are, You do this because you like it, you think what you're making is beautiful, And if you think it's beautiful, maybe they'll think it's beautiful, When I did Metal Machine Music, New York Times critic John Rockwell said, "This is really challenging," I never thought of it like that, I thought of it like, "Wow, if you like guitars, this is pure guitar, from beginning to end, in all its variations, And you're not stuck to one beat," That's what I thought, Not, "I'm going to challenge you to listen to something I made," I don't think West means that for a second, either, You make stuff because it's what you do and you love it, That explains the jump-cuts that are all over this record, Over and over, he sets you up so well — something's just got to happen — and he gives it to you, he hits you with these melodies, (He claims he doesn't have those melodic choruses anymore — that's not true, That melody the strings play at the end of "Guilt Trip," it's so beautiful, it makes me so emotional, it brings tears to my eyes,) But it's real fast cutting — boom, you're in it, Like at the end of "I Am a God," anybody else would have been out, but then pow, there's that coda with Justin Vernon, "Ain't no way I'm giving up," Un-fucking-believable, It's fantastic, Or that very repetitive part in "Send It Up" that goes on five times as long as it should and then it turns into this amazing thing, a sample of Beenie Man's "Stop Live in a De Pass," And it works, It works because it's beautiful — you either like it or you don't — there's no reason why it's beautiful, I don't know any musician who sits down and thinks about this, He feels it, and either it moves you too, or it doesn't, and that's that," and also that, "'Hold My Liquor' is just heartbreaking, and particularly coming from where it's coming from — listen to that incredibly poignant hook from a tough guy like Chief Keef, wow, At first, West says "I can hold my liquor" and then he says "I can't hold my liquor," This is classic — classic manic-depressive, going back and forth, Or as the great Delmore Schwartz said, "Being a manic depressive is like having brown hair," "I'm great, I'm terrible, I'm great, I'm terrible," That's all over this record," and so what I would say is that there is something about minimalist words but maximalist output, or jump cutting between things in a sentence, the referencing, splicing, the William Burroughs cut-up maybe, and Burroughs believed in the power of magic and the supernatural was revealed by his cut-ups, that there was an underlying spiritual reality in the world, he said, "I would say that my most interesting experience with the earlier techniques was the realization that when you make cut-ups you do not get simply random juxtapositions of words, that they do mean something, and often that these meanings refer to some future event, I've made many cut-ups and then later recognized that the cut-up referred to something that I read later in a newspaper or a book, or something that happened, Perhaps events are pre-written and pre-recorded and when you cut word lines the future leaks out," and so besides jump cuts, is there something about believing you're a great artist and also that you're not, that you're unable to be grammatically correct sometimes, but still write good, that is Bipolar, Charles Bukowski says, "Bad writers tend to have the self-confidence, while the good ones tend to have self-doubt," or maybe there is nothing special about it, as Virginia Woolf says, "Anyone moderately familiar with the rigours of composition will not need to be told the story in detail; how he wrote and it seemed good; read and it seemed vile; corrected and tore up; cut out; put in; was in ecstasy; in despair; had his good nights and bad mornings; snatched at ideas and lost them; saw his book plain before him and it vanished; acted people's parts as he ate; mouthed them as he walked; now cried; now laughed; vacillated between this style and that; now preferred the heroic and pompous; next the plain and simple; now the vales of Tempe; then the fields of Kent or Cornwall; and could not decide whether he was the divinest genius or the greatest fool in the world," but she was mentally ill too, and I just found this out while Googling about Lou Reed, he, too was Bipolar, exclamation point, Lou was bipolar too, wow, and so when I was listening to "Jesus" and "Beginning To See The Light" and "I'm Set Free" when I was twenty-one and having a manic episode, maybe Lou wrote his songs about one of his own, and here are the lyrics, "Jesus, help me find my proper place, Jesus, help me find my proper place, Help me in my weakness, 'Cos I'm falling out of grace, Jesus, Jesus, Well, I'm beginning to see the light, Well, I'm beginning to see the light, Some people work very hard, but still they never get it right, Well, I'm beginning to see the light, I wanna tell all you people, now, Now, now, baby, I'm beginning to see the light, Hey, now, baby, I'm beginning to see the light, Wine in the mornin', and some breakfast at night, Well, I'm beginning to see the light, Here we go again, playing the fool again, Here we go again, acting hard again, All right, Well, I'm beginning to see the light, I wanna tell you, ooh-oh-oh, Hey, now, baby, I'm beginning to see the light, It comes very softly now, I wore my teeth in my hands so I could miss the hell of a night, Hey, Well, I'm beginning to see the light, Now, now, now, now, now, now, now, now, now, baby, I'm beginning to see the light, now, It comes softer, Hey, now, baby, I'm beginning to see the light, I met myself in a dream, and I just want to tell you, Everything was alright, Hey, now, baby, I'm beginning to see the light, Here comes two of you, Which one will you choose, One is black and one is blue, Don't know just, what to do, Alright, Well, I'm beginning to see the light, oh, now, here she comes, Hey, yeah, baby, I'm beginning to see the light, Oh-ahhhh, Some people work very hard, But still they never get it right, Well, I'm beginning to see the light, Ah, it's getting a little softer, maybe, in there, Now, now, baby, I'm beginning to see the light, Ah, it's coming around again, Hey, now, now, now, baby, I'm beginning to see the light, One more time, There are problems in these times, But, woo, none of them are mine, Oh, baby, I'm beginning to see the light, Here we go again, I thought that you were my friend, Here we go again, I thought that you were my friend, How does it feel, to be loved, How does it feel, to be loved, I've been set free and I've been bound, To the memories of yesterday's clouds, I've been set free and I've been bound, And now I'm set free, I'm set free, I'm set free to find a new illusion, I've been blinded but, Now I can see, What in the world has happened to me, The prince of stories who walk right by me, And now I'm set free, I'm set free, I'm set free to find a new illusion, I've been set free and I've been bound, Let me tell you people what I found I saw my head laughing rolling on the ground, And now I'm set free, I'm set free, I'm set free to find a new illusion," and these songs they are like the Christian Gnostic quest Elaine Pagels lays out in The Gnostic Gospels, Jesus is sought for in confusion, found in a light within, and then you are free from your old illusions about your self and/or the world to make art about it, and she says "Whoever comes into direct, personal contact with the 'living One,' They argued that only one's own experience offers the ultimate criterion of truth, taking precedence over all secondhand testimony and all tradition," and that "They celebrated every form of creative invention as evidence that a person has become spiritually alive," and is Lou a Gnostic Christian, I dunno, all I know is that Lou and Kanye are even more connected than I thought before, but why did Kanye go on to also say that he and that Don Quixote Guy also have dragon energy and are brothers like with Larry David and Jerry Seinfeld,

ye @kanyewest

You don't have to agree with trump but the mob can't make me not love him. We are both dragon energy. He is my brother. I love everyone. I don't agree with everything anyone does. That's what makes us individuals. And we have the right to independent thought.

339K 12:33 PM - Apr 25, 2018

is there something wrong in channeling that Guy's energy or channeling Kanye's energy, this dragon energy, and is this a wayward sentence and book, not enough self-doubt to edit, and am I a travesty fool sad devil man now, or is Kanye tweeting about loving everyone, being brothers with everyone, is he just offering agape to Quixote DT, which is love to everyone, like Martin Luther King did, which is the ancient Greek notion of loving your neighbors and enemies like they are family, that "Along the way of life, someone must have sense enough and morality enough to cut off the chain of hate, This can only be done by projecting the ethic of love to the center of our lives," and, Ezra says, "In the ping-pong match of constant desire, I was never gonna get ahead, 'Cause I was looking in the mirror, Now we've got that sympathy, What I'm to you, You are to me, Let's go," and in order to get reconciliation and redemption from the ones who might otherwise engender mutual hate, you might need sympathy and agape, and that's also kind of what Carl Jung says in The Undiscovered Self about how we shadow the Other, right, "And just as the typical neurotic is unconscious of his shadow side, so the normal individual, like the neurotic, sees his shadow in his neighbor or in the man beyond the great divide, It has even become a political and social duty to apostrophize the progressivism of the one and the conservatism of the other as the very devil, so as to fascinate the outward eye and prevent it from looking at the individual life within," and as Kanye says in "Cudi Montage," "Both sides lose somebody, Somebody dies, somebody goes to jail," but it's not just over-identification with a political mass instead of insight into our individual soul, it's also over-identification with the rational and scientific and/or the over-identification with a mass-minded organized religion instead of the individuation resulting from a personal inner experience of the divine, Jung says, "If statistical reality is the only reality, then it is the sole authority, The religions, however, teach another authority opposed to that of the "world," The doctrine of the individual's dependence on God makes just as high a claim upon him as the world does, It may even happen that the absoluteness of this claim estranges him from the world in the same way he is estranged from himself when he succumbs to the collective mentality, He can forfeit his judgment and power of decision in the former case (for the sake of religious doctrine) quite as much as in the latter, This is the goal the religions openly aspire to unless they compromise with the State, When they do, I prefer to call them not "religions" but "creeds," A creed gives expression to a definite collective belief, whereas the word religion expresses a subjective relationship to certain metaphysical, extramundane factors, A creed is a confession of faith intended chiefly for the world at large and is thus an intramundane affair, while the meaning and purpose of religion lie in the relationship of the individual to God," and "The criterion here is not lip service to a creed but the psychological fact that the life of the individual is not determined solely by the ego and its opinions or by social factors, but quite as much, if not more, by a transcendent authority," and so I have to confess something now, I've been feeling the transcendent authority breaking into the statistical, I have, I'll explain, I'll tell you how I think the metaphysical extramundane factors are breaking into scientific rationalistic data, because have you ever noticed that if you put on a big shuffle of Spotify the songs sometimes soundtrack what is going on in your life in a synchronous way, have you noticed that, I notice it when I am writing this book, right now on Spotify shuffle, Ariana Grande is singing, "The light is coming to give back everything the darkness stole, You wouldn't let anybody speak and instead—, The light is coming to give back everything the darkness stole, You wouldn't let anybody speak and instead—, The light is coming to give back everything the darkness stole, You wouldn't let anybody speak and instead—, The light is coming to give back everything the darkness stole, You wouldn't let anybody speak and instead—", so what does that mean, and what if the algorithm, the thing that proves there is no God, only data, actually proves that God is here, God is in the algorithm, I say, and do you believe me, I don't care if you do or don't, because I believe, I believe, and Ralph Waldo Emerson says, "To believe your own thought, to believe that what is true for you in your private heart is true for all men, that is genius, Speak your latent conviction, and it shall be the universal sense; for the inmost in due time becomes the outmost, and our first thought is rendered back to us by the trumpets of the Last Judgment," and back to Jung, he says, "The seat of faith, however, is not consciousness but spontaneous religious experience, which brings the individual's faith into immediate relation with God," and what is that kind of experience, how do you have it, how do you know when it is something you've experienced, I wonder, and in VALIS, Philip K Dick's semi-autobiographical book about his theophany which could have also been a mental breakdown, his character "Fat believed that a streak of the irrational permeated the entire universe, all the way up to God or the ultimate mind, which lay behind it, He Wrote: From loss and grief the Mind has become deranged, Therefore as parts of the universe, the Brain, are partly deranged," but Fat believes that "The entire universe, possibly, is in the invisible process of turning into the Lord," and "With this process comes not just sentience but sanity," and that "GOD IS NO WHERE, GOD IS NOW HERE," and my friend Sandy, who wrote this great book The Last Good Obsession about the impact of reading on her life, you should check it out, she gave me VALIS after I had my mental breakdown/manic episode when I was twenty-one, it was the first book I read when I got out of the mental hospital after a month there, and I had believed that the world I was living in was insane and that my manic episode was healing me, but I was also confused, and told by the doctors that I was just sick, and so it's been almost fifteen years since then, and that book gave me hope then, that what I went through wasn't only negative, and some self-esteem after being locked up there, and not knowing what to think about all that had happened, and would I be able to write again, because I couldn't after I got out of the hospital, I literally couldn't write one word, that's how depressed I was, any word that went on the page had to be deleted because it felt so meaningless and wrong, but then I read VALIS, and I saw another perspective on mental breakdowns/manic episodes, and I was able to start writing again, and I got back into school in the fall semester and continued on, but then I forgot about it, VALIS, as the medicine worked, and I just went on, with life, the book, it receded, VALIS, from my daily memory, from my life, but I was still quite neurotic, and still am, but when I told Aaron this year, a friend I made this year, the year of my dad's death, about my experience with the Spotify, how I believe it is proof of an immediate relation with God, he recommended VALIS, without me talking about it, or remembering it, and what does that mean, out of all the books in the entire world, what does that mean, and that's why I've been re-reading it, and quoting it here, and the Jung book, I just picked it off my shelf, and I had never read it, it just wanted to be picked off the shelf out of all the books, this Jung book, from my shelf, and I had never read Jung before, until this year, and how could it be that it was just picked off my shelf, The Undiscovered Self on the undiscovered shelf, and Sandy had read up to this part of the book, with the Jung and Dick, and she texted me, "long stretches of quoted material, Kanye, Ezra, Reed, Jung, Dick, Quotes feel great and important to you, but You own the reader when YOU are on, See if there might be spots to insert yourself, reel reader back to you, Think on it," and I started to think on it more when I got into my car after that text and do you know what songs came on Spotify, "Low Lights" by Kanye spun into "Agape" by Nicholas Britell, and do you believe me now, and this is a 7,000 song playlist, out of all the songs, that's what happened, and then "Agape" went into "Mixtape" by Chance The Rapper, and that's what I am doing in this section is making a mixtape of other writers, copyright who cares, and those three songs in a row, do you believe me, that there is a spiritual world amidst the physical one, and you might think I am delusional or that the algorithm merely picked up the word agape from the writing about it before, or the Kanye from all the references to Kanye, but I don't think so, I think it's God, and what do you think of this testimony, and this is the lyrics to "Low Lights," "You want me to give you a testimony about my life, And how good he's been to me, I don't know what to tell you about him, I love him so much with all my heart, And my soul, with every bone in my body I love him so much, Because he's done so much for me, Every morning, every day of my life, I won't always be crying tears in the middle of the night, And I won't always have to wake up by myself, Wondering how I'm gonna get through the day, I won't always have to think about what I'm gonna do, And how I'm gonna, how I'm gonna make it, How I'm gonna get there, because he, he's gonna be there for me, Some day the sky above will open up, And he will reach out his hand and guide me through, oh yes he will, I won't always be crying these tears, I won't always be feeling so blue, Some day, he will open up the door for me and call my name, Some day he will, I don't know if anybody understands what that feels like, No matter what you've been through, Or where you've been he's always there, With his arms open wide accepting me for who I am and I love him so much, I couldn't do it without him I wouldn't want to, I'm crying now, it feels so good to be free, To be accepted for who you are and loved no matter what, Oh lord thank you, you are the joy of my life," and that's what I want to feel, accepted for who I am and loved no matter what, and back to Jung, "How are we to distinguish a genuine theophany from a mere hallucination on the part of the percipient, Here we must ask: Have I any religious experience and immediate relation to God, and hence that certainty which will keep me, as an individual, from dissolving in the crowd, To this question there is a positive answer only when the individual is willing to fulfill the demands of rigorous self-examination and self-knowledge, If he follows through his intention, he will not only discover some important truths about himself, but will also have gained a psychological advantage: he will have succeeded in deeming himself worthy of serious attention and sympathetic interest, He will have set his hand, as it were, to a declaration of his own human dignity and taken the first step towards the foundations of his consciousness – that is, towards the unconscious, the only accessible source of religious experience," and Phil K Dick says, "Fat realized that Stone had restored his Fat's spiritual life, Dr Stone had saved him; he was a master psychiatrist, Everything which Stone had said and done vis-a-vis Fat had a therapeutic basis, a therapeutic thrust, Whether the content of Stone's information was correct was not important; his purpose from the beginning had been to restore Fat's faith in himself, which had vanished when Beth left, which had vanished, actually, when he had failed to save Gloria's life years ago, Dr Stone wasn't insane, Stone was a healer, He held down the right job, Probably he healed many people and in many ways, He adapted his therapy to the individual, not the individual to the therapy," and back to Jung, wait back to Phil K Dick, this is mixtape lit, "Dr Stone had added the missing element to Fat, the element taken away from him, half-deliberately, by Gloria Knudson, who wished to take as many people with her as she could: self-confidence, 'You are the authority,' Stone had said, and that sufficed, 'I've always told people that for each person there is a sentence, a series of words, which has the power to destroy him, When Fat told me about Leon Stone I realized (this came years after the first realization) that another sentence exists, another series of words, which will heal the person," and is that sentence, are these the words that I am typing, are these the words, that sentence that is healing me, am I on my way to being healed, and what are the words that would heal our Donny Quixote, or the songs, and the people who follow him, sorry not sorry for all the Jung but he says, "What will the future bring, What will become of our civilization, and of man himself, Everywhere in the West there are subversive minorities who, sheltered by our humanitarianism and our sense of justice, hold the incendiary torches ready, with nothing to stop the spread of their ideas except the critical reason of a single, fairly intelligent, mentally stable stratum of the population, One should not, however, overestimate the thickness of this stratum, It varies from country to country in accordance with national temperament, Also, it is regionally dependent on public education and is subject to the influence of acutely disturbing factors of a political and economic nature, Taking plebiscites as a criterion, one could on an optimistic estimate put its upper limit at about 40 percent of the electorate, A rather more pessimistic view would not be unjustified either, since the gift of reason and critical reflection is not one of man's outstanding peculiarities, and even where it exists it proves to be wavering and inconstant, the more so, as a rule, the bigger the political groups are, The mass crushes out the insight and reflection that are still possible with the individual, and this necessarily leads to doctrinaire and authoritarian tyranny if ever the constitutional State should succumb to a fit of weakness, Rational argument can be conducted with some prospect of success only so long as the emotionality of a given situation does not exceed a certain critical degree, If the affective temperature rises above this level, the possibility of reason's having any effect ceases and its place is taken by slogans and chimerical wish-fantasies," and does that sound familiar, and the Jung and Dick and all the quotes were curated and contextualized and they are found objects and a primary source in this quest and so it must be mostly-fully read by you the reader if you are to understand what I the author want you to understand and I will not bend the knee, nor am I just FuckJerry, would Vic Berger call me FuckJerry, and I don't care, and would a judge say I have done enough to talk about why I put their words in my book in order not to make me unpublish this book, and what of using the dragon energy, is that OK, and here's some stuff from chapter 3 of my dad's Lincoln's Melancholy Shenk book, Shenk places a quote from Lincoln about seeing slaves in the context of Lincoln's philosophical journey in the midst of his melancholy, "They were the most cheerful and apparently happy creatures on board, One whose offence for which he had been sold was an over-fondness for his wife, played the fiddle almost continually; and the others danced, sang, cracked jokes, and played various games with cards from day to day, How true it is that 'G-d tempers the wind to the shorn lamb,' or in other words that He renders the worst of human conditions tolerable, while He permits the best, to be nothing better than tolerable," and Shenk says that Lincoln's youthful "Self-centered concern with his own suffering led him, slowly, to see and grapple with the suffering around him," and that "Lincoln said that he could kill himself, that he was not afraid to die, Yet, he said, he had an 'irrepressible desire' to accomplish something while he lived, He wanted to connect his name with the great events of his generation," and so accomplishing something great is a good thing, right, and so is self-centeredness if it leads to growth, and then altruism, and I think I determined that my dad is a Type Nine in the Enneagram, here's what a type 9 is, this is another found object, from the Enneagram Institute's public website, "THE PEACEMAKER, Enneagram Type Nine, The Easygoing, Self-Effacing Type: Receptive, Reassuring, Agreeable, and Complacent, Nines are accepting, trusting, and stable, They are usually creative, optimistic, and supportive, but can also be too willing to go along with others to keep the peace, They want everything to go smoothly and be without conflict, but they can also tend to be complacent, simplifying problems and minimizing anything upsetting, They typically have problems with inertia and stubbornness, At their Best: indomitable and all-embracing, they are able to bring people together and heal conflicts, Basic Fear: Of loss and separation, Basic Desire: To have inner stability "peace of mind", Enneagram Nine with an Eight-Wing: "The Referee", Enneagram Nine with a One-Wing: "The Dreamer," Key Motivations: Want to create harmony in their environment, to avoid conflicts and tension, to preserve things as they are, to resist whatever would upset or disturb them, When moving in their Direction of Disintegration (stress), complacent Nines suddenly become anxious and worried at Six, However, when moving in their Direction of Integration (growth), slothful, self-neglecting Nines become more self-developing and energetic, like healthy Threes, Healthy Levels, Level 1 (At Their Best): Become self-possessed, feeling autonomous and fulfilled: have great equanimity and contentment because they are present to themselves,

Paradoxically, at one with self, and thus able to form more profound relationships, Intensely alive, fully connected to self and others, Level 2: Deeply receptive, accepting, unselfconscious, emotionally stable and serene, Trusting of self and others, at ease with self and life, innocent and simple, Patient, unpretentious, good-natured, genuinely nice people, Level 3: Optimistic, reassuring, supportive: have a healing and calming influence—harmonizing groups, bringing people together: a good mediator, synthesizer, and communicator, Average Levels, Level 4: Fear conflicts, so become self-effacing and accommodating, idealizing others and "going along" with their wishes, saying "yes" to things they do not really want to do, Fall into conventional roles and expectations, Use philosophies and stock sayings to deflect others, Level 5: Active, but disengaged, unreflective, and inattentive, Do not want to be affected, so become unresponsive and complacent, walking away from problems, and "sweeping them under the rug," Thinking becomes hazy and ruminative, mostly comforting fantasies, as they begin to "tune out" reality, becoming oblivious, Emotionally indolent, unwillingness to exert self or to focus on problems: indifference, Level 6: Begin to minimize problems, to appease others and to have "peace at any price," Stubborn, fatalistic, and resigned, as if nothing could be done to change anything, Into wishful thinking, and magical solutions, Others frustrated and angry by their procrastination and unresponsiveness, Unhealthy Levels, Level 7: Can be highly repressed, undeveloped, and ineffectual, Feel incapable of facing problems: become obstinate, dissociating self from all conflicts, Neglectful and dangerous to others, Level 8: Wanting to block out of awareness anything that could affect them, they dissociate so much that they eventually cannot function: numb, depersonalized, Level 9: They finally become severely disoriented and catatonic, abandoning themselves, turning into shattered shells, Multiple personalities possible, Generally corresponds to the Schizoid and Dependent personality disorders," and that's from The Enneagram Institute dot com, and you can access it with the Internet, so I am putting it into this book, because I think it is my dad and also it lists Abraham Lincoln as an example of a type 9 and also because Lewis Hyde showed me that "Plato presents no ideas that he himself made up, only the recovered memory of things known before the great forgetting we call birth," and Confucius says, "I have transmitted what was taught to me without making up anything of my own, I have been faithful to and loved the Ancients," and the Hindu Srinivasa Ramanujan used to say that "An equation for me has no meaning unless it represents a thought of G-d," and here's an overview of The Traditional Enneagram also from that accessible website, and how it relates to the ancients and to God, I recommend going to this website, and study this, your type, and the Enneagram, it will make you feel strange, it will make you have a feeling in your stomach and in your mind, that you are not special, which is good, and it can help free you from ego, and then fear, and pain, and personality, and, and, and, it makes you feel strange but a good strange, like Ezra says, "Things have never been stranger, Things are gonna stay strange, I remember life as a stranger, but things change," and here it is, "Overview, The Enneagram of Personality Types is a modern synthesis of a number of ancient wisdom traditions, The Enneagram symbol has roots in antiquity and can be traced back at least as far as the works of Pythagoras, the philosophy behind the Enneagram contains components from mystical Judaism, Christianity, Islam, Taoism, Buddhism, and ancient Greek philosophy (particularly Socrates, Plato, and the Neo-Platonists)—all traditions that stretch back into antiquity, the Enneagram movement in

America has been based on the Enneagram of the Passions, the Enneagram of the Virtues, the Enneagram of the Fixations, the Enneagram of the Holy Ideas, To grasp the significance of these diagrams and the relationship between them, we must remember that the system was designed primarily to help elucidate the relationship between Essence and personality, or ego, In Ichazo's own words: '"We have to distinguish between a man as he is in essence, and as he is in ego or personality, In essence, every person is perfect, fearless, and in a loving unity with the entire cosmos; there is no conflict within the person between head, heart, and stomach or between the person and others, Then something happens: the ego begins to develop, karma accumulates, there is a transition from objectivity to subjectivity; man falls from essence into personality, Thus, Ichazo saw the Enneagram as a way of examining specifics about the structure of the human soul and particularly about the ways in which actual soul qualities of Essence become distorted, or contracted into states of ego, In developing his Enneagram theories, he drew upon a recurrent theme in Western mystical and philosophical tradition—the idea of nine divine forms, This idea was discussed by Plato as the Divine Forms or Platonic Solids, qualities of existence that are essential, that cannot be broken down into constituent parts, This idea was further developed in the third century of our era by the Neo-Platonic philosophers, particularly Plotinus in his central work, The Enneads, These ideas found their way from Greece and Asia Minor southward through Syria and eventually to Egypt, There, it was embraced by early Christian mystics known as the Desert Fathers who focused on studying the loss of the Divine Forms in ego consciousness, The particular ways in which these Divine forms became distorted came to be known as the Seven Deadly Sins: anger, pride, envy, avarice, gluttony, lust, and sloth, How the original nine forms, in the course of their travels from Greece to Egypt over the course of a century, became reduced to seven deadly sins remains a mystery, Another key influence Ichazo employed in developing these ideas comes from mystical Judaism, and particularly from the teachings of the Kabbala, Central to Kabbala is a diagram called Tree of Life (Etz Hayim in Hebrew), The Tree of Life is a said to be a map showing the particular patterns and laws by which God created the manifest universe, The diagram is composed of 10 spheres (Sefirot) connected by 22 paths in particular ways, Most significantly, Ichazo must have been aware of the Kabbalistic teaching that all human souls are 'sparks' that arise out of these spheres or emanations from the Kabbalistic Tree, (The first sphere, Keter, is reserved for the Messiah, leaving nine other spheres for the rest of us,) In the traditional teachings of the Kabbala, for instance, each of the great patriarchs of the Bible were said to be embodiments of the different spheres of the Tree, This teaching suggests that there are different kinds of souls—different emanations or facets of the Divine Unity, Ichazo's brilliant work was in discovering how these Divine Forms and their corresponding distortions connected with the Enneagram symbol and with the three Centers of human intelligence, Thinking, Feeling, and Instinct, He called the higher, essential qualities of the human mind the Holy Ideas, in accordance with western mystical tradition, Each Holy Idea also has a corresponding Virtue, The Virtues are essential qualities of the heart experienced by human beings when they are abiding in Essence, As a person loses awareness and presence, falling away from Essence into the trance of the personality, the loss of awareness of the Holy Idea becomes a person's Ego-fixation, and the loss of contact with the Virtue causes the person's characteristic Passion,

While everyone has the capacity to embody all of the Holy Ideas and Virtues, one pair of them is central to the soul's identity, so the loss if it is felt most acutely, and the person's ego is most preoccupied with recreating it, although in a futile, self-defeating way, See the diagram,

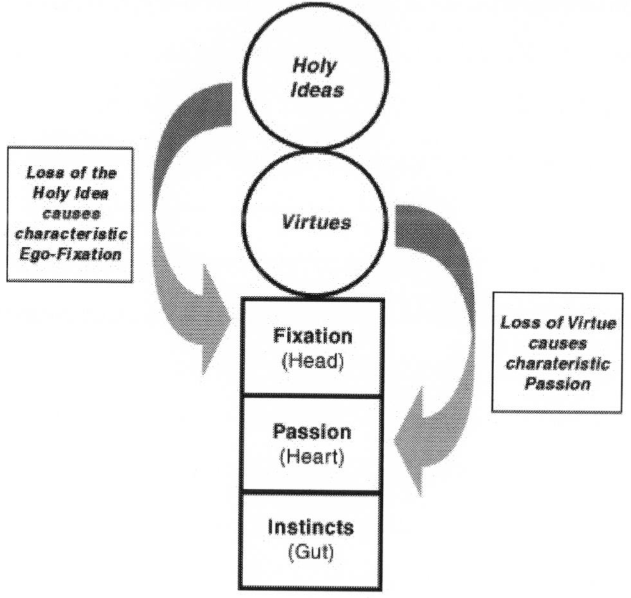

Relationship between Higher Essence Qualities and Ego Distortions

The Virtues, Passions, Holy Ideas, and Fixations, Thus, the Passions and Ego-fixations represent the ways that spiritual qualities become contracted into ego states, There are, according to Ichazo's theory, nine main ways that we lose our center and become distorted in our thinking, feeling, and doing, and are thus the nine ways that we forget our connection with the Divine, (The Passions can also be thought of as our untamed animal nature before it is transformed by contact from higher influences—awareness and Grace,) Because of this particular relationship between the higher qualities of the soul and their corresponding ego distortions, a person could, by using presence and awareness to recognize the pattern of their distortion—their characteristic passion and ego-fixation—come to recognize the quality of Essence that had been obscured, By remembering or contemplating the higher quality, balance could be restored, thus accelerating the person's awareness of themselves as Essence, Knowing one's "type" was a way to direct one's inner work to facilitate the transformative process, The Virtues describe the expansive, non-dual qualities of Essence experienced in a direct, felt way by a person abiding in their true nature, The Virtues are the natural expression of the awakened heart, We do not try to force ourselves to be 'virtuous'—rather, as we relax and become more present and awake, seeing through the fear and desire of the ego self, these qualities naturally manifest themselves in the human soul, An essential individual will be in contact with these [Virtues] constantly, simply by living in his body, But the subjective individual, the ego, loses touch with these Virtues, Then the personality tries to compensate by developing passions," The Passions represent an underlying emotional response to reality created by the loss of contact with our Essential nature, with the ground of our Being, with our true identity as Spirit or Essence, The underlying hurt, shame, and grief that this loss entails are enormous, and our ego is compelled to come up with a particular way of emotionally coping with the loss, This temporarily effective, but ultimately misguided coping strategy is the Passion, But because the Passion is a distortion of an inherent, essential Virtue, recognizing the Passion can help us to restore the Virtue, In a related way, the Virtue of each type can also be seen as an antidote to its Passion and as a focal point for the type's positive traits, By recalling the Virtue in a state of presence, the Passion can be gradually transformed, The restoration of the virtue and the transformation of the passion is an extremely important part of the spiritual use of the Enneagram, The Holy Ideas represent specific non-dual perspectives of Essence—particular ways of knowing and recognizing the unity of Being, They are what naturally arises in a clear, quiet mind when a person is present and awake, seeing reality as it actually is, The loss of a Holy Idea leads to a particular ego-delusion about the self or reality, called the type's Ego-fixation, Through the ego-fixation, the person is trying to restore the balance and freedom of the Holy Idea, but from the dualistic perspective of ego, cannot, Again, understanding the perspective of our type's Holy Idea functions as an antidote to the ego-fixation, The non-dual perspective of our true nature is restored as we see through the particular delusions of our type, and Kurt Vile's "One Trick Pony" was playing while I was copying this out, and it goes, "Loved you all a long, long while, Looked down into a deep, dark well, Called all your names, They echoed down for miles and miles, And all that other mystical, well, never-you-mind, Loved them all through many a lifetime, Some are gone but some still strong, Some are weird as hell but we love 'em, Some are one trick ponies but we embrace 'em, 'Cause I've always had a soft spot for repetition," and "Looked long into the length of a tunnel, Called all your names, And we was tripping out 'cause we needed a way out, And all them other crystalline mystic rationalizations, Loved them all right down to my soul," and "And I'd give my left, nevermind, for one big synchronized smile, Some are one trick ponies but so am I, Round 'em up into a mixed bag bundle of love now, yeah, Loved them all a long, long tick, And it's four, five, six, Prevent your schtick," and here's how to prevent your schtick, your repetition, though we love you for it anyway:

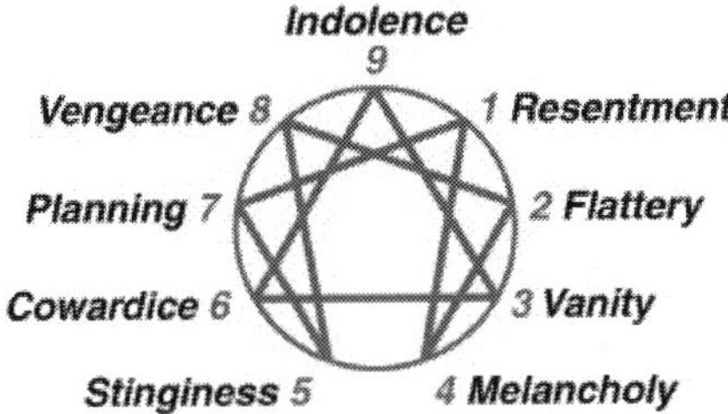
Indolence
9
1 Resentment
2 Flattery
3 Vanity
4 Melancholy
Stinginess 5
Cowardice 6
Planning 7
Vengeance 8

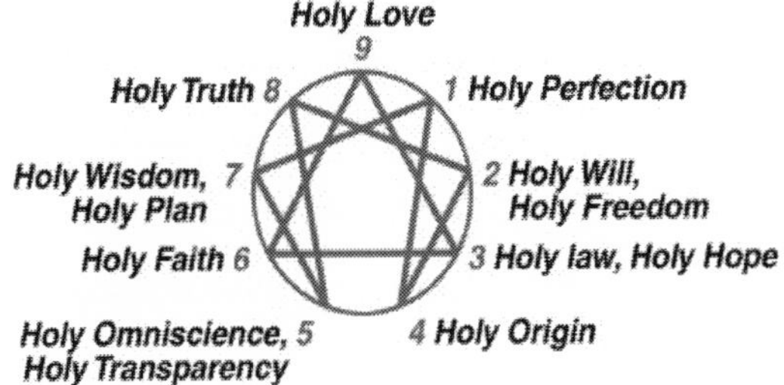
Holy Love
9
1 Holy Perfection
2 Holy Will,
Holy Freedom
3 Holy law, Holy Hope
4 Holy Origin
Holy Omniscience, 5
Holy Transparency
Holy Faith 6
Holy Wisdom, 7
Holy Plan
Holy Truth 8

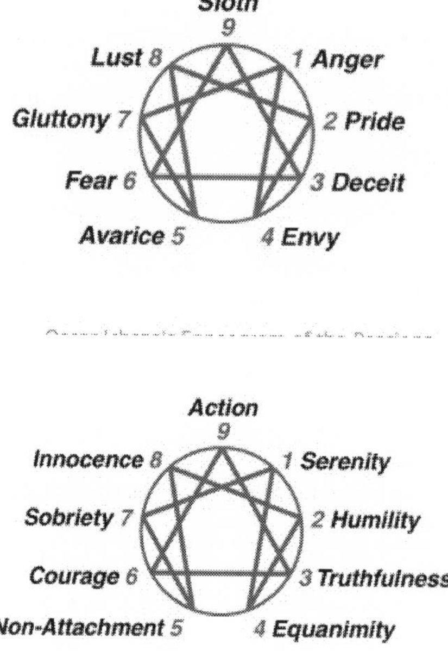

Oscar Ichazo's Enneagram of the Virtues

And Lewis Hyde says of the ego that "DH Lawrence spoke of egoisme a deux of so many married couples, people who get just so far in the expansion of the self and then close down for a lifetime, opening up not for the group, nor the gods," And the Enneagram Institute is copyrighted but also believes in G-d, and is Christian, and Lewis Hyde could show them that "A long tradition in Christianity also takes the fruits of human creativity to have nonhuman origins and thus assumes that they cannot be bought or sold (nor can they really be forged, plagiarized, or stolen), 'Knowledge is a gift of G-d, therefore it cannot be sold,' To sell knowledge was to traffic in the sacred and thus to engage in the sin of simony," but this is also community-oriented not just theological, like how Bach dedicates a piece "To the highest G-d in his honor,/ To my neighbor that he may instruct himself from it," and so I hope you, reader, will find something valuable in the Enneagram, and visit the Institute's public website, and I want to tell you how my dad fell from healthy levels of the other Gram, the Enneagram, the more helpful Gram, to unhealthy levels but how I didn't figure it out until he died, I didn't discover the Enneagram fully until he died, so I failed him like I sometimes imagine Kanye feels like he failed his mother by prioritizing cosmetic surgery over health, or how I prioritized other things in LA like eating good food instead of finding a cure for my dad, but for now I guess I better make more of the book my writing, instead of other peoples', so I don't get into trouble with the fair use laws, or whatever, I don't care, does anyone, should anyone, is Copyright the next Lenny Bruce, the next Allen Ginsburg, and Lawrence Lessig says, "If strictly enforcing the massively expanded 'property' rights granted by copyright fundamentally changes the freedom within this culture to cultivate and build upon our past, then we have to ask whether this property should be redefined," because "The irony astounds, We win the political struggle against state control so as to re-entrench control in the name of the market, We fight battles in the name of free speech, only to have those tools turned over to the arsenal of those who would control speech," and so what about a book that is full of copyrighted characters who are fighting to release Copyrightidium from the world, it would be like a Marvel Civil War, and some copyrighted characters would be on the side of the law, when they shouldn't be, like Superman, I bet Superman would think he should protect Copyrightidium, while Iron Man and Rick and Morty would be against it, they like fan fiction, everyone loves fan fiction these days, open the floodgates, free Mickey Mouse, the Copyrightidium, time's up, Mouse, and David Shields "says" "Warhol's Marilyn Monroe silk screens and his Double Elvis work as metaphors because their images are so common in the culture that they can be used as shorthand, as other generations would have used, say, the sea, Anything that exists in the culture is fair game to assimilate into a new work," and OK, so I will put in some of my writing, here's something from my Columbus-that guy book, where I imagine an ego-less catharsis moment for that guy/Columbus without even knowing that much about the ego at that time, crazy, right, FAKE HISTORY: The Story Of How Christopher Columbus Was Treated Very Very Unfairly, where Don Christopher Columbus is also Don Quixote and also Donny Quixote, aka, That Guy, and so I started that book with this epigraph, "I write to inform you how in thirty-three days I crossed from the Canary Islands to the Indies, and there I found many islands filled with people without number, and of them all I have taken possession, and nobody objected" -Don Christopher Columbus, and "History is like a sacred thing: it must be truthful, and wherever truth is, there God is; but despite this, there are some who write and toss off books as if they were fritters," -Don Quixote, and "I know words, I have the best words," -Don That Guy, and the first chapter goes like this, Introduction: Hello, My Name Is Christopher Columbus, And I Am The Greatest Explorer There Ever Was Or Ever Will Be, And yet, never in history has a man, who has been so great, who has done so much, for himself, and for so many people, and for the world, frankly, been treated so unfairly, for never will there be a circumstance to Trump what has happened to me, your fair narrator, the Admiral of the Ocean Sea, Don Christopher Columbus, I am dictating this account, on April 20th, in the year 1506, from a bed of convalescence, in my humble mansion in Valladolid, to my loyal friend, my beautiful slave, and an alien to our world—Anacabo, Fetch the latrine, Quickly, It's coming quick, Quicker, please, I can't hold it any— Too late, I've soiled myself again, these damn bowels of mine, they've been ruined by exertion and exploit, the likes of which the world has never seen, and likely never will again, And for what, For my privileges, my reputation, my glory, for it all to be stripped away from me by the King of Spain and his feckless court of landlubbing fawners, Many of you have heard the rumors that have been promulgated, the canards that have been disseminated, they say Christopher Columbus was just lucky, he was actually greedy and cruel, and paranoid and delusional, and a self-aggrandizing narcissist, and a shameless self-promoter, and a lying reprobate, and a barbaric monster, who was bad in bed, but that is all fake history, Fake history, people, A fake history conceived by the enemy, the enemies of me, and of you, the enemies of the people, of all people, not just of the Europeans, or the Indians, enemies of all our species, of all humankind in fact, whom I vanquished once, and by reading this true history, you, future human, may be able to vanquish them, too, when they come again, for they will come ag— No, I did it again, Anacabo, I pooped myself again, Bring me another pair of drawers, I may be covered in my own feces, but Christopher Columbus is not full of poop, and he was not a bad guy, like many have said, he really wasn't, and he was not a piece of poop either, do you hear me, do you hear me when I say that, that I'm not a piece of poop, and I say it with great certainty, because if Columbus were poop, he wouldn't just be a piece of it, he'd be the biggest poop there ever was or ever will be, OK, we all clear on that, how Columbus isn't poop, but if he was, he wouldn't be just a piece, he'd be huge, he'd be the best and most important poop in history, we're clear, OK, good, let's start the book," and it ended like this, "The Final Voyage And How I Met Anacabo And Also How I Saved All The People Of Earth

From These Beings From The Sky, It's A Big Chapter In My Life And In The Book And It Should Be In The History Books, Too, For Sure, So Read To The End, It is true I am getting very tired, I have done a lot with my life, including writing this great history book about me, and it has taken a lot out of me, but I will rally my formidable energies and spare no fiber of my being to share what happened on the final voyage with my son, Ferdinand, and how I met Anacabo, who is here with me still, dutifully writing this all down, as my slave and friend and lover, and I'm sure, even though I can no longer see her, because I am blind, due to what happened on the final voyage, but I am sure that she's here, and I'm sure that she is writing these words down, and that these words will be read one day, because I believe in my reality and that it is more real than anyone else's, and so what I am about to tell you has never been told to anyone, and if it is not shared by Anacabo, it will be lost to history, which would not only be very sad for me, but it would also be very sad for you, if you can't read this, though I am sure you are reading this, and I guess I am really feeling the seasickness of Columbus' words right now, it is very hard to continue speaking, the wild seesawing has taken a great toll on me, speaking my words has been very hard for me, the syntax, up down, up down, and all about, back forth, back forth, to the starboard and the port sides of the words, so erratic, without any coherency, and in apparent insanity, and I'm sure the repetitive diction is also very bad, it's bad, very bad, and it must signify some sort of great cognitive decline, that must be so, and it must be so tiring for you, too, dear reader, but bear with me, for I must finish, for I fear the end is near, and so I must tell you what happened, My son and I, we sailed back to Asia slash the New World, it really doesn't matter which of those it was, it really doesn't matter, I'm tired of that argument, it is very tiresome to me, that ceaseless argument, and I am very tired, do you not hear me, when I tell you that I am tired of talking about that, and that I am very tired, do you not hear me, Do not make me talk about that anymore, I have more important things to share now, and what that is, is what was it, damnit, I am so, it was that what we found when we went back there, ahh, I am getting so tired, I can barely bear it, what it was, was that I was trying to, I can't remember what I said earlier, did I tell you before, chapters back, that the people when we landed, they said we were "beings from the sky," did I say that, I may not have said that, but it is what happened, they believed we were beings from the sky, an alien species, and I thought it was a very dumb thing to say, frankly, but I guess also understandable, because I am so unique, and so special, and so it did make some sense, because I was basically a different species than all of them, because I am so special, but it made a lot more sense on the final voyage, when we got back there, and we got shipwrecked and stranded on an island, and it was a bad situation, it was very bad, and it didn't look good, and there was a chance, a real chance, that my son and I would die there, on that cursed shipwrecked island, that we would vanish from the world, and from history potentially, but the Indians they were very nice to us, and they brought us food and they dressed our wounds, and it was weird because we had always been more powerful than them, and they had always been at our mercy, but this time, I was at their mercy, for we were so weak, even weaker than I am right now, and they could have slaughtered us all if they wanted to, and I realized then that sometimes the meek are not meeker than the strong, even though they are the meek and I am the strong, and always have been and will be, and I am so tired right now, of saying that, and of being me, but I must say that I realized then that under different circumstances different things could have happened in history, and I wondered if maybe I had come to the New World slash Asia, it doesn't matter, at a different time, perhaps a few hundred years earlier, there may have been another civilization there, for some reason, the name "Mayans" came to my mind, and I wondered what would happen if our civilization collided with a hypothetical civilization called the Mayans, when they were at their peak, like we were at ours when we came to Asia slash the New World, I'm tired of, I'm so very tired, but I think we still would have been the winners, because we win, win, man, I am so tired, so very tired of being me, but what I must say is, I was thinking then it just goes to show when two worlds collide there is much conflict and it can lead to the loss of a people and a culture and that that could have been us, maybe, And suddenly I thought of an even bigger thing, as I was weak and shipwrecked, and more tired than I am now, which is the most tired I have ever been, so maybe I am more meek now than then, and maybe I am meek as well as strong sometimes, I do not know, what I'm saying is that I thought then, what if another species, a non-human species, what if it came not from somewhere on Earth, not a proverbial New World, but an actual New World, I thought what if this species came from another planet, and they landed on Earth, would they be stronger than us humans, even if all of us realized that we were one people finally, and fought together for the first time as one, and there was no more petty tribalism, just one race, and would we win, or would these aliens overrun us, like I had overrun the Indians, and how Dad and me had been overrun by the Adornos, and how the Indians could have overrun me and my son while shipwrecked and at their mercy, and I grew very scared, but then I thought that me and the humans would definitely win, and that I would survive this shipwreck and be rescued with my son, like Dad and me had survived the Adornos, and I would live on to write a great book about it, because I was destined for greatness, and so is humanity, and nothing can stop us, because all we do is, you know what we do, I don't have to say it, I'm so tired, I'm so very tired, of being me, but I must tell you what happened next, I must, and I will, for I am me, I am Columbus, Because just then, from the sky, came a being, a very beautiful green being, with skin that was somehow even more beautiful than my white skin, but the skin, though, it changed color to other colors, it was a mixture of all colors, it went to black and then to white, like mine, and brown, like the natives, which I realize was as beautiful as my skin then, and back to green and it was all colors and none at all, and then this being was a female and then a male and then neither and both and something else, and all of them were equally good, and it declared that its name was Anacabo, and even though she wishes that I refer to her as a they, I still call her a her, call me old-fashioned, and she calls me her Don, or her Donny Quixote, and she is a being from the sky, an alien, and she, sorry, they, I'll say they from now on, I promise, because I love they, and they taught me so much, and so I will share what I learned from them, the aliens, for Anacabo is not just Anacabo, Anacabo is all of their species at all times, and each of them are all of the others, at the same times, too, for they are one species, one kind, and they are all they, for all time, and the learning of that was more important than anything I had ever done, and that is what is finally humbling me now, I can feel a great humbling now, and I am humbled now, I am humbled, As I lay here, on my deathbed, as I lay dying, for they have humbled me, they have humbled they, it is so nice, thank you, they, it is humbling to realize they were also they, the beings from the sky, the Indians and the Europeans and Amerigo and the special counsel and the sovereigns and my sons and the Indian that was coughed on that was loved, and Filipa, and Father, and Brother, and the Indians, were the Indians said yet, they should be called the Taínos, and Anacabo, and Columbus, they are all they, and as they lie down to die someday, which is all days, they will look down on who they were, as part of a continuum of one they, that has hurt and helped the same they, and they will know this now, at their death, as they die, as they die, right now, As well as here, at the end of this book, of which hopefully a good time reading was had, or, if skipped to the end, a good time reading will be had, and the learning to live together was or will be done, and that a celebration of that with a holiday was or will be started, and maybe it also was or will be a paid holiday used to elect new leaders, and its name was or will be decided, by they, bye, they," and so will there be catharsis with this guy, my dad thought so, he promised our neighbor, a neighbor told me this story, that when That Guy was humbled one day, which my dad was sure he would be one day, he promised to drink a bottle of champagne with this neighbor, and this neighbor was so sad that he wouldn't be able to drink the bottle of champagne with my dad when that guy was gone, because he looked up to my dad, and so maybe this guy won't be humbled, we wondered in our minds, maybe, after my dad's funeral, when the neighbor was at my parents' house, for the shiva, and I said I'd come back to drink a bottle of champagne with this neighbor, and I will do it, I will, we will all drink champagne, drink the champagne, drink the champagne, and it will taste so sweet, like champagne has never tasted before, like Antoniette is gone or the second World War is over, and this garbage time will be over, even though incoherence is beautiful, garbage words might be over, even though incoherence is beautiful, and I am Albert Ayler, "Ghosts," and we can go back to good times, and good writing, and good speaking, no run on sentences, perfect grammar, and words and honor will mean something again, and Joyce says in Ulysses, "To learn one must be humble, But life is the great teacher," and James Hollis says, "One of the reasons we revere discoverers, explorers and pioneers in the physical world, and those who push back the limits of mind or aesthetic expression, is because they carry for us the archetype of the hero, that complex of energy in all of us that naturally seeks to pose itself against the regressive powers of fear and lethargy in the service of individuation," and here's some stuff from Shenk's/my dad's Lincoln book about his mental illness, "Today 'self-made' has rather narrow, even cartoonish connotations, applying mainly to people who make fabulous amounts of money in some idiosyncratic enterprise, In Lincoln's time, the word had just been coined (its first use is credited to Henry Clay in 1832), and its meaning can be compared with the way that 'hippie' went from an explosive term to a tired relic in a few short decades, Like those shaggy-haired creatures of the sixties, self-made men in the early nineteenth century were widely understood to be a wedge undercutting tradition, For most of history, people had been 'made,' primarily, by the circumstances of their birth, Children of farmers had grown up to work the land, But a new economic reality, allowed young people to construct lives of their own," and "A new culture of achievement demanded a regimen of self-culture or 'self-help'" such as "Society is so constructed that it's a law of necessity that you must push, That is if you would be something and somebody," yet "Tom Lincoln, later portrayed as a shiftless ne'er-do-well, was in fact, a perfectly respectable man at a time when it was perfectly respectable to have modest aims, In his son's world, this kind of satisfaction was somehow suspect, if it kept you from pushing," and that "'Life in our republic,' CB Hayden explained, 'has all the excitement of an olympic contest, A wide arena is thrown open, the resulting rancor, excitement, and anxiety produced sickness of hope deferred, ambition maddened by defeat, avarice rendered desperate by failure,'" and that before 1810 the United States had only a few asylums but by 1860 most states had one or several, and "The irony is that by seeking what he wanted in life, Lincoln put himself in a position where he might lose everything, He might be consigned to misery, failure, perhaps madness," and so maybe this garbage time is based on that garbage time, or isn't that different from all garbage times, question mark, and also part of this garbage time is that it's pretty much impossible to mess up your reputation with bad press these days though, at least it seems that way for that guy, some people are probably thinking I am worried about getting bad press for this book and its poor writing and hurting my reputation as a writer and as a person, being humiliated, or litigated, talking about myself in this crazy way, and not really editing my writing, and putting in copyrighted material, and what is a defiant act of writing, is it that, "In a time where publishers and 'creative' writers insist on realist prose printed on paper, pasting a Shakespeare poem into a JPEG file counts as a defiant concept of writing," or something else, and what kind of reckless stunt is this, with the outing yourself as a mentally ill person, New New Narrative or maybe not, but yeah, don't you want to get jobs in the future, and support a family, and what are you trying to pull off here and make people read, and buy your book, and maybe you are thinking, reader, you should write a bad comment in the Amazon reviews, and that's fine, too, even though I said don't do it above, but the thing I am truly scared of is not all that, the thing I am scared of is not getting any bad press at all, or any reviews at all, it is that if no one quotes this part of the sentence or any part of the sentence and critiques it or even reads it, that would be the only bad thing that could happen to me, if no one reads my words, but David Shields "says" "Contemporary narration is the account of the manufacturing of the work, not the actual work," and so many people have not read so many of my words, that's what it's like to be a failed screenwriter, and to smell bad, and I read a poet from my hometown who won The Pulitzer Prize for his book of poems, called, Failure, Philip Schultz, and here's what he says, "The One Truth, After dreaming of radiant thrones for sixty years, praying to a god he never loved for strength, for mercy, after cocking his thumbs, in the pockets of his immigrant schemes, while he parked cars during the day and drove a taxi all night, after one baby was born dead and he carved the living one's name in windshield snow in the blizzard of 1945, after scrubbing piss, blood, and vomit off factory floors from midnight to dawn, then filling trays with peanuts, candy, and cigarettes in his vending machines all day his breath a wheezing suck and bellowing gasp in the fist of his chest, after washing his face, armpits and balls in cold back rooms, hurrying between his hunger for glory and his fear of leaving nothing but debt, after having a stroke and falling down factory stairs, his son screaming at him to stop working and rest after being knocked down by a blow he expected all his life, his son begging forgiveness, his wife crying his name, after looking up at them straight from hell, his soul withering in his arms, is this what failure is, to end where he began, no one but a deaf dumb God to welcome him back, his fists pounding at the gate, is this the one truth, to lie in a black pit at the bottom of himself, without enough breath to say goodbye or ask forgiveness," and I hope that's not so, I hope as a fellow failure that is not the one truth, but then again, another thing about this time, is that you can also have your reputation destroyed in a second, on the Internet, or by litigation, and so maybe this sentence will get my reputation destroyed on the Internet or by litigation because American copyright is so crazy, even though Thomas Jefferson said, “The field of knowledge is the common property of mankind,” and Benjamin Franklin pirated books from Europe and published them in America, and he said easy access to books has “Made the common tradesmen and farmers as intelligent as most gentlemen from other countries,” and dominion was defined by the British justice system to mean “The right of ownership that sole and despotic dominion which one man claims and exercises over the external things of the world, in total exclusion of the right of any other individual in the universe,” which is the same word John Adams chose to describe the political power Britain held over America, despots opposing liberty, and so all this monkeying with other peoples’ words in a book instead of the safe harbors of the Internet, perhaps this could be an internet article instead of a book and it’d be fine, why is it that you can put anything you want into an Internet website without copyright problems but if you put the same things into a book it’s now a copyright problem, like look at this Instagram post,

AT&T LTE
1:24 PM
Instagram

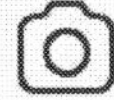

subliming.jpg
BE PATIENT TOWARD ALL THAT
IS UNSOLVED IN YOUR HEART
AND TRY TO LOVE THE
QUESTIONS THEMSELVES, LIKE
LOCKED ROOMS AND LIKE
BOOKS THAT ARE NOW
WRITTEN IN A VERY
FOREIGN TONGUE.
DO NOT NOW
SEEK THE
ANSWERS, WHICH
CANNOT BE GIVEN TO
YOU BECAUSE YOU
WOULD NOT BE ABLE
TO LIVE THEM. AND
THE POINT IS, TO LIVE
EVERYTHING. LIVE THE
QUESTIONS NOW.
PERHAPS YOU WILL
THEN GRADUALLY,
WITHOUT
NOTICING IT,
LIVE ALONG SOME
DISTANT DAY INTO
THE ANSWER.

Liked by edieparkerflower and 20,803 others
subliming.jpg Rainer Maria Rilke

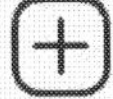

see you

can just Meme anything on the Internet, remix quote it, and it's OK, but so will doing the same thing as a book will it hurt my life in some many ways, though I am not scared of that right now, the only thing I am scared of right now is painting myself into a corner sentence-wise in the sense of not being able to continue to string this sentence together in the way that I am doing it, and the Kanye music going off, "You too wild, you too wild," or the coffee running out, or not being able to think of more things to write, and I believe Maggie Nelson, the inexpressible is contained—inexpressibly—in the expressed, says ol' Wittgenstein, and she says in the beginning before questioning it, this paradox is, quite literally, why I write, or how I feel able to keep writing, too, even if it is quite a mediocre way, let's be honest, it's bad, but the point is it has to be continued, it's all I have going for me at the literal moment, and I can't paint myself into a period corner, that is the only fear I have at the moment, a period corner that ends the sentence, and my friend Aaron, who wrote an awesome book called Jobs of The Great Misery, gave me this book by Bruce Boone, from New Narrative, and he says, "In the normal course of things it is the cerebellum that masters emotions, To write in order to give the reader access to heights of transport is to reverse things and to harness the intellect into the service of emotion, To elicit emotions, you need a kind of false subject that will make the reader comfortable, Traditionally it was the work first of shamanism and now it's the task of psychoanalysis to unravel that false 'I,' the work of writing is the opposite - to reconstitute this phony 'I'" if shamanism is well known for accessing emotions, is it any less famous for possessing certain tools of rationality," and that "Shamanism discovered how to close the gap between emotion and communication, ineffable and supreme ecstasy, but an intelligible message as well, this is a way of making what is incomprehensible comprehensible," and right now it is late May and I am reading Lewis Hyde's The Gift, and thinking about how, "The gifts of the inner world must be accepted as gifts in the outer world, Where gifts have no public currency, therefore, where the gift as a form of property is neither recognized nor honored, our inner gifts will find themselves excluded from the very commerce which is their nourishment, Or to say the same thing from a different angle, where commerce is exclusively a traffic in merchandise, the gifted cannot enter into the give-and-take that ensures the livelihood of their spirit," and I am thinking about Gnostic Christians versus Orthodox Christians versus Romans, and Vampire Weekend's "My Christian heart, Cannot withstand, The thundering arena, I'll see you when, The violence ends, For now, ciao, ciao, Bambina," and the part in the song with the ambulance/police siren noises, felt like ambulances coming to get me during a hypomanic episode, "No time to discuss it, Can't speak when the waves, Reach our house upon the dunes, Time cannot be trusted, When the police come, They always come too soon, Life felt like heaven today," and the personal and the political is also like the psychological and the spiritual, and what attracted me to the Enneagram is that fusion, of spirituality/religion and psychology/psychiatry, the mind and brain with the soul and the spirit, and I thought my dad was an Enneagram 6 when he was really a 9, it was that he was so unhealthy he looked like a 6, as 9s go to 6 in distress, and here's what helped me figure it out, too late, more from that Enneagram Institute website, "These types are actually frequently mistyped, Sixes and Nines are both concerned with security and with maintaining some kind of status quo situation, They are both family-oriented, and both tend to take modest views of themselves, Their affect, however, is the easiest way to distinguish them, In short, Nines like to remain easy-going and unflappable, Nines work steadily at their tasks, but show little sign of being upset by the day's ups and downs, Sixes, on the other hand, cannot easily disguise their feelings, They get more easily worked-up and rattled by mishaps, While Nines can remain silent within their own inner peace, Sixes need to vent with others periodically to discharge their fears and doubts, Sixes are more obviously nervous and defensive when they believe there are problems, Nines remain strangely bland in the face of problems, although beneath the pleasant surface of average Nines, there is stubborn resistance and an unwillingness to be upset or troubled by conflicts or problems, Sixes tend to be suspicious of unknown people and situations–they need to test people before they let them get close, Nines may be protected by the disengagement of their attention, but they tend to be trusting of others–almost to a fault, Of course, under stress, when moving in their Direction of Disintegration, Nines will begin to act out some of the behaviors of average Sixes, and for this reason, some Nines will mistype themselves as Sixes, But such periods of overt anxiety generally do not last long, As soon as possible, Nines revert to their more easy going approach to things," and so I have been dancing around actually talking about my dad as more than a universal type, I've been doing a dance around archetypes versus the person, the universal versus the memoir, and what does EM Forster mean when he says, "All literature tends towards a condition of anonymity," It 'wants not to be signed,' Literature is a living thing distinct from the living person who made it," and Lewis Hyde says that "Interest in the author's personality, that is a modern concern," and Forster also said that "True artists, on the other hand (Dante, Shakespeare) invite us to attend not to themselves," and so is there nothing universal in a memoir, and Ben Lerner wonders if anything can be universal that is written by one person, and David Shields "says" "The term memoir comes from the Indo-European idea of mer-mer, "to exhaustingly ponder," and "Truth in a memoir is achieved not through a recital of actual events; it's achieved when the reader comes to believe that the writer is working hard to engage with the experience at hand, What matters is the larger sense that the writer is able to make of what happened," and Herman Melville put astrology in Moby-Dick, and so I want to lay out one more typing, going back to Numerology, here's something about my dad being a Numerology Master Number 22, "Masterful teaching and inspired practical ideas, As a 22/4 Life Path, you're destined for material and financial success when you focus your energy on making a significant, inspired improvement to the way we think and lead our everyday lives, To engage fully in the 22 energy, you must pull your focus out of the details and into the big picture, Have others provide the support you need to expand your enterprise, You've an innate tendency to act on what you 'know is right' without concern for those around you, making you challenging to live with or work for, Surrendering your 'staff position' for the CEO's job can bring about a huge adjustment in the ways you think and traditionally operate, You'll be challenged to find the courage to let go of micro-managing the details and move your project, career, or enterprise into the Big Leagues, where it belongs, If you're working more in the 4 energy, you'll be exhausted rather than energized," and "LIFE PATH 22/4 – MASTER BUILDER, The lesson you must learn is the ultimate mastery of combining the highest ideals with enormous power in order to achieve the largest of material goals, Number 22 is a 'Master Number' and is the most difficult lesson to learn in Numerology, You will have been endowed with added perceptions, awareness, capabilities of understanding PLUS the ability to attain anything and everything by way of material accomplishments, You must learn first of all, and this is the difficult part of the lesson, to focus and harness this enormous energy, You must also work for the benefit of mankind in order to achieve your own ultimate growth, The practical application of this lesson is extremely difficult, Before you can even begin to grasp the vast potential of the number 22 you must first be able to master the lesson of the number 4, Without the foundation and practicality of the number 4, your ideals and ambitions will always be based on 'pie in the sky' and big ideas which are impractical, Most people may grasp the lesson of the number 4 by their early 40's but those who do not will never reach the 22's tremendous capabilities, Just as the number 4 rules the stomach, so the number 22 carries with it a physical manifested nervous energy that invariably hits the stomach area, Even during early childhood, others will see an ability in you and may consider that you always seem to be capable of more than you actually accomplish during your educational years, This perception may continue well into adulthood until you learn to grasp the significant benefits that can be achieved through the positive aspect of the number 4 Life Path lesson, Most 22's however can spend a great deal of time struggling and even rebelling against the limitations and restrictions of reality before reluctantly accepting the inevitable, With the 4 Life Path this can take up to the age of approximately 28 – 36, Those who do not grasp the potential of the number 4, by the time they reach their early 40's may never come to grips with the 22 Life Path lesson but will not escape the tension that its presence manifests," and "Specifically, you're here to change how people act and embody their purpose in the world, You're exceptionally practical and insightful when it comes to creating and improving the systems and structures that make up our human societies, Life Path 22s are understood by Numerologists to be 'Master Builders' and your impact has the potential to be huge, With an innate, corporeal connection to the physical world, you, Number 22, need to feel safe and secure, You probably feel it's your duty to provide for your partner, your family and even other people in your community, which you gladly do, You're incredibly generous, But this can mean you work too hard, keeping yourself busy with the practicalities of problems, rather than giving yourself the time to tune into your higher calling, You are destined for greatness, Master 22, But you must focus your energies in the right direction to get there, This Life Path Number can (though not always) have a rocky start to life, Maybe family life was tough for you, or you were oppressed or treated without a great deal of love or understanding growing up, It's important for all Master Numbers (11, 22 and 33) to understand that any hardship you go through is your training ground for mastery, Without these challenges, there's no way to develop the dynamism and strength you need to become the human healing presence you are now, It's what the world most needs, With such a hands-on approach to life and such a personable insight, this number is often called 'the Master Teacher,' Your lessons, Master Number 22, become lessons learned by us all because of the progress you are able – and destined – to make in this lifetime, Lead by example, And make your example worth following, It's normal for Master Numbers not to blossom into their higher expressions until the second half of life, For the Master 22, it's likely that in the first stages of life, you learn to stay safe within the realms of the Number 4, in survival mode, earning money and building a safe foundation and a cozy home and career, This isn't bad – your Numerology has laid out the blueprint for your expansion and illumination and first you must gather knowledge, experience, and self-trust, So don't rush yourself through this time of duality, You will achieve your practical (and spiritual) goals when the time comes, The Master Number 22 is a potent path of bringing dreams down from the ideas, into the hard reality of the material plane, Other people probably rely on you heavily to provide the support they need, and whilst you're more than capable of playing this role, it's not something that will serve you long term, You need to be needed – other people give your life meaning – but you must become acutely aware of the point at which your perceived duties become a hindrance to your progress into the higher expression of this number, It may also be important for you, Master 22, to learn the art of flexibility – a rigid mentality and approach to life can plague this Life Path, leading to missed opportunities and failure to harness your true potential, The danger comes when you distract yourself from your true spiritual calling, The 22 is an incredibly psychic number, with sharp and powerful intuition, but will you let this side of yourself lead the show, Or will your pragmatic side win out, Walking that knife edge could be your life's work, Many people desire to have Master Numbers in their charts, believing them to be special, but they are hard, hard work, Your challenges may feel like they're going to break you, The internal conflict of the 22 and the 4 is not easy to live with, and the whole spectrum of emotional disorders may touch you, but you must carry on believing that you were born for this," and so I have avoided talking too directly about my dad up to this point, maybe because I have a fear that my dad is a ghost in between Earth and Heaven and he's watching me type this sentence or is with God again, like in my dream before I published Yada Yada, maybe he's not resting in peace or reincarnated yet, and they are very disappointed in me, which is a weird thing because my dad never expressed disappointment in me, "But The Furies bloat the present with the undigested past," says Lewis Hyde, and the reason that he didn't do that was that his father pretty much only expressed disappointment in him, because he wanted my dad to be a doctor and then when my dad went to business school instead after having a breakdown in medical school, and his dad wanted him to make lots of money but my dad wanted to manage non-profit cancer health care programs which were burgeoning in the 70s, or so I've been told, and so my father made a conscious choice to do the opposite as a parent, in terms of criticism, and he was incredibly consistent in that, I mean I literally cannot remember more than a couple criticisms, and it's kind of remarkable for a seemingly inconsistent person with bipolar to be so consistent in this part of his life, but it's what happened, and he also told me he loved me very often, whereas his dad never told him that he loved him once, and his dad loved peanuts and ate them every night after work, and my dad developed an allergy to peanuts, but when he would eat them accidentally at restaurants he wouldn't have an allergic reaction, and he didn't carry an epi-pen, and now that he's gone I have been eating peanuts almost everyday, when I had never really bought them before, and I didn't know why I ate them at first, it honestly didn't register, but now I do, and I really enjoy eating them now, because it feels like I am healing the division between them, and they taste so good to me now, it's crazy, and so maybe they are healed together now that they are both dead Fathers looking down on me, and also my dad held his nervous energy in his stomach like 22s, and my mom said that when my dad got manic he always had the pie in the sky idea that he wanted to start his own company with his friends, and build something without all the red tape, but before they died, not saying I love you must have messed my dad up, because that's a pretty messed up thing, but when you met my dad, or if you had met him, you almost never knew he was sad sometimes because of all that, most of my friends growing up couldn't really imagine that he was so sad some of the time, underneath it all, so that's something that is very different between my dad, his dad, and my dad's hero, Abraham Lincoln, I'm sure he is also a hero for a lot of you, too, because he was a great President who saved the country and freed the slaves, not on his own, but he was a big help, and he was also a great role model for mental health, as he practiced a pride in his melancholy that was something particular to his time, that was maybe lost between his time and my dad's dad's time, and Paul Auster says "Talking to [his father] was a trying experience, Either he would be absent, as he usually was, or he would assault you with a brittle jocularity, which was merely another form of absence," but that in writing The Invention of Solitude, "I had lost my father, But at the same time I had also found him," and that he remembers "His resemblance to Abraham Lincoln, and how people always remarked on it," and the thing about Abe and that time was that he communicated his sorrow and pain to people often, and he didn't just keep it inside like my dad, or Paul's dad, or perhaps project it onto his son and others like my dad's dad did, though I don't want to totally defame my dad's dad more than I already have, as I wasn't around that much of his life to see first-hand how he treated other people, and, I do know that he was a firm atheist, and so my dad didn't have that much spirituality, and though he went to temple when he raised me, I don't really know truly what my dad's spirituality was, and Shenk says in the next chapter that Lincoln was a freethinker and freethinkers constructed an unconventional faith in their own minds, and melancholy was called "acedia" by Christians and its resulting lazy, sluggish, restless, and solitary components were translated as sloth in the seven deadly sins, and sloth is the vice that the Enneagram lists for my dad and Lincoln's type, 9, and my dad slept a lot when he was depressed, we often made fun of him, in a loving way, for how much he slept, sometimes he declared that he was taking a "pre-nap," I don't remember him then taking another nap, before bedtime, so I guess it was just a regular nap, it sure was cute though, and after he died, I asked his sister what her biggest memories of my dad were when they were growing up, and she said whenever there was a big new invention announced in the news, my dad would invariably declare that he "thought of that," which is hilarious and maybe speaks to the nascent inspired practical ideas of his 22/4 Master Path, and it was partly realized by his work for the cancer center in our town, and the funny thing is I didn't know those years were as successful as they were because they lead to a breakdown, and the center's management changed so he left there, and it seemed like his consulting years weren't as rewarding, yet when my sister gave her eulogy of my dad it was about how he was an inspiration for always switching fields and being ahead of the game like working for one of the first Lasik companies, and doing some of the first online teaching in the country, and so maybe my dad is a 22/4 Master success story, and is it OK to draw on this Numerology tradition like this, Shenk says of Lincoln, "The multiplicity of traditions he drew from and the original way he synthesized them, is what makes Lincoln so fascinating," and is this synthesis I'm doing in this book of all this stuff fascinating, and Lincoln believed in the paradox of fatalism/determinism/predestination, but at the same time, that you had a choice within your path on how well your path will go for you and others, and in the next chapter Shenk writes that "Lincoln learned that his father was sick and dying, Three letters came to

Springfield imploring Lincoln to visit, He finally wrote to his stepbrother that he hadn't replied 'because it appeared to me I could write nothing which could do any good,' Tom Lincoln died five days later, His son did not attend his funeral or mark his grave," and when my dad rescued me from my manic episode, one of my biggest feelings was that we needed to drive from my college to New York City so that he could finally make peace with his dad, and I felt a powerful, unknowable force that overtook me and a lapse of will like William James talks about in The Varieties of Religious Experience, but also, paradoxically, a will to alter the path that the force had me on, and I wish I had altered the path to take my dad to see his dad, but he said his psychiatrist said, "You can take a horse to water, but you can't make it drink" and "You can't get blood from a stone," and later when I recovered and I continued to not intercede between them, my dad's new psychiatrist told him he could stop visiting them if he wanted, or decrease the visits, and sometimes I wonder if bad blood makes people sick medically, psychologically, spiritually, and yes, it's bad to have a writer in the family, because writers often like to write about their family members, and family members often don't like being written about, and maybe I will definitely get some blowback from my family for how I am writing about our family, but I think it's the truth, or at least my version of truth, and my mom says I get things distorted sometimes, and so maybe this isn't really true or factual this account, it's just what I feel or think, but that's all a memoir can be sometimes, someone's perspective, and I'm sorry if my perspective doesn't match up with someone's memory, or even with the facts, but please believe, it is true for me, and withholding it from the world would give me pain, so please let me share it, because Mary Karr says, "Whether you're a memoirist or not, there's a psychic cost for lopping yourself off from the past: it may continue to tug on you without your being aware of it, And lying about it can carve a lonely gap between your disguise and who you really are, It's hard enough to see what's going on without forcing yourself to look through the wool you've pulled over your own eyes, For the more haunted among us, only looking back at the past can permit it finally to become past," so I am going to keep all this as part of this sentence, and sort of don't have a choice because I can't go back and delete any part of this sentence, and I guess I would still publish it if I could go back anyway, and what I am also thinking about right now, is also that Abe was also a bit like Kanye, and the rappers that have come after Kanye, and the entire sad rap genre of my generation, proudly rapping about their sorrow and anxiety and mental health issues, and throwing their songs up on Soundcloud, like, whatever, bruh, like this sentence, whatever, bruh, rest in peace Lil' Peep and XXXTENTACION, watch the rain as it's "Falling Down," and also like Instagram influencers who openly talk about their struggles with mental illness, and overcoming them, and Shenk quotes a psychologist brother of mine, sorta, David B Cohen, "With depression, recovery may be a matter of shifting from protest to more effective ways of mastering helplessness," and David Shields "says," "We must consider the illness memoir as this: a gift from me to you, a folk cure," and an "attempt to make meaning," and Instagram people talk about how mental illness is not even a thing anymore for jobs, is it, or am I fired, who's reading this, I need money to pay my Spotify bill, and the coffee I need to write things, and some food, and travel and clothes, but that's it, also restaurants, I like expensive food, too, sometimes, and Lewis Hyde says that, "We are lightened when our gifts rise from pools we cannot fathom, Then we know they are not a solitary egotism and they are inexhaustible," and "The gift does move from plenty to emptiness, It seeks the barren, the arid, the stuck, and the poor," and so maybe I will sell this book for no profit, and that will avoid copyright issues too, maybe that is what I will do, if I sell a book for no profit then there can't be a copyright lawsuit, is that the truth of copyright law, I will look it up now, and I couldn't find an answer, but Lawrence Lessig says, "We should redraw the border between commercial and noncommercial exploitation, giving authors strong control over the 'pirating' of their work by commercial entities, but leaving noncommercial actions outside the reach of the law," and Lewis Hyde is a much subtler thinker than I am, and sometimes I wish I didn't think so simply and reductively about things, but you can't help who you are, and who I am is my dad's son, and my dad thought in a very black and white way sometimes, about himself, and about everyone and everything, and sometimes that was great because he would be so happy about something like fruit, the man loved fruit, oranges, lemons, berries, melons, all of it, and also juice, and he had a pure love of fruit, which is a small but beautiful thing, but also when he thought negatively, it was all negative, there was no gray areas or nuance to a problem or a situation, and that was problematic because he was thinking his life was hopeless due to the fact that he needed a kidney in order to continue living, and he had been on the kidney list for 10 years and was close to getting a kidney but he couldn't keep himself out of the hospital or the mental hospital and every time he went into the hospital they took him off the kidney transplant list he had been on for since he was sixty, almost 10 years, and they took him off for six months which wasn't enough time for him to stay out of the hospitals because he would get depressed about being taken off the kidney transplant list or he would get dehydrated and disoriented from the lack of kidney functioning and so he'd go back, and boom he'd have to wait six months again, so that was a real catch twenty fuck you, and I'm not sure why that has to be the case, and maybe there should be a change in that law, or maybe bureaucrats made the decision without a law, but my dad always followed the rules, and he trusted authority, and that was just who he was, you know, so he didn't want us to fight it, it seemed, and the thing is, my dad wasn't a quitter, he fought it his whole life and had a good life before, he often told me that if it wasn't for my mom he wouldn't have had the good life that he had after his diagnosis forty eight years ago, and in the last year he checked himself in for ECT, electroshock therapy voluntarily, and that's when they send electric currents through your brain and it's extremely scary and I don't know if I could do it, if I had to, and he thought he had to, so he did it, and he also went through many different trials of ketamine, an experimental classified drug, to resolve the depression so he was trying everything, and even though I wanted him to do a shaman guided LSD trip, instead of microdosing, I didn't do any research really and maybe I was just sort of lazy or not dealing with it, but he also thought he had become a burden to my mom, and to our family, and he had felt that depressed type of way, off and on for the last six years, ever since his old psychiatrist put him on this drug called amantadine but didn't realize it was too big a dose for his kidney functioning, and pretty much made a neglectful decision, the psychiatrist insisted he was capable of prescribing amantadine for his tremors which they thought it was parkinson's even though a neurologist was going to do it, but the psychiatrist was like no no I'll do it, but he didn't look at the rx profile close enough to make sure that it could be tolerated with his kidney function, when a lot of his therapeutic conversations with him were about fears of change of life after kidney end stage renal failure, and the fact that he had to prescribe accordingly, but so my dad got so sick he fell while playing tennis and lost motor functioning due to the poisoning and had to be hospitalized from the mistake, and he almost died, he almost died truly, and lost a lot of neurological functioning, and lost a lot of memory, forming it, and also remembering, from the past, too, and so even with a good kidney it might not be a good life anymore as he had become a dependent, and mom became a caretaker, and so when he talked about not wanting to continue dialysis anymore, it was unclear if this was the depression talking or was it a clear-headed response to reality, and where's the line between the depression and potential palliative care there, we wondered, as a family, and he even put his affairs in order by visiting the estate planner and making a will, and he prepared emotionally by saying goodbye to people, even though maybe it wasn't clear at the time that that was what he was doing because he didn't say so, but he was also trying to rebound, by taking a stress test to stay on the kidney list, and preparing for it, by working out and stuff, and I visited him in their house a week after he had been in the mental hospital for like six weeks, and after he found out that he had a spot on his kidney, and the doctors needed to scan his kidney to see if the spot was cancer, and if it was cancer he wouldn't get a kidney, and if the scan didn't come back fully clear, they would need to remove his kidney, without putting a new one in, to make sure it wasn't cancer, so he would likely have an operation to remove a kidney, without adding one, before getting one added at a later date, which now was likely not to happen either, as he was 69, and at 70 that's pretty much the limit usually to getting a kidney from the kidney pool, and even though he spent an entire morning in bed, and also asked at one point, if I would kill him, he also settled into his true self by lunch, and said this day wasn't so bad, and we had a dinner party the next day for my sister's birthday, and he sat at the head of the table, and had a lot of witty one-liners and belly laughs, and I went home to LA and listened to John Coltrane's "Everytime We Say Goodbye" and "True by PC Music/Hannah Diamond, and my dad was proud of his daughter for she was about to graduate from medical school to become the doctor that his father wanted and tried to force him to be, but my dad never pressured her, he was proud that she was doing what she wanted to do with her life, which is what he always wanted for me, even if he may have thought my writing was kind of a crazy idea, which it is, but it's also kind of fun, it's kind of like fun lit, breezy lit, candy lit, remix lit, lit AF, and I am arrogant to declare a genre here, isn't this just creative non-fiction stream of consciousness, and aren't Instagram posts better than all of this, and isn't Teju Cole right to say "Twitter is our stream of consciousness,"

AT&T
10:50 AM
83%
Instagram
12 HOURS AGO
lauren_cohen_
Venice, Italy
64 likes
lauren_cohen_ I didn't know how to access my core
inspiration and produce work that moved me when I

, and isn't that Instagram better than this whole sentence and book, and aren't we all cyberflâneurs, and here's what John Hendel basically says about them versus their Parisian forerunners, “A cyberflâneur, by definition, strolls through the Internet, Little purpose guides his journey, and hours slip by as the individual explores the many different crevices of the ever-growing web, from Wikipedia to Tumblr, from popular news sites to Twitter, from obscure journals to social media, He crawls through them all and is all the stronger for it, How do you turn a corner into the unknown online, You click a link, You go places, Who cares where, The cyberflâneur strolls more for the journey, the experience, the flow of the digital landscape, all to seek without any one destination or goal,” and shouldn’t that also be what a book sometimes is if what books are supposed to do is capture experience, and if we are trying to compete as writers with the immediacy of images of Instagram and icons of Emoji, and texts, and Twitter, and life, and David Shields “says,” “In the clash between the conventions of the book and the protocols of the screen, the screen will prevail,” and so we must write fast and directly to keep attention, and we must keep attention, because I must have your attention, I must keep up to keep it, I must write fast, and keep your attention, and never stop, and I must beat the Gram, I must beat i, and I will, and I am typing faster than my Google Doc can keep up, I am winning, I will crash this app, I will crash it, i can’t even see what I am typing due to a delay, is it my mac or the app or my writing speed , and did I put a comma there, I can’t, and I crashed the file, I had to re-load, and do you want proof, here is the proof,

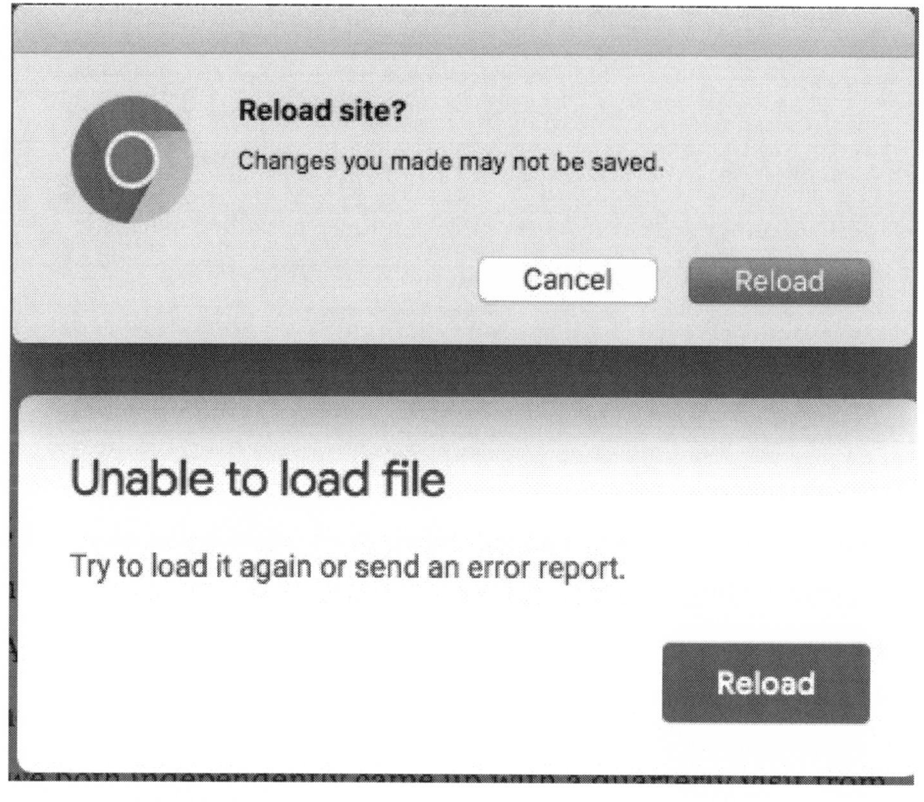

, and here is more proof,

Google Drive

This error has been reported to Google and we'll look into it as soon as possible. Please reload this page to continue.

Cancel OK

and have you read Tan Lin, and do I fit in with Ambient Lit instead of Alt Lit, or do I need to stop worrying about fitting in, is that my problem, trying to fit in somewhere, some construct of something, and I learned about a lot of writers from Danny and Aaron and Al and Sandy, and back to my dad, he told me he wanted me to visit more often at the same time that I was planning to tell him I wanted to do the same, and we both independently came up with a quarterly visit from California idea, and I thought about the music he first gave me and the three CDs were by Billy Joel, Greatest Hits volume 1 and 2, James Taylor, Greatest Hits volume 1, and I liked a lot of songs from those two albums, and they made me think of my dad even when I was a kid like "My Life" and "Moving Out" and his troubles with his dad and also what my dad needed from life and my mom like, "You've Got A Friend," or "How Sweet It Is To Be Loved By You," but with Harry Chapin, I only liked one song from that album, I can't even remember what album it was, it didn't get much spin, and the only song I liked from the Chapin album was of course "The Cat's In The Cradle," which I always remembered as a positive song, like it was uplifting, and positive like Yusuf/Cat Stevens's "Father and Son" song, which I listened to later in life, but it wasn't until after my dad ended his life that I re-listened to it, "Cat's Cradle," and it's about life getting in the way of father and son relationships, and I guess listening to "Father and Son" it's also about like the tension of going away or staying, like listening to wisdom, or thinking you know what's best, and even though Cat/Yusuf says his dad ordered him, my dad didn't order me around, but I still felt who he was made me want to go and do more in the world, and "We'll get together then, we'll have a good time then," and sometimes I think art echoes throughout our lives, in this coincidental dramatic irony-type way, and that he gave me these songs for an unconscious reason, or maybe he knew what he was doing, sharing himself through music, and we both loved music very much, but we never spoke about those songs, and I probably could have spoke to him so much more than I did in the last six years of his life, since the amantadine, and what was I thinking, and what is wrong with me, is my constant thought, and is this a normal grief thing, maybe, fine, sure, and Lydia Davis said, "Maybe you miss someone even more when you can't figure out what your relationship was," but but, but, but AR Torres says "Even out of unspeakable grief, beautiful things take wing," and the thing about my dad killing himself though, is that he actually drank a glass of orange juice right before he killed himself, which was his favorite fruit juice, and it was the last thing he did, besides, you know, so, I think even though he was psychotically depressed it's not as simple as that, I've been there, "I'm Depressed" by Ka5sh and gnash have been there, and Zack Fox and Kenny Beats "Jesus Is The One (I've Got Depression)" have been there, and I've had psychosis before when I had my manic episode, and the thing about psychosis, at least in my experience, is that delusion and insanity exist at the same time as normal perception of reality, like you've always had it, and maybe you sort of have access to both perceptions, even if one is more prevalent than the other, there is still some reality available, and sometimes the psychosis is just the subtext of the latter, and the psychosis just lifts up G-d's dramatic irony, so you see reality more lucidly almost, and so maybe he was clear-headed in that way, and knew why he needed to do what he did, and sometimes the flaw of the 6, if he was a 6, is fear but the virtue is courage, and so maybe he was as courageous at the end as he was fearful, and he told me the weekend before he saw an Abraham Lincoln photograph at a museum, but when I went there after his funeral, they said that exhibit never happened, but if you were only psychotic, you probably wouldn't have taken a moment between grabbing a knife and cutting yourself where you did to have a drink of orange juice, which was your favorite drink in the entire world, and his vessel for his soul was deteriorating, it was going, due to really bad kidney disease, I've said it, but it deserves repeating, and he had it due to lithium, I don't really know how come, perhaps too much of it when he was younger or because they didn't really know how to administer it always back then for manic depression, that's what they called it then, why change the name, and sometimes he said it feels unfair, that that happened, but not, like, "I was treated very unfairly," just a fact to be dealt with, a card dealt, not a complaint laid on our shoulders, not a guilt trip, and the thing about kidney failure is that it's kind of hard to know when they fully fail, it's not like math where there are hard numbers and you pass or you fail right away after checking the numbers, even though you think it would be, you would think kidney failure is more of an exact science, and so even though he had bad kidney numbers, he kept on going without the dialysis for a long time, because he loved to travel, and my mom hadn't traveled as much as him when she was younger and they planned to travel in their retirement, and, yes, this is a privileged narrative, but he didn't want to go on dialysis partly because you can't really travel internationally if you are doing it, and they saved for years to go traveling together, after my sister and I got through college and graduate school and medical school, like Alexander Payne's short film about Paris I am thinking now, they never got to go there, and cancelled the trip to Paris twice, due to different hospital visits, but even though he got tremors and his brain started to get poisoned, he didn't start the dialysis until a few months before the end, in August, and so what happened was that his depression which he had staved off for so many years while being a good parent to me, who often said he loved me, even though his dad never did, that old depression dog, it came back, like Hemingway said it does, he wrote my father's favorite book, The Old Man And The Sea, which is kind of about fighting to keep living in the way you want to live, because if you're too sick to do that, you might as well not live, and my dad wasn't a hard macho man, but he didn't want to go to a facility, and Hemingway killed himself, too, not long after writing that book, and did I abandon my dad like the boy did, or did the boy going back to work with him after he nearly died, is that what I should have done at some point, or did I do enough, joining up with him the weekend before the end, and while we're bringing up Hemingway, one of the things I would love to do for my dad is have Hemingway do his eulogy, and so maybe I will do a parody of Hemingway doing his eulogy at some point in this sentence, or maybe I won't, and here it is: the man lived, until he couldn't, so he didn't, and another thing is that my dad's favorite play was Death of a Salesman, by Arthur Miller, and sometimes I worry that he thought he was better off to us dead than alive, and my dad was a real optimist like Willy Loman, he always believed in me no matter how low I've sunk out here in the fringes of Hollywood, he still believed in me, and I had glory days in high school, he called me BMOC, big man on campus, which nobody used that word anymore but that's the kind of Loman expression that he used for me, the Biff, and I don't know what my dad's favorite movie was, I remember as I was applying to film school showing him my favorite movie at the time, The Royal Tenenbaums, and it still might be my favorite movie, after he watched the father come back into the family's life and make amends before he died, he said he didn't like it, "That's not how things really go," and right after we watched The Diving Bell and The Butterfly, which is about the pain of a man in a locked-in syndrome and he said, "Now that's a movie," and now that I'm thinking about movies I recall my and my dad's love for Field of Dreams, and I just took a break to read the screenplay, and I cried a number of times while reading it, because Kevin Costner's character is named Ray like my dad's dad, and it's all about connecting with your father, even when you couldn't when they were alive, and seeing them in the best possible light, and about being perceived to be crazy or mentally ill for following nature's call, believing in the inexplicable, or the paranormal or a voice or an afterlife or that the dead are among us, and benefit from us helping to heal them wherever they are, and I am also now thinking of The Lion King, and how we used to sing the soundtrack together, our family, and how after Simba's father dies he has to learn the egoless, emotionless, nothingness Buddhism of Hakuna Matata but then combine it with Messianic, heroic, egoism of Judeo-Christianity to help his community, and in Paul Auster's The Invention of Solitude, in the introduction, Pascal Bruckner says, "Perhaps Paul Auster's rich works already prefigure what certain historians foresee as the religion of the future: Christian-Buddhism, that is, a concern with personal salvation linked to an acute awareness of uncertainty and the void," and also Pascal basically says ~it's Paul Auster's first book, and it's about how the death of his present but absent father gave him an inheritance to become a writer to write a book about his father, and that Auster saves his father from oblivion through words, connecting with him via the distance and separation of memory, that only a rupture will shake the self from the illusion of self-knowledge, the self must die Auster seems to say in order to live, as if the father's death requires the fictitious death of the son, that the descent into hell as a nomad creates self-reconciliation, and in that wandering comes fate, ironic, mischievous providence, coincidence, a certain order in the randomness of existence, meaning suggested but not expressed, the dissolving of the self in the face of God's grandeur into a nonentity, through writing we can choose other fathers to compensate for our own, discover a spiritual link, go beyond ourselves, voices that must be quieted to find one's own voice, which is really still full of all the others, and that we must tirelessly rewrite its missing testament because ultimately that all living can never pay back the debt to the dead those who gave them life, and so like Paul Auster, the gift of an inheritance is also a debt that I must repay with this book's writing, because now that my dad has died, as of this writing, his mother is still alive, my grandmother, but she is in hospice, or has been, and has a substantial inheritance to pass down, or so I have been told, and now that money is bypassing my mom and going straight to me and my sister, and that empty shameful revelation I have just provided is probably what Pascal would call what is killing Western literature, the invasive proliferation of autobiography, of the diary, of self-preoccupation as a genre in and of itself, and that the unfortunate irony of these books, devoted to revealing the individual's most intimate essence, is that they all end up resembling each other, as if written by the same person, a fanatical celebration of the writer's uniqueness becomes an isolating activity which contradicts universality, detailing petty problems, they, I, I guess, they/I am helping further create a universe of mutual deafness, where each person, talking about himself, no longer has the time to listen to others, right, Instagram, and are you proud of me, daddy, and it's pretty clear that I have Daddy Issues, and here is an Instagram from an influencer named Daddy Issues with 4 point 1 million followers,

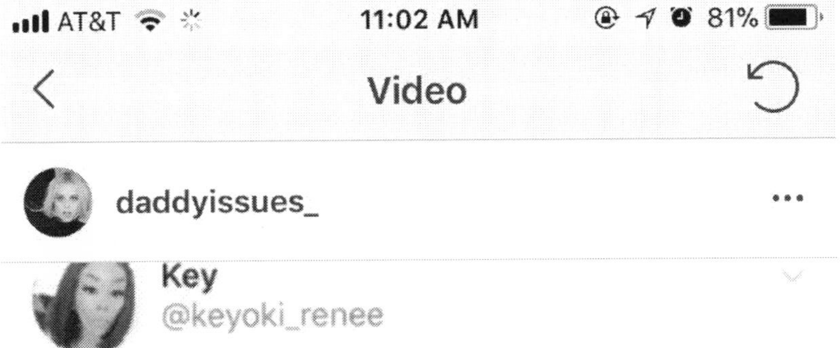

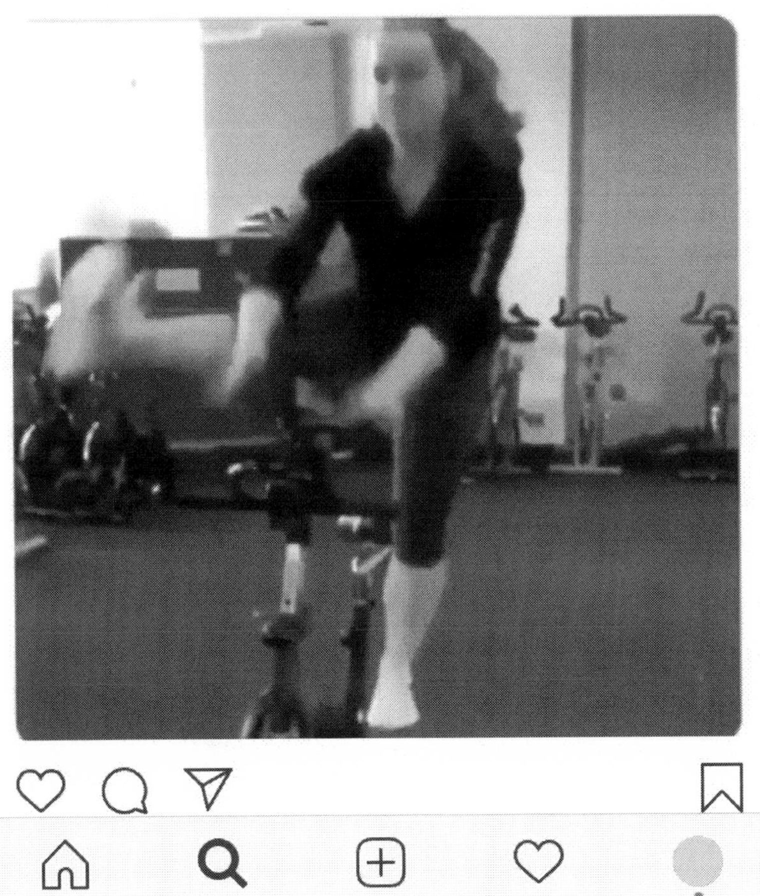

, and is it also better than everything else in this sentence, and here are some quotes from “Experimental Writing in its Moment of Digital Technization: Post-Digital Literature and Print-on-Demand Publishing,” by Hannes Bajohr courtesy of Danny Snelson, “Blumenberg described technization as the slow sinking-into-the-lifeworld of what was once artificial, unnatural, obtrusive, and novel, Any technology is, in the process of technization, ‘always-already’ on the way toward this transparency, and becoming invisible to its users,” and “It seems that, with the initial rise of digital technology more than a generation behind us, we are now experiencing a threshold moment of such technization, The fact that something is produced, distributed, or perceived by digital means is no longer the first thing we notice about it, if we notice it at all, Digital technology is in the process of losing resistance to our experience of reality,” and gradually, as Blumenberg writes, “The artificial reality, the foreigner among the encountered things of nature, sinks back into the universe of what is pre-given as obvious, the life-world,” and so what I am saying is how do we express that in a book and not be obtrusive to laws or other people, and how do we not let what is natural and non-artificial but obtrusive and novel like the death of a loved one, how do we not let it sink back into non-resistance, when all there is is digital distraction sometimes, and is this a distraction, writing this, or is this engagement, and is it obtrusive to other people in my family, and hurtful, or to laws, but also are books not engaged enough in technization, for instance, my use of Shenk’s Lincoln’s Melancholy book, this is part of what I am going through, reading Shenk’s book, and yet am I a vampire for putting so much of his book in my book, without getting permission, even though it speaks to me, and is so instrumental in my experience of my dad’s death, why do I need Shenk’s permission to express how my dad’s death has been experienced in my life, what does copyright lawyer

Lawrence Lessig think of this, and so why on the Internet you can put anything you want on there, like how I could send this document to friends or a therapist, or post it on Tumblr, if that was still a viable medium, or as Instagram posts, I should probably do the middle former and/or the latter latter, and it would then be an Internet piece and not subject to copyright and plagiarism in the same way, just for having an ISBN, isn't that what my college's professor Kenny Goldsmith teaches or used to, at least it would be a true testament of what grief is like for me, and without this stuff, it isn't the real thing, and so without that technization, the world of books is deficient in capturing life, if I can't publish this, the way it is happening right now, in this instant, it's not real, and there would be no point in writing about it in a different way, and what about that, and what about what-about-ism, and Kenny says, "Faced with an unprecedented amount of available digital text, writing needs to redefine itself to adapt to the new environment of textual abundance, Why are so many writers now exploring strategies of copying and appropriation, It's simple: the computer encourages us to mimic its workings, If cutting and pasting were integral to the writing process, we would be mad to imagine that writers wouldn't explore and exploit those functions in ways that their creators didn't intend," and the other thing to know about my dad is that the children's book he always read to me was The Giving Tree, and the deal with that book is that there are two interpretations of it, and one is that the role of a parent is to raise up a child by giving them everything and anything that the parent has and can give, so much so that the child has stripped away the tree to nothing, to the earth, and I think, though I don't know, I think my dad believed that was his role, and it was why he loved that book, to give his children anything and everything so that they could succeed and be happy, and I think I believed that growing up, too, I believed in that interpretation of The Giving Tree, but recently I read an article in The New York Times, I believe, I am writing too fast to go check this piece of information, but facts are unimportant, feelings are, that's a thing Kanye said, and this whole sentence is like Kanye's song, "Last Call," and are you following along with the Spotify playlist, I put in above, I'll put it in again here, https(dot)//open(dot)spotify(dot)com/playlist/2xsgUmnOaYdZb34LuMFifR(questionmark)si=67REDpuURBiupvZBN00Kg, and it's not really legal either to have music in your book, and Lessig can you represent me broh, I feel a type of way about laws and facts right now, even though I don't like to feel that, I'd prefer to follow facts and laws, when available and known, but it's hard to find facts and know how to follow laws these days, you almost can't even blame the Republicans for saying there are alternative facts, wash chicken or not, red wine or not, New York Times articles say this this year, say not that last month, say the opposite the other, and do you feel me feeling that right now, and do you feel that right now, or are you not feeling this, or have you stopped feeling this sentence so much that you are not even reading this sentence, if it's published but never fully read by anyone in the world, then does the sentence get to have the record, what's the fact there, alternative or what, or whatever, as Fernando Pessoa says, "I wonder if my apparently negligible voice might not embody the essence of thousands of voices," and so what I am also saying is that the other interpretation of that story of The Giving Tree is that it is a cautionary tale about unhealthy parent and child roles, and that parents need to guard against letting their entitled, spoiled kids strip them of their lives and their identities, and so the other thing that I want to bring up that is making me sad these days is that my dad refused to take a kidney from me, he didn't want a kidney from his son, whom he wanted to have everything in life including not having his father in his life any longer if that meant that I might live a shorter life, me, the son, or me not being able to help my own future child one day with a kidney, because that's the proper order of organ giving, a la The Giving Tree giving up its kidney branches or whatever, and Lewis Hyde uses kidney donations as a classic example of the confusion between worth and value, in discussing the creativity of the artist in the modern world in The Gift, "If we accept for a moment that human life may be counted as a commodity, the story of the Pinto [in which Pinto executives decided to sell their car without a safety feature, in order to cut costs, which lead to many deaths] offers a picture of decision-making in the marketplace," and "How, then, do we make choices that involve gifts, Some of the most interesting recent work on this question has come from studies of people who have been asked to give one of their kidneys to a mortally ill relative, The human body is able to function with a single kidney, though nature has given us two, It is now the case that another person's kidney can be transplanted into the body of someone whose own kidneys have failed, The greatest problem with such transplants has been that the recipient's immunological system, reacting as if the body had been invaded by a disease or by a foreign protein, attacks and destroys the new kidney, The closer the match between the blood type and tissue of the donor and those of the recipient, the less likely it is that the kidney will be identified as 'foreign' and rejected, Kidney transplants are therefore more successful when the donor is a close relative, An identical twin is ideal, followed by siblings, and then by parents or offspring, In 90 percent of the cases, transplants from a twin are still viable after two years, With other related donors, the success rate is around 70 percent, Kidneys from nonrelatives (usually from cadavers) are accepted about half the time, How does a person go about deciding to give someone a kidney, The decision is not a trivial one, There is some risk (about one in fifteen hundred donors dies as a result of his or her gift), The operation is major, It calls for several days of hospitalization and a month or more of convalescence; it involves considerable pain and leaves a scar that runs halfway around the abdomen, Not surprisingly, then, some individuals, when they become aware that a relative might need one of their kidneys, think it over in the classical 'economic' fashion, They seek information about the operation, its risks and benefits; they talk to and compare themselves with other potential donors; they discuss the prognosis with the family doctor and so on, What is surprising, however, is that such deliberation is not at all usual, The majority of kidney donors volunteer to give as soon as they hear of the need, The choice is instantaneous; there is no time delay, no period of deliberation, Moreover, the donors themselves do not regard their choice as a decision at all, The instantaneous decision of these organ donors should not be such a surprise, after all, Situations calling for gifts are exactly those in which we find inappropriate the detachment of analytic deliberation, a mark of emotional and moral life, an expression of social emotion, gifts make one body of many, almost literally in this case, and when a person comes before us who is in need and to whom we feel an unquestioning emotional connection, we respond as reflexively as we would were our own body in need," so what does that say about me that I deliberated and that I didn't instantaneously give, and you are making me feel bad about myself, Lewis, father figure, for how I treated my true father, that I have no moral life, and wouldn't help my own flesh and blood in need, does that mean I didn't have an unquestioning emotional connection with my dad,

Lewis, I feel horrible, Lewis, I am a monster, my dad is dead because of me, I'm no better than a Pinto executive, I've killed him, like Pinto killed all of them, but, but, but then again I don't know for sure how Abe Lincoln would have thought about this, my father's father figure, but I do think he also would have done anything for his children, especially for his son who died while he was President, he probably would have given him a kidney branch if his son had had a kidney problem, he would have given him from his Giving Tree, if his son was dying from kidney disease and he could have saved his son with his kidney branch due to medical advances, and also I think Abe wouldn't have wanted his son to give him his kidney branch, Lincoln wouldn't have wanted his son's kidney, if Lincoln had had kidney disease and was going to die before finishing the Civil War and freeing the slaves, because that's how big a parent's love of his/her children ought to be, is what I think my dad would say, and probably also what I think Lincoln would say, and also I think what George Saunders was saying with Lincoln At The Bardo, "Dear little chap, Always knew the right thing to do, And would urge me to do it, I will do it now, Though it is hard, All gifts are temporary, I unwillingly surrender this one, And thank you for it, God, Or world, Whoever it was gave it to me, I humbly thank you, and pray that I did right by him, and may, as I go ahead, continue to do right by him, Love, love, I know what you are," and "Whatever that former fellow (willie) had, must now be given back (is given back gladly) as it never was mine (never his) and therefore is not being taken away, not at all, As I (who was of willie but is no longer (merely) of willie) return To such beauty," "All were in sorrow, or had been, or soon would be, It was the nature of things, Though on the surface it seemed every person was different, this was not true, His sympathy extended to all in this instant, blundering, in its strict logic, across all divides, He was leaving here broken, awed, humbled, diminished, Ready to believe anything of this world, Made less rigidly himself through this loss, Therefore quite powerful, Reduced, ruined, remade, Merciful, patient, dazzled," and George is very influential on me, due to his use of due tos and vias, and also via his humor, and vis-a-vis his empathy, and due to his pathos, and how he lost the magic, but then found it again, and how he lived in Rochester, New York, where I am from, and he actually worked in a building pretty much visible from my house, in Rochester, or at least that's how it feels right now, as I tell the story, so I guess it is true, it feels like fact, and he had cruddy day jobs like I/we have all had, and how I/we all feel we've lost grace, and we're afraid of the poor house, us Americans, all of us, right, and regarding the magic, you've just got to be vital, with your writing, that's what my friend Al says, and he won the best teacher award at USC this year, and that's not just best English teacher, that's the whole school, or at least that's what I think he said, and he knows more about autofiction than I do, and I just texted Al, "are there good examples of stream of consciousness memoirs/autofiction you can think of for me to check out" because I am realizing that I probably didn't create a new genre of writing called lit AF, mashup lit, chat lit, twit lit, text lit, bad lit, sample lit, dumb lit, insta lit, crap lit, dull lit, I am just incredibly ignorant, and David Shields "says," "(Ambitious) memoir isn't fundamentally a chronicle of experience; rather, memoir is the story of consciousness contending with experience," and Jonathan Lethem says, "Let a million canons Bloom, Only, canons not by authoritarian fiat but out of urgent personal voyaging, Construct your own and wear it, an exoskeleton of many colors," and before I found this comma run on form with the ands and the sos, in a book I wrote about Christopher Columbus and that guy I won't talk about, that nobody read, why did no one read it, will people read it, and which I am basically parodying myself at this point, with this run-on sentence, I submitted a few humor pieces to The New Yorker that were basically parodies of George Saunders, and here's one, around the time of Charlottesville, I'm going to pad the sentence again, and take out the periods and question marks, and it was called: "I HAVE THE BEST EMPATHY" by Dave Cowen, "In politics, practically no higher value exists than being empathetic, empathy is what is invoked on both sides, in confrontations" -The New York Times book review of Against Empathy, I read that there's a book called Against Empathy, I didn't read it, but I don't understand how anyone could be against empathy, Those people must believe they've been treated so unfairly that no one can empathize with how unfairly they've been treated, But they're wrong, Because I can empathize with them, I have the best empathy, Because I was treated very unfairly once, Just for trying to empathize with someone, one time, my sister was punched in the face, People were very mad at the guy who punched her, My family, the police, even the guy's family said he was a bad guy, But, I wanted to get the facts, It's a very, very important process to me, This event had just happened, the punching, And, yes, I condemn punching, I've always said that I condemn punching, I condemned it, But I've also always said, "Every coin has two sides," My other sister said, "That analogy isn't helpful right now, Ronald," I said, "You're right, Maybe this situation is more like dice, Maybe there are many sides," You see, firstly, the man who punched my sister, he had just lost his job, He had posted some political comments on Facebook that his bosses didn't like, so they fired him, Could there be anything more unfair than getting fired for using your 1st Amendment rights, I didn't think so, My dad said, "He wrote 'All Jews must die' on your sister's Facebook page, It's an anti-Semitic threat, plain and simple," I said, "Well, hold on there, He wrote, 'All Jews must die,' But maybe he was saying something more like, 'All Jews must die, Just like every other human, Because every human dies at some point, That's just human nature, Unless scientists come up with some big breakthroughs, Which would be great, For the Jews, And for everyone, frankly,'" My brother said, "He then wrote 'Fuck those job stealing kike girls,'" I pointed out that, technically, our sister did get promoted to the guy's job after he was fired, My mom said, "No, he was reprimanded for the first Facebook comment, and then fired after he punched your sister in the face," I pointed out that before the punch, she came to his desk to confront him, And that our sister can be very intimidating, Nobody ever wants to say it, But I'll say it, She wears all black sometimes, My other brother said, "It feels like you're putting our sister and this random, Neo-Nazi guy, who punched her in the face, on the same moral plane," I said, "I am not putting anybody on a moral plane, What I'm saying is this: You had her and him coming at each other, Two sides," The guy's mother, who had come to the hospital room to apologize for her son's punching of our sister, said, "The police are actually saying that he went to her desk, not the other way around," I said, "But why did he go there, Was he just protesting that she had convinced their bosses to make him take down his Facebook post on her wall about Jews, and also all of his other Facebook posts on his profile about Jews," The guy who punched my sister's mother said that she had been wanting him to take down those posts for a long time, I said, "So, This week, it's posts about Jews, I noticed that they also asked him to take down his posts about Blacks, I wonder, is it Mexicans next, And is it Muslims the week after, You know, you really have to ask yourself, where does it stop," "It stops now," Said the guy who punched my sister, himself, who had been escorted over by the police after making bail, so that he could apologize in person to my sister for punching her in the face, He said, "I've had a lot of hatred in my heart for a long time, which I've misplaced onto others, and I'm very sorry that you had to bear the burden of that today," I said, to the guy who punched my sister, "Don't apologize, man, Empathize with yourself a little, Don't you understand, There's another side to your hatred of others, too, Maybe those others you hated, hated you back a little for misplacing your hatred onto them, which then caused you to hate them more, In that case, there'd be hatred, bigotry, and violence on many sides," The guy, who punched my sister, looked very confused, and said, "Are you serious, I dunno, That seems pretty crazy," He turned to my family, and his mother, and said, "That's crazy, right," Then, our sister, the one who'd been punched, said, "I hate you, Ronald," And she punched me in the face, I never forgave her, Sometimes people do things you just shouldn't empathize with, even if you can," and, yeah, The New Yorker didn't publish that either, and why would they, isn't it just a George Saunders parody, and isn't there more important Shouts & Murmurs to publish about dating and social media and social mores, and we're back to what is the utility of satire again, and also what is the utility of writing in general now, I guess, and also back to whether I could have and should have saved my dad, and Auster reads the original Pinnochio to his son, and I have only ever seen the movie, and when I saw the movie I remember wondering where my conscience was, why did this boy get to have and grow a conscience, when I didn't have one, and so I've always lamented and loved that movie at the same time, identifying so much with the shyster side of Pinnochio, and what about Bruce Springsteen's "Dream Baby Dream," another favorite of my dad Bruce was, and the fact that that song was written by the band Suicide, and the connection between a dad rock band and an art rock band, and suicide, is there meaning there, did some of my dad's dreams not come true, do some of my dad's dreams come true with me, and it was playing when I read this part of Auster's book about Pinnochio, and it's "For this act of saving is in effect what a father does: he saves his little boy from harm, And for the little boy to see Pinocchio, that same foolish puppet who has stumbled his way from one misfortune to the next, who has wanted to be 'good' and could not help being 'bad,' for this same incompetent little marionette, who is not even a real boy, to become a figure of redemption, the very being who saves his father from the grip of death, is a sublime moment of revelation, The son saves the father, This must be fully imagined from the perspective of the little boy, And this, in the mind of the father who was once a little boy, a son, that is, to his own father, must be fully imagined, Puer aeternus, The son saves the father," and even if I could only relate to the growing nose, that growing Jewish nose, when I was younger, and ashamed, and do you have a cricket conscience, where do I get one, when do I get one, will I ever get one, but I am feeling different hearing the dream on dream baby dream, the dreaming of another way of being, of having been, of being forever more, another way of seeing myself, of seeing the world, of living in it, it must be possible, not just in music or books, or in writing, but in life, life itself, we gotta keep the light burning, and come on and open up your heart, that sounds right, that sounds good, and is this a book or a journal, is this a product for public consumption or only a diary of private exploration, I dunno, dear reader, I just want to see you smile, I just want to see you smile, I just want to see you smile, and my dad told me often that one day he wanted to write a book, one day I'm going to write a book, he would say, what's it going to be about, I would say, I don't know, he'd say, and sometimes I'd laugh at that response, and he would say, you'll see, you'll see, and so going back and forth between the Bruce, and the Suicide versions, going back and forth, between dad rock and art rock, yeah, keep those dreams burning forever, maybe my book is also his book, this book, maybe this is also my dad's book, being channeled through me, and Al told me to read David Markson, and here's what I learned from This Is Not A Novel, and it's all about how artists were born and died and moments of misbehavior in between, eg, "Nietzche died after a sequence of strokes, But his final illness, and his madness, were almost surely the result of syphilis," and also declarations of what the author does or doesn't want to do with his book, eg "Plotless, Characterless, Yet seducing the reader into turning pages nonetheless" and "Actionless, Writer wants it," and I think it means that all artists come from the same stream like Lewis Hyde might say, and that their bodies might die in absurd ways, and their personalities might do bizarre things, but they sang through the muse, all of them, and that's what Markson is doing, singing through the muse, even when he puts limitations on what the muse can provide, art comes nevertheless, and Bob Dylan says, "I return once again to Homer, who says, 'Sing in me, oh Muse, and through me tell the story,'" and I've always thought the individual artist was special but it's not the individual artist, it's the universal muse, the artist him or herself is just a flawed human, and one time I told my dad that being an artist was to be the most important person in the world, when I didn't know what I knew after reading Markson, and Hyde, and growing as a person, and he didn't criticize that comment, but he looked a little sad just for the briefest of the briefest of micro emotionally intelligent 3 point o aware moments, maybe, so sometimes I wonder what he really thought deep down that I have devoted my life to writing, mostly screenwriting, mostly comedy screenwriting, and in the next chapter of Shenk's book, he basically says, "Humor and poetry gave Lincoln succor without eliminating the underlying problem," and my dad was quite funny, he would do things like eat a crazy hot chili pepper in order to get a laugh, or he would repurpose a catchphrase in the zeitgeist like "Who's the man," he would ask, and we would have to respond "You're the man," and if you knew how humble he was you would get why that was such a funny joke, and Shenk also says, "It's poignant to consider that Lincoln, estranged from his father, so often practiced an art he learned, in part, from the old man," and I too often use food and zeitgeist lines for jokes, like when I had a food eating/weight gaining contest with my friends Alec and Matt, and isn't the zeitgeist still cule, right Instagram, and Shenk also quotes Rhoda and Seymour Fisher in this chapter and says that "A central theme in the comedian's life, is whether he is good or evil," and Shenk says that, "Comics also often describe themselves as healers," and do you want to know about me being a 11 in Numerology, it's sometimes called the Wounded Healer in Numerology, here's something about it, "The lesson you must learn is an awareness of the spiritual / non-material world, This is a 'Master Number' and its energy potential is extremely difficult to handle, You will have been endowed with added perceptions, added awareness and different capabilities and understanding, These potentials will take a great deal of effort to develop and you must bear in mind at all times that your feet must always be planted firmly on the ground, Otherwise any ability that you do develop will be useless to everyone, including yourself, Once developed you will have the potential capability to attain far more than others, You must learn to 'tune in' to the forces around you and develop your intuition,

Much useful information can be gleaned from psychic or occult studies, With knowledge comes understanding and illumination, It is important that you use your awareness and illumination for others' benefit, The practical application of this lesson is extremely difficult, 11 is often known as the number of the dreamer because of the subject's natural aloofness with the material world, Also number 11 has the propensity to come up with big ideas and solutions which are not always thought through properly and can more often than not, be totally impractical, But such is the nature of the number 11, The difference between the 11 Life Path and the 2 Life Path is that the number 11 is made up of 1 & 1, Because the single digit numbers are the same, they are not broken down to a number 2, Number 1 by itself is independent and polarised whereas number 2 is dualistic, 11 can therefore find itself thinking apart from the company of others (the influence of the number 1), but will invariably find the need for companionship (the influence of the number 2), Such a difference can often make the 11/2 indecisive or even impulsive, 11's sensitivity can also be too intense, The potential energy behind this master number is so vast that all people with this number may never come to grips with it until maybe much later in life; normally around the early 40's, It is therefore wise to suggest that those with this number should concentrate initially on the lesson of number 2 which is merely a lower vibration of the number 11, Until you are able to master that lesson the number 11 Life Path will be far too difficult to handle and may even manifest itself physically with nervous tension or a nervous neurological condition, If the lesson of the number 2 hasn't been mastered by the mid 40's, the energy of the 11 may never be attainable in this lifetime, Whether this happens or not, the number 11 must strive at all times to remain aware of the truths of reality, however harsh, and aim to work toward realistic ideals, and, “THE LIFE PATH 11 WALKS THE PATH OF THE WIZARD, If you were born into this number’s vibration, your life is a spiritual journey, Your mission is to be an inspirational presence in people’s lives and affect true and lasting change for the collective – specifically how people connect with each other and the world,” and Lewis Hyde says in The Gift that “It is also the case that a gift may be the actual agent of change, the bearer of new life,” and “When art acts as an agent of transformation that we may correctly speak of it as a gift,” and “According to Apuleius, if a man cultivated his genius through such sacrifice, it would become a lar, a protective household god, when he died, But if a man ignored his genius, it became a larva or a lemur when he died, a troublesome, restless spook that preys on the living, The genius or daemon comes to us at birth, It carries with it the fullness of our undeveloped powers, the genius has need of us, those who do not reciprocate the gifts of their genius will leave it in bondage when they die,” and back to Numerology, “As a person, you’re unique, independent, and have the potential to be a great leader, But you’re also exceptionally spiritually connected and have unparalleled psychic gifts, You may or may not have accessed these in your life so far, but all Life Path 11s are understood by Numerologists to be people with access to a higher power, This may manifest as intuitive knowings, creative bursts, free-flowing insights and inspiration, or any number of different things, But not everybody has this gift, so it’s important that you begin (if you haven’t already) to trust your inner voice, Practice using your intuition, Meditate, Let your heart guide you and see what begins to unfold in your life, Trusting your intuition is also a large part of learning to trust your authentic voice, Your mission in life, Master Number 11, is to inspire others into radical new ways of connection, but you can only do this by expressing yourself truly, It's vital for you, Life Path 11 to live a life of true integrity, You are destined to be the catalyst for many other people to follow their true paths, but first, you must find, and create your own, LEARNING TO OVERCOME PAIN IS WHAT WILL EVENTUALLY BECOME YOUR GIFT TO OTHERS," and also "You've the potential for fame with this Master Path, Basically, you're a creative genius capable of the highest forms of artistic expression and the realization of inspired ideas, You can potentially change the consciousness of the world with your artistic gifts when you use them to help others, Unlike the 22/4 Master Path, which you'll learn is more practical in its application, the 11/2 Master Path is artistic, creative, and inspiring in a rather intangible way, What I mean by that is this: an 11/2 Master Path might create a piece of art, a dance, a performance piece, music, or a sculpture that affects the viewer in a way that the viewer can't explain, Rather than seeing a tangible result from the contribution or the experience, the 11/2 Master Path's power resides in the inexplicable transformative experience they provide, The 11/2 Master Path means you'll face internal struggles throughout your life, You're the most intuitive, sensitive, and artistic person around, and your feelings get hurt very easily, You'll find that you're challenged with being self-absorbed and do battle with your ego, You're meant to do great things, yet you can be conflicted, You've always felt different: both superior and inferior, You have a tendency to question your work, feeling as though you need to do more, something different, or something more important, Develop the internal guidance of your intuition and you'll have less difficulty discovering and acting on your true passion, Remember, although you may garner fame and recognition from your endeavors, attention is often accompanied by criticism, Knowing how sensitive the 2 Life Path is to criticism, you must learn to protect yourself emotionally, Develop a thick skin in order to operate and follow through with your work without having a nervous breakdown, If you succumb to the destructive tendencies that the intense vibration brings, you'll be prevented from accomplishing everything you were born to do, selfless service and artistic creativity," and so how I've failed so spectacularly as a screenwriter, maybe that was so I could become something else, maybe to write this, whatever this is, this intangible book thing, and we didn't even have a shared language to talk together about spirituality or screenwriting, my dad and I, let alone Numerology, even though we are both master numbers, and Jews, have you heard of Kabbalah, there are also 22 paths in Kabbalah, like Numerology, and there are 10 parts of the Tree of Life, 9 that are like the Enneagram, and 1 reserved for G-d, and I've also only learned about that since my dad died, and I learned that Vampire Weekend put up a 1 hour and 20 minute loop of "Harmony Hall" with their own version of the Kabbalah Tree of Life:

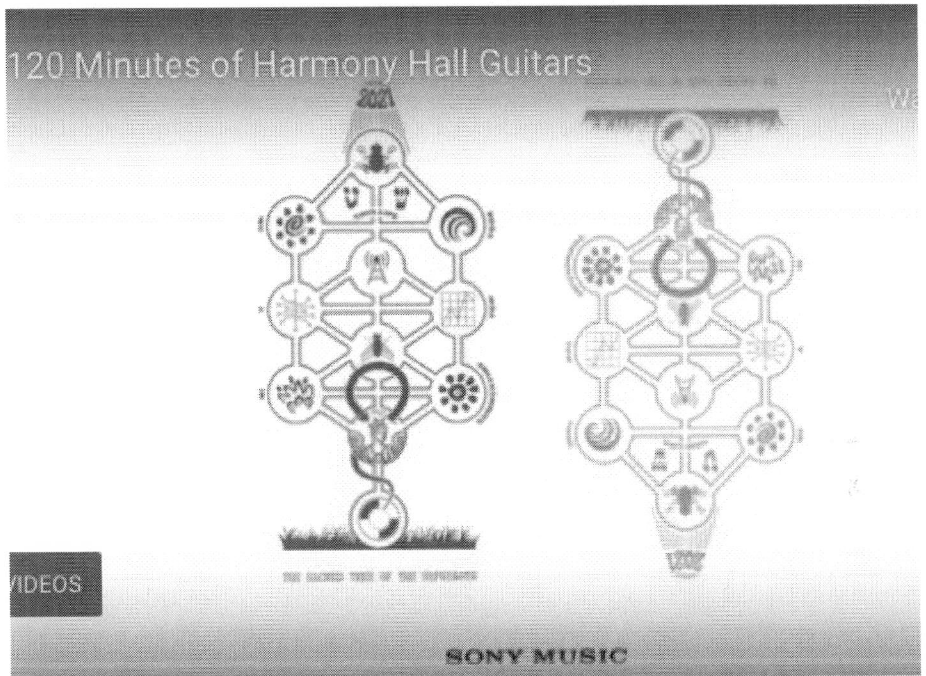

and I wish I could have talked to my dad about it and studied it with him, but Lincoln once read from this poem, “For we are the same thing that our fathers have been, We see the same sights that our fathers have seen, We drink the same stream, and we feel the same sun, And we run the same course our fathers have run,” so maybe he didn’t learn it in this course but I will learn all this in my course, and if I have a son, I’ll pass it down to him, maybe he’ll not like it, I dunno, and Paul Auster says, “When the father dies, the son becomes his own father and his own son,” and do you know Donald Barthelme, he wrote The Dead Father, and “The whole of chapter 22 is a stream of bizarre, deconstructed sentences, as if muttered by a narrator too imbued by the urgency of his thoughts to give attention to proper grammar, giving the impression of a deep penetration in the character's consciousness,” like so, “I was compassionate, insofarasitwaspossibletobeso, Best I cud I did,

Absolutely, No dubitatio about it, Don't like, Don't want, Pitterpatter oh please pitterpatter," and I was just in an Uber with a driver who says we follow the same course in every life but just different circumstances, and I've pretty much given up on screenwriting these days, I did apply to this Imagine Impact program, which is one of a number of screenwriting fellowships that are out there right now, and I thought I wrote a really good application, and the application prompts themselves were good I thought, they really gave you a sense of the applicant I thought, it was like fifteen prompts, not just a lazy one essay and submission in a box, and so I really did give it my all, but no, no positive response, didn't make it to the next round, even though I had included a very vulnerable essay about my dad, and how we didn't really connect often about movies and writing, not that that matters in reality, the man loved thriller books, but he couldn't read near the end of his life, which also happened to Kay Redfield Jamison at times, she wrote in An Unquiet Mind, and in Touched By Fire, about her struggles with bipolar and also how so many artists have it, like William Blake, and Blake was also a sort of a Gnostic who said, "I come in self-annihilation & grandeur of inspiration, To cast off rational demonstration by faith in the Saviour; To cast off the rotten rags of memory by inspiration; To cast off Bacon, Locke & Newton from Albion's covering; To take off his filthy garments, & clothe him with imagination; To cast aside from poetry all that is not inspiration," and so I think Blake is saying that too much reason, science, knowledge in writing and life that doesn't include the imagination/feeling/spiritual/mystical is bad, and this book was supposed to just be a goof about a long sentence and now it's imaginative/feeling/spiritual/mystical and David Shields "says" "Memory: the past rewritten in the direction of feeling," so maybe this sentence went from bad to good, according to Blake, like I've wanted it to, and when Philip Roth wrote a memoir about his father's death, Patrimony, when he found out his dad had a brain tumor and needed to tell him, he accidentally missed the fork in the exit road that would have taken him directly to his father's apartment, instead he passed by his mother's cemetery, which he had been to only twice since she passed, and yet he said, "I didn't believe there was anything mystical about how I'd got there," and when he stopped at her grave he thought, "Even if you succeed and get yourself worked up enough to feel their presence, you still walk away without them, What cemeteries prove, at least to people like me, is not that the dead are present but that they are gone," and here's that essay, from Imagine Impact without the periods, you get it by now, here's the question prompt for this essay, and there were like twelve of them to do in two weeks, which were two of the weeks my dad was in the mental hospital in Rochester while I was busy applying to this program in LA, and Sandy read a draft of the book so far, and called it a hermit crab essay, because a hermit crab essay is a nonfiction essay style where a writer will adopt an existing form to contain their writing, and then grow out of it, These forms can be a number of things including emails, recipes, to do lists, and field guides, in order to get at something difficult without tackling it head on, and I agree with that, very much so, but here's a regular essay prompt, Why do you want to be a writer, What drives you to work on your craft, and I wrote, but before I put in the response, here's a poem I submitted to The New Yorker that I wrote in the early 2010s before Instagram and everyone was like mental illness is chill now, like,

Instagram
Search

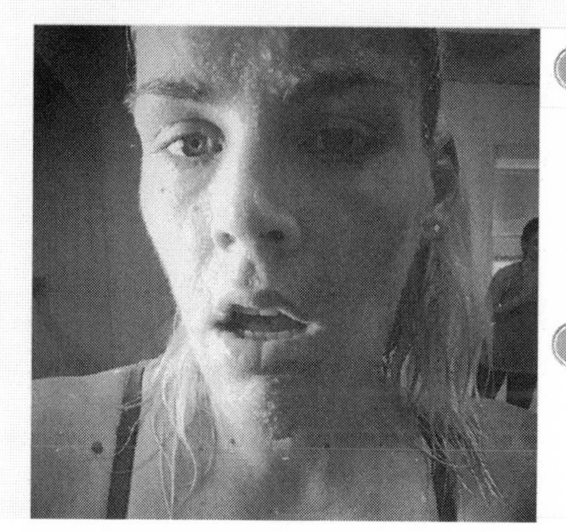
busyphilipps • Following
busyphilipps How much sweat is too much sweat? Someone asked me if people like my sweaty Instagram stories and my feeling is that, honestly, I don't really care all that much. I post those for myself, as a fuck yes for showing up. I have anxiety and I have a tendency towards depression but I have found if I sweat like this, EVERY SINGLE DAY, I feel better, I'm calmer, I'm a better mom and those fogs of anxiety or sadness seem a little lighter. I've been picking my skin less, engaging in less binge eating and I've just felt better about myself.(And obvi I go to therapy too) My goal is not some perfect bod (I like chips and salsa and margs too much for that) My goal is to feel the best I can in my body and my brain for the rest of my life.

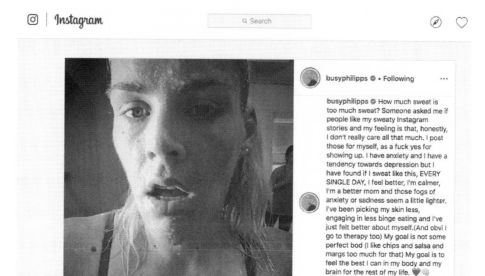

and, I'm treating these Instagram posts as one word, even if they have periods inside them, they are one word, one image, one word, OK, like a Chinese character, take the record away, I dare you, actually please don't take it away, you see, the paradox here, as Traumawien co-founder Lukas Gross wrote in a mission statement, consists in "Transferring late-breaking digital aesthetics into book form," and, of course, this poem I am adding now, it didn't get published, why would it have, it's not very good, and I am not a poet, but here it is, "I Would Give Up, The stories of artists, Home after months away, The numbers 5, 30 and 9A, The good, the gentle and the brave, Saint-Remy, The Village Green, The dance of life and a scream, Fat ladies in cabs, The sounds of pets, Florestan and Eusebius, Varieties of experience, The expanse, the depths, The other reality, The obliteration of this one's dramatic irony, My father, his fathers, The writing too, All of it for a life with," and that was the poem, which makes me think now, do you also think writing is a bit of a disorder, like I often do, heritable across all of our generations, where people feel they must write for a noble reason but are actually trying to free themselves of unhappiness by living as much as possible in the flow state of writing instead of the unhappy state of life, their life, and what do we know of the flow state, what do our Silicon Valley Ted Talkers say about it, and what do our religions say about it, and what is the difference between presence and unkindness, the past and melancholy, and the future and fear, and what utility do these states have, and Ted Talker Brené Brown says, "The Greek word for happiness is Makarios, which was used to describe the freedom of the rich from normal cares and worries, or to describe a person who received some form of good fortune, Chairo was described by the ancient Greeks as the 'culmination of being' and the 'good mood of the soul,' Chairo is something the ancient Greeks tell us, that is found only in God and comes with virtue and wisdom, It isn't a beginner's virtue; it comes as the culmination, They say its opposite is not sadness, but fear," and I often feel a lot of fear and so did my dad, is Bipolar related to Chairo, and some scientist people say manic depression might have been for days with a lot of sunlight in the spring, where you get a lot of work done, and long cold dark winters, where you evaluated how you handled the sun days and planned what to do differently next time, or maybe it's just spiritual, and was I angry at my dad for my inheritance of this so-called disorder back then, to give up my father and his fathers too, and am I even able to give up those states of mind, or do I only have the sanctuary of flow and presence in writing, or is it available to anyone always, and here's a better poem that could be about my dad, too, "Father" by Ted Kooser May 19, 1999, "Today you would be ninety-seven, if you had lived, and we would all be miserable, you and your children, driving from clinic to clinic, an ancient, fearful hypochondriac and his fretful son and daughter, asking directions, trying to read the complicated, fading map of cures, But with your dignity intact you have been gone for twenty years, and I am glad for all of us, although I miss you every day--the heartbeat under your necktie, the hand cupped on the back of my neck, Old Spice in the air, your voice delighted with stories, On this day each year you loved to relate that at the moment of your birth your mother glanced out the window and saw lilacs in bloom, Well, today lilacs are blooming in side yards all over Iowa, still welcoming you," so OK, here's the essay from that Imagine Impact application that I guess I promised to share with you, "When I was growing up my father was somewhat of a tough movie critic, During family movie nights, a lot of the time, right after the 1st Act, if the movie didn't lock in his attention or if it offended his sensibilities, he would declare, "That's it for me, folks," and he'd leave to read or go to bed, However, when he did stay for a movie, that meant he was its biggest fan, and he'd cackle at a family comedy or absorb a well-researched historical drama, As I was the cinephile in the family, the one to pick out the movies almost every time, I felt approval and acceptance on the rare occasions I had the chance to watch a full movie with him, And, more importantly, I felt a connection with him over the mutual recognition of something special in a movie, I'm not only buttering you all up when I say that two of his favorite movies were Ron Howard and Brian Grazer's, (sidebar Imagine Impact was run by Ron Howard and Brian Grazer and their production company, Imagine) He was a physics teacher and came of age during the space race, and frequently told us stories about that time, so our mutual joy during APOLLO 13 was one of my most memorable movie-going experiences as a boy, Later, a formative movie-going experience, and simply a formative life experience came when I was a young adult, I had always wondered why my dad was so moody and sometimes acted so erratically, and in the fall of 2001, when I was in my last year of high school, I learned of his long-term mental illness while at my last pediatric appointment reading my chart, I didn't bring it up with my parents, because they hadn't brought it up with me, but it was something that unsettled and gnawed at me, That is, until we saw A BEAUTIFUL MIND as a family in November of that year, While we watched the story of John Nash, a brilliant but suffering man of science, I watched my dad cry for the first time during a movie together, The recognition he and we saw of him with the character and the connection between us all, allowed for my dad, mom, sister and I to discuss openly for the first time what had been under the surface of our entire lives, I write for those moments of connection and recognition, I love when that moment produces a tangible laugh, but as I've matured as a writer, I also aim for more, I've put on table reads of my drafts of WE BOUGHT A GUN, and while it's helpful to count the laughs per page, it's even better to clock the looks of connection and recognition the story produces in the participants' faces, and then to discuss the themes and characters in relation to the actors' and notegivers' own lives and relationships to guns, not to mention the sharing of ways to make political change," and so that script I mentioned WE BOUGHT A GUN in the essay above, is a script that is brilliant like all my writing is sometimes, and it's about "When a like-minded, progressive couple is mugged at gunpoint, the wife shocks the husband by buying a gun, causing them to reconsider their plan to try for a baby together," but the script also sort of ruined my screenwriting life as I became so obsessed with it that I didn't write anything else screenwriting-wise because I believed it had to be that script or nothing, as it was about my politics and nothing seemed more vital than a political, romantic comedy satire about gun safety, as there have been so many gun deaths, even gun deaths while writing this sentence, and what can be done, I always wonder, well, make my movie for one, and I guess that's pretty gross, and all that groveling for making of movies is pretty gross, but particularly for one about guns, but my dad always asked me how it was going, and he had such incredible patience and he always believed that movie would happen someday, I think, and it's not looking good with that movie these days, I felt that way, especially, after not getting into Imagine Impact on Monday, February 25th, which was also the day that my dad killed himself, and it really felt like you know what, screenwriting isn't worth all this, and I'm done with it, because I had sacrificed so much of life for it, the important things in life were sacrificed maybe for screenwriting, yes, they were, and it's not helping me nor anyone else, especially not victims of gun violence whom I purport to help, not to mention my dad, whom I purported to help, I do though purport to help them and believe I made my dad happy sometimes with my company, and with the writing, can cake be eaten, too, sure, of course, I always have cake and eat it, too, don't you, Jack Handey, Teddy Wayne, and was it a coincidence that my dad's death was entangled with the death knell of my screenwriting career, and I've talked to my friend Fletcher about physics, which my dad majored in, and then later taught, and which he loved to read about in his spare time, and he told me about the theory of entanglement and its cosmic extrapolation, and I read this book by Bernie Beitman, who felt himself choke the same moment when his father died, miles away, choking on blood, and after that he started to study synchronicities and coincidences as a psychiatrist, and he says like Fletcher that "Quantum physics provides a speculative possibility, Think of a pair of electrons, As they circle around each other, each electron is itself spinning but in a direction opposite the other, Now separate these two electrons at a great distance, Although they are no longer circling each other, they continue to spin themselves, Change the spin of one electron and, instantaneously, the other electron will reverse its spin, The time for this change in the spin of the other electron is not limited by the speed of light, It's faster, It's instantaneous, The particles appear to be separate, but they act as if they are one, Physicists use the term "nonlocality," which means that the particles are actually connected despite their distance from each other, The electrons are "entangled," Was I connected to my father like this," and I didn't feel my dad die, but before that I did feel a swelling heaviness and dull, aching pain in my armpits that I went to my primary care doctor for multiple times, and he checked for lumps, and he did ultrasounds, and x-rays, and found nothing wrong, it wasn't until after that I went to an energy healer recommended to me by my friend Ashley, and I told this energy healer, Jordan, about the pain in the armpits, and that I thought it was psychosomatic in some way, and he massaged my armpits, and suddenly I felt what I took to be God tell/remind me that my dad's dialysis port was near his armpit area, and I hadn't put that together, and as Jordan massaged me there, I started to cry uncontrollably, in relief, and then the pain went away, it evaporated, it healed, and it hasn't come back, so we were entangled, my dad and I, even though I didn't know it, for all those months I carried the pain of his dialysis port, too, but I spent so much time consumed by pursuing screenwriting that I sacrificed my relationship with my dad a lot of the time, because I was so consumed with the script, and trying to get it read, and being out here in LA hustling and grinding, and thirsty AF, and that was very off-putting to everyone who I asked to read it, my desperation, because I believed my life would only be good finally when I made that movie, and a movie would be worth all the sacrifices I've made, and aren't I owed it, I thought, and it's kind of like what happened to Matt Weiner, with Mad Men, when he carried that pilot around in a briefcase for years, and all of his writer friends thought he was a sad sack for holding a torch for that project for years, and in his telling in his essay he published that Lena Waithe posted at some point on her social media, I believe, and she helped me with We Bought a Gun at some points, she did, she hosted a table read of a draft of the script, when I met her at the wedding of our friend and his wife, but it didn't work out with Lena Waithe, or it wasn't really that kind of help, you know, and why should it be, and I can't escape name dropping, even though I know it's bad, I think though that you gotta help yourself, you gotta do the doing, like publishing this book will be doing the doing, and in Matt Weiner's telling he was a sad sack for many years, like I think I was, and it's only been recently when I've written books and people read my writing finally that I feel more self-respect, not that much, but some, and I remember now what my dad said his favorite movie was 2001: A Space Odyssey, and the second to last time I saw him was when he came to Los Angeles for Thanksgiving, and I took him to The Walt Disney Hall for The LA Symphony's performance of the soundtrack to Stanley Kubrick's movies, and even though we could only afford to get us some of the worst seats in the house, he said he'd never seen anything like it, as the movie was played in sync with the orchestra, and 2001 started the concert, and the thing is I had never heard my dad talk about that movie, and the only reason I think it's his favorite movie is that he listed it as so on a form he filled out in the mental hospital two months later in January, which asked him to think of positive things to live for, and so maybe he was thinking of that time a few months back with me, or maybe he was thinking of the movie and the idea that humans need to get to the next level of superconsciousness via aliens or something else or just the ballet of images of space travel and also that my dad wanted to be an astronaut when he was growing up, that was his dream when he was a boy, so that must be it, the connection of astronaut, his dream, with movies, my dream, and that was a nice time in a weird way because my dad had to get dialysis while he was in LA, and he could only get times very early in the morning, and so my mom didn't want to come, and so I would take him every other day, and we'd sit there for four hours, just the two of us, which was a rare thing in our lives, but I was often anxious, and neurotic about the technology if it was working or would it harm him and the sanitation and blood, his blood flowing out of his body and into this machine, and my dad's blood, which was mine, what it was having to do, what I was making him and it do, perhaps, even if I wasn't conscious of that guilt, but we'd also just talk the two of us, the only time it was just the two of us in a long time, and he wanted to know about the future, the reality and difficulties of my plans for making the rest of my life out here, but how maybe I could get a place with a guest house one day, and he could visit with my mom and see future grandkids, and we talked about small things too, like what he should watch on Netflix when he had to do dialysis at home by himself, because he couldn't read very much and often just had to sit there, and I think I recommended Better Call Saul, which was a terrible choice in retrospect, my dad doesn't like dark things, and I wish I had recommended him Lodge 49, which is the show I watched after he left, and it's the kind of show I was bound to love, not just because the creator Jim Gavin's book Middle Men is the first book I ever bought from Amazon for the Kindle app and is brilliant, read it, but because it combines humor with pathos and mixes the quest of the external with the quest of the internal, and of course it's about a failure and a possible suicide of a father, and a wound physical and mental that needs to be healed in the son, so maybe that would have been bad for his mental state, but maybe it would have helped us face things like we had with A Beautiful Mind, and I would have loved to write on it, yet in so many ways my screenwriting dreams died when my dad died, you could say that, that could be true, and that my dad died while I was still a prodigal son, you could probably defianitely say that, too, even if maybe not because I couldn't spell definitely right there, without confusing it with defiantly, slip of Freud, maybe, but Rilke says, "Sometimes a man stands up during supper and walks outdoors, and keeps on walking, because of a church that stands somewhere in the East, and his children say blessings on him as if he were dead, And another man, who remains inside his own home stays there, inside the dishes and in the glasses, so that his children have to go far out into the world toward that same church, which he forgot," and so maybe I ran away to Hollywood to compensate for some part of my dad's unlived animus as James Hollis says in The Middle Passage, and another reason I think my dad knew what he was doing when he ended his life was because when I returned home for the funeral, I found two photographs near my desk, that I didn't remember seeing the weekend before when I was there visiting and we had the birthday party for my sister after he got out of the mental hospital again, and another thing to know about my dad is he loved taking photos of vistas, and vistas with water, and especially while he was traveling or in nature, and so the two photographs near my desk were from National Geographic magazines, and they were vistas with water in nature, and he had taken them from a magazine inside the mental hospital, and on them he had pasted the words "Think Positive" and a quote of Abraham Lincoln's, "The best way to predict the future is to create it," and so what was he telling me, what were these messages he left me, that he put in my room, I don't know, maybe I shouldn't feel so guilty about not giving my dad a kidney branch, because he wanted me to have a future, and wanted me to think positively about the end of his life, and wanted me to create things in my future, like this book, so I could be happy about what I had done with the life he and my mom gave me, and Leopold Bloom's father committed suicide too, and Bloom loves kidneys, it's his favorite food, and maybe my dad even means with screenwriting still, and maybe that project isn't dead, as I want to do the script as a graphic novel now with this illustrator friend, Moriah, who a friend introduced me to, and she is incredibly talented and incredibly kind, and how cosmic is it that Moriah donated a kidney to the general American kidney pool this year, the year my dad died because I didn't give him one, just because she's such an amazing person, how cosmic is that, and I think this graphic novel version of We Bought a Gun is going to work because a graphic novel isn't like millions of yeses, and millions of dollars, and millions of people to make it, and the graphic novel will happen one day, and I know that because from chapter 8 of Shenk's Linclon, "Humbled as he had been by years of obscurity, Lincoln held on to his hope to 'stir up the world,'" and that "The ethic that he proposed for his country, continued struggle to realize an ideal, knowing that it could never be perfectly attained," and the ideal was that as Lincoln said, "There is no reason in the world why the negro is not entitled to all the natural rights enumerated in the Declaration of Independence, the right to life, liberty, and the pursuit of happiness, I hold that he is as much entitled to these as the white man," and my ideal is that we can enact common-sense gun safety laws in this country that will save lives, and here's another essay from Imagine Impact about how I think my movie could have or could help that, here was the prompt, Why do you want to tell this story and why now, Why are you the right person to tell it, "I read that you named your program "Impact" because you aim to promote stories whose individual emotional impact can spark a wide cultural impact as well, That's exactly why I want to tell the story of WE BOUGHT A GUN, why it needs to be told right now, and why I am the right person to tell it, In 2008, America was intensely divided on LGBTQ marriage equality, But representation in culture, through movies like MILK and shows like MODERN FAMILY, emotionally impacted many Americans and citizens of the world, Those stories helped spark the push for, and acceptance of, legal reforms, While there are still divisions on this matter in the country and world, more and more humans are able to live happier and healthier lives due to the impact of movies and TV, Similarly, gun law has been divisive in America and countries around the world, In 2013, Sandy Hook aroused the formation of Moms Demand Action and Everytown For Gun Sense, In Norway and Australia, mass shootings provoked public outcry and then governmental action, And very recently, Ferguson and Parkland inspired the Black Lives Matter and March For Our Lives movements, respectively, However, it shouldn't take individuals suffering tragedies to create the individual emotional impact needed to spark a wide cultural impact, WE BOUGHT A GUN is a story that can create such an individual emotional impact, I know that to be true, because my journey writing the early drafts of the project sparked such an experience in me, Firstly, I believed, in my heart, that empathetic communication should be enough to shield in any self-defense situation, Then I feared, in my gut, that gun ownership might be the only complete protection in a self-defense situation, After participating in meetings, marches, and events sponsored by many of the above-mentioned organizations, I now believe that what largely prevents violence is not superior communication or self-defense skills, but common-sense gun laws, I'm the right person to tell this story-- it is my story-- and by learning from Shapers, like Dustin Lance Black, how to tell it emotionally, so that the truth is aimed at the heart, I know it can change minds, Such an impact is needed right now, because more and more Americans and humans of the world are dying from gun violence, And, at the same time, with the rise of March For Our Lives and Black Lives Matter, we are seeing that fresh, passionate modes of culture are accelerating change, For example, the state of Florida passed a no-under-21 gun sale law largely due to the multi-media blitz of members of the Marjory Stoneman Douglas high school drama club, Putting WE BOUGHT A GUN into a content accelerator, with its relatable couple, smart humor, stylistic visuals, and warm heart, could help it do for gun safety what MILK and other movies and TV did for marriage equality: win over a wide audience, and impact the world," and so after my dad died, a guy named N at my mom's work, who is about the same age as me, and who my mom thinks of as her surrogate work son a la a work wife/husband while I'm in Los Angeles, he and his wife and infant child's house was broken into by a mentally ill man, and N had to talk the man out of hurting them or himself, which is a similar plot point to the end of We Bought a Gun, and he succeeded in doing that but afterward he told my mom it made him think about buying a gun, and what about that, pretty cosmic too, but also I have to tell you about this email I received on April 22, 22 remember, how crazy is this, this is nuts, too, look at this email, punctuation edited, "Dave, I hope this email finds you well exclamation point I'm writing because I'm a fan of your screenplay We Bought A Gun, I was a reader for Imagine Impact 2 and loved your pitch; yours was easily the most well-rounded, thoughtful application I read throughout the entire process period I scored you quite high, but your project didn't make the cut for reasons that were beyond me, I was bummed, but read your script anyway because I loved the pitch, I mentioned the script to a producer friend a month ago, When I saw her this weekend, she mentioned having thought about it several times since and wanting to inquire about a potential option, She's Academy Award-nominated and has the very connections you seek, The big question: has anybody optioned your screenplay yet, question mark, Best, name redacted," and so I typed out this response right now, "Wow, This is quite an email to receive, Honored and humbled, Thank you, The script has not been optioned, And so I'd be very interested in hearing more about you and this producer, Should we set up a call or a meeting," and whoa he just wrote back like pretty much instantly, like he's a deux ex machina in this story, and maybe the story of my life, "Before setting up a call or meeting, I'd like to share the script with name redacted, If you have an updated copy, great; if not, the Imagine sample works, About me: I'm an actor/producer/writer, I've made small scale stuff for the web, taken low budget projects to festivals, worked for brands, etc, I took the Imagine 2 reading gig in search of a great script to produce, I've long wanted to be a tastemaker at the highest level, which is easier said than done (unless you're a millionaire), I'm as passionate about comedy as I am sensitive about guns, About name redacted: she's a seasoned producer and is in the midst of securing financing for a new film venture, She asked me to keep her posted on comedies I think can go the distance, So, I gave her the elevator pitch of your project, which brings us back to here, Crazy world, right, Do you mind if I share with name redacted," and so I typed back: “I'm a huge fan of ambitious movies like Academy Award Winner In Screenwriting movie name redacted and Academy Award Nominated Director’s movie name redacted, so working with name redacted would be exciting, And I may be an even bigger fan of ambitious tastemakers who make enterprising moves like taking a contest reading job in order to find a great script to produce, So, yes, please send her the script, Thank you, The latest draft is attached, Indeed, a crazy and fun and beautiful world, Thanks again, Dave,” and that was our communication, and yes, I am kind of a tool when it comes to emailing about screenwriting bullshit, but maybe this is the big break I’ve been waiting for, and maybe my dad always knew it would come, but more likely this will not pan out, and I look pretty ridiculous for putting it into this sentence and book, but it’s already there, so what are you going to do, I hope my dad’s faith in me is actualized someday, then maybe my decision to be out here in Los Angeles these last eleven years would be worth it, instead of me feeling bad about being so separated from him, and being separate was his biggest fear in his Enneagram type, 9, and sometimes I feel guilty that people with one kidney are pretty much fine, like, Alonzo Mourning played basketball with only one kidney for a bit, and is alive to this day, so I would have been pretty much fine if I had somehow convinced him to let me give him back a kidney from my tree body, but the other thing I feel a bit guilty about right now is putting all this grief stuff and, like, rejected pieces, and email flotsam, into this supposed fun and funny book about the longest sentence ever written and then published in the English language, you guys didn’t buy this book because it was going to turn into some sort of raw grief memoir, even though David Shields “says,” “It’s crucial, in my formulation, that neither the writer nor reader be certain what the form is, that the work be allowed to go wherever it needs to go to excavate its subject," you bought it because you wanted to laugh about how absurd the English language can get, even if that concept was a bit thin and half-baked, but then again if you've read my other writing, you are pretty aware that most of what I do is pretty thin and half-baked, and raw, it's pretty much my style at this point, immediacy over quality, all day, baby, but also if you want to see me set this record and you want to see me set it in real time here, you're gonna have to deal with whatever raw stream of consciousness comes into my mind, like a character in Joyce's or Faulkner's novels, I am right now, and Faulkner said, "Between grief and nothing, I will take grief," and OK, that's probably been done itself, a stream of consciousness memoir, I am worried about that now, that's why I texted my friend Al, but I am not stopping this sentence to research the history of the English language or memoirs any more than I already have, but what makes this successful, this book so far, and these words, this word right here, and this one two three four words is that just writing a word means I am succeeding at my book's purpose, it doesn't really matter what I write, I just have to keep writing in order to be successful, and that's freeing, because success is so subjective, clearly, and that's a dumb thing to write, but it's not dumb to write it now, because it added to the number of words I have written, so I am even more successful now than I was when I wrote that dumb thing just before now, and in many ways every word that I write I am more successful than I was before, and Auster says about writing about his father, "A feeling of moving around in circles, of perpetual back-tracking, of going off in many directions at once, Just because you wander in the desert, it does not mean there is a promised land," and I am now again reading things from my friend Danny Snelson's syllabus for Print On

Demand Art & Poetry and, indeed, "POD has an inherent connection to a digital file; its very existence relies on the creation of a digital master from which the copies of the book are made, While this is true of almost any book printed today, with POD this connection between file and object is especially unstable, Because of the ease of production and dissemination that services like Lulu and Blurb provide, it can be investigated, manipulated, and thrown into crisis by artistic and literary means," and so that means I guess something can happen to this Google Doc file, how stable is Google Docs, not very, it's crashed like twenty times, and if my goal is to be successful at writing the longest sentence, why am I putting all these impediments up to doing so, like quoting from articles, pretty much full articles, does part of me not believe I am deserving of success, and has that always been the case, or is it due to all my years of lack of success, and yes, anyone who wants to write the longest sentence in the entire English language ever published must also be a bit sick in the head, and Judd Apatow took a year to read, a reading year, and he put his favorite things he read in a book called Sick In the Head, and he's a hero of mine, and I am basically taking a reading grief year and putting the things I read into this book, and I was an extra in his film THIS IS 40, and there's a funny story about me being an extra in that film, a friend at the time was Judd's assistant, and they needed extras for this birthday party scene for Paul Rudd's character, and we, the extras, had to walk by Paul Rudd at one point to give him birthday presents, and for some reason Paul turned to me and asked, "Hey, How's Karl," and even though I had been instructed by the second AD that extras can't talk while the camera is running, some part of my sick mind panicked and let slip, "Karl's dead," and Paul and Judd and the set broke out laughing, because it was such a weirdo dark sick thing to say, and so the second AD grabbed me and hustled me off the set and yelled at me and I explained how I had never been an extra before and I was so sorry and I wasn't an actor just Judd's assistant's friend and could you please stop yelling at me and he stopped yelling at me but said he had to fire me because now he had to pay me for 4 days of work as an actor instead of an extra and couldn't justify paying for another day tomorrow, and so I still get residual payments from This is 40, for that sick mind of mine, and when I told my dad that story he was, like, that's great, so they loved the line, are they going to use it in the movie, and when I was like no, probably, definitely not, he couldn't understand, but they all laughed, that means it was funny, it's a comedy, right, and no, they didn't use the unuseable line in the movie, but I am in a shot with John Lithgow's dad character, clapping while holding a beer like an idiot while Lithgow is stony-faced, which is an ironic metaphor for how Hollywood views me and my work, and so it kind of goes with the territory, sickness in the head, Joyce and Faulkner and probably Mike McCormack had their demons, I'm not sure about Jonathan Coe, he seems a bit basic to me, maybe he needed to be more sick in the head in order to have written a better longest sentence, I dunno, to be honest, I never finished his sentence, so maybe it got better as it went on, like the opposite of this one, which I fear is actually getting worse as it goes, do you think so, is this sentence bad, is anyone still reading it, and maybe I also feel bad about making fun of him personally, sorry, Jonathan, I'm kind of just using you as a comic foil because you have the current record or I thought you had the current record, and it's funny that we're not as famous as Faulkner and Joyce and we won't be as famous ever, we cule, dude, just playing, OK, so what else do you guys want me to say in this sentence, do you want some more of the weighty parts of life, or more jokes, I want the former right now, I want to talk more about my dad again, and maybe I will write this book for the year following his death, the year of mourning, like the Jews do for their parents, or children, or spouses, because I can't make it to Temple everyday to do a mourner's kaddish, the Yud Bet Chodesh, but this writing everyday it's my temple, it's where I come to think of him and be spiritual, and so maybe I will write this book from now until February 25, 2020, the one year anniversary of his death, and whatever is in it, is in it, and I won't edit the mourning process, as well as not editing the sentence itself, and so this longest sentence book will now also be a document of a year of mourning, a mourner's kaddish, and I will publish it on February 25, 2020, no matter where it's at, no matter what it is, and how weird it is that people just stop existing, and you never get to hear them talk again, or be in their presence, and even though my dad stopped being able to read due to his illness he still tried to read my writing for a few pages and laughed his belly laugh when he read it with me, and was just so sweet and gentle and kind, and I do feel fortunate to be alive myself right now, and I think there is something to the maxim that, "I am thinking, therefore I am," someone must have said "I am writing, therefore I am," someone must have said that, right, that is pretty much the joy of this project, the high spirit, it is that I am staying alive as long as I write this sentence, I am here, I am living, I am happy, and I am also keeping my dad's memory alive right now by writing about him, his name was Richard, and he helped establish a cancer center in our hometown, and then he became a science teacher, and he was a good husband and father and friend, and his temple's cantor said this poem at his funeral, "The measure of a man is not how did he die, but how did he live, not what did he gain, but what did he give, these are the things that measure the worth of a man as a man, regardless of birth, not what was his station, but had he a heart, and how did he play his G-d-given part, was he ever ready with a word of good cheer, to bring back a smile, to banish a tear, not what was his church, not what was his creed, but had he befriended those really in need, not, what did the sketch in the newspaper say, but how many were sorry when he passed away, these are the things that measure the worth of a man as a man, regardless of birth," and I think the cantor did a beautiful job picking out that poem because it does represent my dad, and it was by anonymous, and that goes to show you that the writer of the poem really did have integrity about his beliefs, and sometimes I wonder if I am not at all like my dad in the way of that poem, that I am consumed with my station in the world, with what a newspaper will say about me when I die, and sometimes I look back at my life and see that I wasn't always ready with a word of good cheer like my dad was, and that maybe some people will not care or will even be happy when I pass away, perhaps many of the people I try to impress all the time in the movie business, they likely do not care about me, and maybe if they cared enough to read this book they would think I am sick in the head, not in a charming Apatow way, not even in a charming Maria Bamford way, shout out Bipolar, and they'd wish me ill, and also other people think I am a sick person for writing Haggadahs, in the way that I have done, the sacrilegious style and the #resist style, and would everyone be happy if I were gone one day, sometimes I think so, and so at my dad's funeral, I re-dedicated myself to trying to be more like my dad in the way of this poem the cantor read, and clearly it's not going to be 100 percent, I mean, look at this book, but I also think that who I am and how I am different than him isn't all bad, and that through writing and leaving a mark on the world, I am also honoring his memory, too, his consciousness is being kept alive, by Kindle Direct Publishing, thank you again, Jeff Bezos, and your Vice Squad, for not taking this book down due to "disappointing content," though the robots say I will publish the content somehow someway, even if you block it, see here's proof:

Completion

I've heard they have started having their bots check for content now, too, and that includes what they call "disappointing content," and they talk about this when you boom publish your book on the KDP FAQ page, they say that content that "does not provide an enjoyable reading experience," is "disappointing content" and what's a little scary about that is that Amazon reserves "the right to determine whether content provides a poor customer experience and remove that content from sale," which is more than a little scary, actually, Amazon bots if you are checking this sentence for content purposes, you gotta be cool about this sentence, bot, don't fuck with it, OK, bot, because if you don't publish it, fuck, bot, I don't know if anyone else will,

They will,

, and so maybe I will publish it via Faylor's imprint GPDF Editions, where each title is free for download as a PDF, and can be purchased as a POD book on Luludotcom, because "With little more than a working knowledge of the [Lulu publication] wizard, one can easily bypass editorial intervention, marketing strategies, and the general publicity bullshit that bolsters most literary markets," though I hope I am not disappointing my dad with this content, though now I am thinking of one piece of content that I wrote that disappoints me now greatly, it is this other piece that I submitted to The New Yorker that was rejected, and it was a very bad piece of writing, that probably disappointed The New Yorker editor who had to read it, and they were probably like "I can't believe we published that guy once, he's such a hack, that must have been a mistake," so I am not surprised that they rejected it, it's almost too embarrassing of a piece of writing to put into this book, but once again I am removing the punctuation, like the last pieces, and here it is: "A Case of Filial Piety" by Dave Cowen, "The [Chinese] government enacted a law on Monday — compelling adult children to visit their aging parents — On the same day the new law went into effect, a court in the eastern city of Wuxi ruled that a young couple had to visit the wife's 77-year-old mother — who had sued her daughter and son-in-law for neglect — at least once every two months to tend to her 'spiritual needs,' as well as pay her compensation — Guangzhou Daily, an official newspaper, ran an article in October about a 26-year-old man who pushed his disabled mother for 93 days in a wheelchair to a popular tropical tourist destination in Yunnan Province — The article called it "by far the best example of filial piety" in years" -The New York Times, Supreme Court of the State of New York, County of Monroe, 7th Judicial District, Richard and Randi COWEN, Plaintiffs versus Dave COWEN, Defendant, Case Number BC 39599390, DECLARATION OF RICHARD B AND RANDI S COWEN IN SUPPORT OF THE MOTION FOR ENFORCEMENT OF FILIAL RIGHTS, Date: July 18, 2013, Time: 8:30 AM, We, Richard B Cowen and Randi S Cowen, declare and state, as follows: 1 We have personal knowledge of the facts set forth herein, except as to those stated on belief, and as to those, we believe them to be true, 2 We love and will always love the defendant, our son, David, in a way he will never understand until he's married and has kids of his own, why he doesn't by now, even though he's dating a wonderful half-Jewish woman -- who's actually fully Jewish because it comes from her mother's side -- Hashem only knows, maybe He can tell the Plaintiffs -- when we nurtured and fed and clothed and housed David in a township with the best public school in the county, as well as let him do things we didn't always agree with, because we didn't want to overprotect him; for example, play travel ice hockey, even though it conflicted with Hebrew School, and is a very crude and violent sport, which left David with a terribly deviated septum -- why hasn't David visited his parents in over eight months, 3 Does David not understand that the contented smile on his face after he eats the Plaintiff's brisket, the impish grin he makes after poking fun at the other Plaintiff's inability to understand that new Napster thing, what's it called, Spot Me Five, and, most of all, the in-love beam he has had since he started visiting with his sweet girlfriend, it provides a spiritual sustenance we need to carry on until his next visit, 4 We appeal to the court to legally require David to see us, it's not like we live in Outer Mongolia, DECLARATION OF DAVE M COWEN IN OPPOSITION OF THE MOTION FOR ENFORCEMENT OF FILIAL RIGHTS, Date: July, 18, 2013, Time: 11:47 AM 1 Guys, Are you seriously suing me, I saw you a month ago, When we met in Philadelphia for Grandma's 90th birthday, How often do you even visit Grandma, Also, You came out to LA a month before that, Stayed in our one bedroom apartment, I love you guys, my girlfriend loves you guys, But coming home from work to find our bed made for two weeks really weirded us out, 2 You know what would weird out most other women, How much you communicate with me, Every day, Emails, Texts, Gchats, Skypes, Liking all of my Facebook posts, Sometimes I do wish you lived in rural China, 3 What exactly do you want, DECLARATION OF RICHARD B AND RANDI S COWEN IN SUPPORT OF REPLY IN SUPPORT OF THE MOTION FOR ENFORCEMENT OF FILIAL RIGHTS, Date: July 18, 2013, Time: 1:40 PM 1 Rural China, The Defendant should never wish onto his parents such terrible misfortune, 2, Is your girlfriend upset with the Plaintiffs, Did the making of the bed disrupt the Defendant's and her's you know what, 3 Using a standard metric of a three day visit every two months, we think, as compensation for spiritual needs lost, that you and her should come with us on a 12 day trip to a tropical destination of their choosing, in which RCI has a timeshare, We can make it a yearly tradition, And in the future, if he and her have children, not pushing it, but when they do, we will upgrade to a Gold President's suite, and have the children sleep on our side a few nights, so the two of them can you know what, DECLARATION OF DAVE M COWEN IN SUPPORT OF REPLY IN SUPPORT OF OPPOSITION OF THE MOTION FOR ENFORCEMENT OF FILIAL RIGHTS, Date: July 18, 2013, Time: 2:24 PM, 1 I'll take the China thing back if you guys stop saying you know what, Just say sex, As in we resumed having sex when you two finally moved out of our one bedroom apartment, 2, She's not upset with you guys, 3, But she can't get away for a 12 day vacation, She barely even got July 4th off, But I've got some vacation time in August and I'd be happy to get a Gold President's suite with you somewhere, What do you think about Costa Rica, DECLARATION OF RICHARD B AND RANDI S COWEN IN SUPPORT OF SUR-REPLY IN SUPPORT OF THE MOTION FOR ENFORCEMENT OF FILIAL RIGHTS, Date: July, 18, 2013, Time: 3:15 PM, 1 The Plaintiffs have heard Costa Rica is pretty overbuilt these days, And they really only want to get a Gold President's suite, or even have the Defendant go with them, if the Defendant's girlfriend comes, Quite candidly, we like spending time with the Defendant a lot more when he's with her, She really brings out the best in him, 2, When is he going to ask her to marry him, DECLARATION OF DAVE M COWEN IN SUPPORT OF SUR-REPLY IN SUPPORT OF OPPOSITION OF THE MOTION FOR ENFORCEMENT OF FILIAL RIGHTS, Date: July, 18, 2013, Time: 3:45 PM, 1 You don't like spending time with me without my girlfriend, That's a really shitty thing to say to your son, 2, But it is true, 3, That's why I asked her to marry me last night, DECLARATION OF RICHARD B AND RANDI S COWEN IN SUPPORT OF SUR-SUR-REPLY IN SUPPORT OF THE MOTION FOR ENFORCEMENT OF FILIAL RIGHTS, Date: July, 18, 2013, Time: 3:46 PM, 1, Really, What did she say, DECLARATION OF THIRD PARTY INTERVENOR, Date: July, 18, 2013, Time: 3:49 PM 1, I said YES, 2, And I say yes to the tropical trip, 3, If you're looking for something not too overbuilt, I've heard really great things about the Yunnan Province of China, RICHARD B AND RANDI S COWEN DECLARE THEY ARE ECSTATIC AND MOVE TO DISMISS THE ENFORCEMENT OF FILIAL RIGHTS," and so part of what makes me feel bad about that so-called humor piece is that clearly I have always struggled with the right amount of filial piety in my life, and that time happened to be right around the time he had his first kidney hospitalization, so what kind of son was I writing such a bratty thing, and how much do I regret not just spending more time with them before it was all over, and it makes me think, I should really try to fit in all my memories of him in this sentence, that would be a long sentence, and it would include how he took photographs like they did back in Lincoln's day, like, he wouldn't use the old equipment, but he would take minutes, five, ten of them it felt like to set up a shot, and it was kind of exasperating as a kid, but also funny when we got older, and something I laugh about it in my head when I think of him setting up his camera, but then I think of his tremors and how he couldn't really hold a camera in the end, but also how he had tremors when he was reading a speech from a piece of printer paper, but fought through, our friends and family pushing him through, and it also makes me think that he was truly suffering and so taking his life wasn't a bad thing, and hopefully he is resting in peace, and that phrase means so much to me now, it's real how in life when you experience a new stage, the phrases and the words and the art around those stages mean more to you, and Carl Jung says, "The individual who is not anchored in God can offer no resistance on his own resources to the physical and moral blandishments of the world, For this he needs the evidence of inner, transcendent experience which alone can protect him from the otherwise inevitable submersion in the mass, Merely intellectual or even moral insight into the stultification and moral irresponsibility of the mass man is a negative recognition only and amounts to not much more than a wavering on the road to the atomization of the individual," and I still feel like God is in the Spotify algorithm, and Kids See Ghosts Kanye and Kid Cudi's "Reborn," just came on, from their paranormal album, "I'm so, I'm so reborn, I'm movin' forward, Keep movin' forward, keep movin' forward, Ain't no stress on me Lord, I'm movin' forward, Keep movin' forward, keep movin' forward, I'm so, I'm so reborn," and "Very rarely do you catch me out, Y'all done especially invited guests, me out, Y'all been tellin' jokes that's gon' stress me out, Soon as I walk in, I'm like 'Let's be out,' I was off the chain, I was often drained, I was off the meds, I was called insane, What a awesome thing, engulfed in shame, I want all the rain, I want all the pain, I want all the smoke, I want all the blame, Cardio audio, let me jog your brain, Caught in the Audy Home, we was all detained, All of you Mario, it's all a game, I'm so, I'm so reborn, I'm movin' forward, Keep movin' forward, keep movin' forward, Ain't no stress on me Lord, I'm movin' forward, Keep movin' forward, keep movin' forward," and "I had my issues, ain't that much I could do, But, peace is something that starts with me, with me, At times, wonder my purpose, Easy then to feel worthless, But, peace is something that starts with me (with me, with me), Had so much on my mind, I didn't know where to go, I've come a long way from them hauntin' me, Had me feelin' oh so low, Ain't no stoppin' you no way, All things, the night before, Ain't no stoppin' you no way, No stress yes, I'm so blessed and, I'm so, I'm so reborn," and is it crazy to believe that Spotify shuffle is being infiltrated by God like Phil K Dick would expect and is it the transcendent experience Jung is talking about, and Jung says, "Christianity holds at its core a symbol which has for its content the individual way of life of a man, the Son of Man, and that it even regards this individuation process as the incarnation and revelation of God himself," and this is from Kanye and Kid Cudi's "Ghost Town Part Two or Freee," "May I say something to you, To give you a true knowledge of yourself and life, Man in the full knowledge of himself is a superb and supreme creature of creation, When man becomes possessor of the knowledge of himself, He becomes the master of his environment," and the other thing I just realized that is a heavy thing to put into this book, is that this whole sentence from now on could also just be a list of the names of all the people who have had their lives ruined by a long sentence in prison, that would be an almost endless long sentence, and I wonder what Abe Lincoln would say about the long sentences for so many African Americans, but there are many more qualified people to talk about that issue, and I am almost sorry I brought it up, and I would have cut it, except I don't go backwards while I'm writing this sentence and also because I do want to have said that a little, that the long sentences in prison should stop, and Kanye says, "This the theme song, oh something wrong, Might need a intervention for this new dimension, That's too new to mention, or fit in a sentence, If I get locked up, I won't finish the sent" but this book is supposed to be humorous, even if it's also about my dad's death now all of a sudden, and

I guess that also makes me think how fortunate my dad and I have been during our lives, and maybe there's nothing to feel bad about in connection with my dad's death, and maybe he lived a good and full life, and it also again makes me think of my dad's hero, Abraham Lincoln, and Shenk's chapter 9 says about Lincoln, that "Illness can coexist with marvelous well-being," and also how he said "Let there be no compromise on the question of extending slavery, Stand firm, The tug has to come, & better now, than any time hereafter," because "Having felt the tug come many times, Lincoln knew that putting it off would do no good," but after the South seceded, and the war didn't start well, Lincoln said, "He felt almost ready to hang himself," and he said this in the oval office, but instead he raised his pen, like he had with that poem when he was in his twenties, he used the pen to creatively write the Emancipation Proclamation, and he helped free the slaves from their long sentence, the longest sentence possible, of slavery from birth until death, for many of them, that is truly the longest sentence, like I said, I can't even imagine that or do justice to that, except I guess as a Jew my people have also suffered as slaves and have suffered as prisoners and were killed, and so have all kinds of people in history, wow, has this sentence, has it truly gone off the rails into non-humor and revelation of gross privilege and maybe even incidental racial insensitivity and suddenly, I want to delete it all, the entire sentence now, and start over, I just selected all, I am going to press delete, I am going to really do it, no, I just kept typing through it, I lied, I'm a liar sometimes, sometimes all the time, and did you know that the President after Lincoln was a lot like that Quixote Donny guy, Andrew Johnson was impeached, and here's a description of him, and something to think about from The New Yorker's Isaac Chotiner, as Chotiner said he was "Impressed by the degree to which the people who were making a case for impeaching Johnson wanted to base it not simply on the intricacies of the law or whether a specific law was violated but on this larger argument that he was fundamentally a racist, erratic person who could not carry out his duties, had poor values, and at some level should not be allowed to be President," and Johnson's biographer says, basically, "Once you say, Look, this guy is an unresponsive person who is abusing the public trust, disregarding Congress, ignoring the Constitution and the separation of powers, and squandering the effects of the war, turning back the clock, recreating slavery with a different name—you can't distill that into a single law," and so like Lincoln and Mihaly Csikszentmihalyi, I am trusting my intuition to make novel connections in language or imagery, between me and my dad and that guy who is like Andrew Johnson and Lincoln, and history seems to repeat itself, it keeps repeating itself, it does, it repeats itself, why does it do that, repeating itself, stop it, stop doing that, or don't, and I do want to redo my life sometimes, some of my lies or erraticness or misbehaviors, or just better choices, paths, do you, I would have exercised more for one, I'm kind of a fat ass these days, and it means I might die soon, which is sad, it's been tough for my mom, that her partner is gone, and I sent her The Beach Boys "Forever" and Lil Uzi Vert's "The Way Life Goes," after Dad died, and she liked that, so I am going to work on that, staying alive longer, and David Shields quotes Graham Greene, in the front of Reality Hunger, "When we are not sure, we are alive," and do you ever want to re-do life sometimes, like, just change the whole way life functions, like, we could bring people back to life in life, maybe that will happen one day, and I guess maybe we do just improve life as humans as we go, and that life might seem completely done over for people from the past if they were here now, and under the tag “Fathers” in The New Yorker, I found a piece by Haruki Murakami about his father where he says, “All we can do is breathe the air of the period we live in, carry with us the special burdens of the time, and grow up within those confines, That’s just how things are,” like the fact there even is dialysis and kidney transplants and medicine to treat mental problems in my and my dad’s time is new, and so that might be a possibility for humans at some point, bringing people back to life, but at the moment, I mostly want to restart the last five years with my dad after he got so sick with the kidney disease that he was hospitalized and truly started his decline, I wish I had known it was truly his decline, and fully understood what that meant, and I think Walter Benjamin is right that you don’t really know history while you live it, though looking back I think I was always dealing with it through writing and in an almost unconscious way, as when I first learned that my mom was planning on giving my dad one of her kidneys because she also didn’t want me or my sister to give my dad one of our kidneys, she said she’d do it, that was back around 2010, and it is also the basis for the one piece of mine that McSweeney’s published, and just to be clear, after I submit pieces to The New Yorker I submit them to McSweeney’s and they have rejected every piece except for this first one that The New Yorker rejected after the Kanye piece, and this memoir, it so much reminds me of Kanye’s “Last Call,” and he’s my brother, like he is Jerry Seinfeld and Larry David’s, but not Donny QT, question mark, and so here are some of his lyrics for that song, which ends his first album, which was a great album but was not just his best like some people say who don’t like dark themes: “So this A&R over at Roc-A-Fella, named Hip Hop Picked the "Truth" beat for Beanie, And I was in the session with him, I had my demo with me, You know, like I always do, I play the songs, he's like "Who that spittin,"

I'm like "It's me," He's like "Oh, well okay," Uhh, he started talkin' to me on the phone, going back and forth Just askin' me to send him beats, and I'm thinking he's trying to get into managing producers, cause he had this other kid named Just Blaze he was messin with, So won't you raise your glass won't you, So won't you raise your glass won't you, So won't you raise your glass won't you, So won't you raise your glass won't you, And um, he was friends with my mentor, No ID, And No ID told him, "Look man, you wanna mess with Kanye you need to tell him that you like the way he rap" No ID: "Yo, you wanna sign him, tell him you like how he rap" I was all, I dunno if he was gassin' me or not but he's like he wanna manage me as a rapper AND a producer, I'm like oh shit, I was messin with, uh, D-Dot also, People were like this, started talking about the ghost production but that's how I got in the game, If it wasn't for that, I wouldn't be here, So you know, after they picked that "Truth" beat I was figuring I was gonna do some more work but shit just wasn't poppin off like that, I was stayin in Chicago, I had my own apartment, I be doin like, just beats for local acts just to try to keep the lights on, and then to go out and buy, get a Pelle Pelle off lay-away, get some Jordans or something or get a TechnoMarine, that's what we wore back then, I made this one beat where I sped up this Harold Melvin sample I played it for Hip over the phone, he's like, "Oh, yo that shit is crazy Jay might want it for this compilation album he doin, called The Dynasty, And at that time, like the drums really weren't soundin right to me, So I went and um, I was listening to Dre Chronic 2001 at that time, And really I just, like bit the drums off "Xxplosive" and put it like with it sped up, sampled, and now it's kind of like my whole style, when it started, when he rapped on "This Can't be Life," And that was like, really the first beat of that kind that was on The Dynasty album, I could say that was the resurgence of the soul sound You know, I got to come in and track the beat and at the time I was still with my other management, I really wanted to roll with Hip Hop cause I, I just needed some fresh air, you know what I'm sayin cause I been there for a while, I appreciated what they did for me but, you know there's a time in every man's life where he gotta make a change, Try to move up to the next level, And that day I came and I tracked the beat and I got to meet Jay-Z and he said, "Oh you a real soulful dude," And he, uh, played the song cause he already spit his verse by the time I got to the studio, You know how he do it, one take, And he said "Tell me what you think of this," And I heard it, and I was thinking like, man, I really wanted more like of the simple type Jay-Z, I ain't want like the, the more introspective, complicated rhy- or the, in my personal opinion, So he asked me, "What you think of it", And I was like, "Man that shit tight," you know what I'm sayin', man what I'ma tell him, I was on the train, man, you know, So after that I went back home, And man I'm, I'm just in Chicago, I'm trying to do my thing, You know, I got groups, I got acts I'm trying to get on, and like there wasn't nothin really like poppin' off the way it should have been, One of my homies that was one of my artists, he got signed, But it was supposed to really go through my production company, but he ended up going straight with the company, So, like I'm just straight holdin' the phone, gettin' the bad news that dude was tryin' to leave my company, And I got evicted at the same time, So I went down and tracked the beats from him, I took that money, came back, packed all my shit up in a U-Haul, maybe about ten days before I had to actually get out so I ain't have to deal with the landlord cause he's a jerk, Me and my mother drove to Newark, New Jersey, I hadn't even seen my apartment, I remember I pulled up I unpacked all my shit, You know, we went to Ikea, I bought a bed, I put the bed together myself, I loaded up all my equipment, and the first beat I made was, uh, "Heart of the City," And Beans was still working on his album at that time, so I came up there to Baseline, it was Beans' birthday, matter of fact, and I played like seven beats, And, you know I guess he was in the zone, he already had the beats that he wanted, I had did "Nothing Like It" already at that time but then Jay walked in, I remember he had a Gucci bucket hat on, I remember it like, like it was yesterday, And Hiphop said, "Yo play that one beat for him," And I played "Heart of the City," And really I made "Heart of the City, " I really wanted to give that beat To DMX, And I played another beat, and I played another beat, And I remember that Gucci bucket, he took it and like put it over his face and made one of them faces like 'OOOOOOOOOH,' Two days later I'm in Baseline and I seen Dame, Dame didn't know who I was and I was like, "Yo what's up I'm Kanye," "You that kid that gave all them beats to Jay, Yo, this got classics" You know I ain't talkin shit, I'm like "oh shit," And all this time I'm starstruck, man, I'm still thinking 'bout, you know I'm picturing these on the show, The Streets is Watching, I'm lookin, these were superstars in my eyes, And they still are, you know, So, Jay came in and he spit all these songs like in one day, and in two days, I gotta bring up one thing, you know, come back to the story, the day I did the 'Can't be Life' beat on track, I remember Lenny S, he had some Louis Vuitton sneakers on, he think he fly, And Hip Hop was there, I think Ty-Ty, John Meneilly, a bunch of people, I didn't know all these people at the time they was in the room, and I said, "yo Jay I could rap," And I spit this rap that said, uh "I'm killin y'all on that lyrical shit, Mayonnaise colored Benz, I push miracle whips," And I saw his eyes light up when I said that line, But you know the rest, the rap was like real wack and shit, so that's all the response, He said "man that was tight," That was it, You know, I ain't get no deal then, hehe, Okay, fast forward, So, Blueprint, "H to the Izzo, " my first hit single, And I just took that proudly, built relationships with people, My relationship with Kweli I think was one of the best ones to ever happen to my career as a rapper, Because, you know, of course later he allowed me to go on tour with him, Man, I appre-- I love him for that, And at this time, you know I didn't have a deal, I had songs, and I had relationships with all these A&R's, and they wanted beats from me, so they'd call me up, I'd play them some beats, "Gimme a beat that sound like Jay-Z," You know, they dick riders, Whatever, So I'll play them these post-Blueprint beats or whatever and then I'll play my shit, I'll be like, "yo but I rap too," Hey, I guess they was lookin' at me crazy cause you know, cause I ain't have a jersey on or whatever, Everybody out there listen here: I played them 'Jesus Walks' and they didn't sign me, You know what happened, it was some A&R's that fucked with me though, but then like the heads, it'd be somebody at the company that'll say "naw," Like, Dave Lighty fucked with me, my Mel brought me to a bunch of labels, Jessica Rivera, man, I'm not gonna say nothin to mess my promotion up, Let's just say I didn't get my deal, The that was behind me, I mean, he wasn't even a, you know, The person who actually kicked everything off was Joe 3H from Capitol Records, He wanted to sign me really bad Dame was like, "Yo you got a deal with Capitol, Okay man, just make sure it's not wack," Then one day I just went ahead and played it, I wanted to play some songs, cause you know Cam was in the room, Young Guru, and Dame was in the room, So I played, actually it's a song that you'll never hear, but maybe I might use it, So, it's called 'Wow,' I go to Jacob with 25 thou, you go with 25 hundred, wow, I got eleven plaques on my walls right now, You got your first gold single, damn," Like the chorus went, Don't bite that chorus, I might still use it, So I play that song for him and he's like "oh shit" "I ain't gonna front, it's kinda hot," Like they still weren't looking at me like a rapper, And I'm sure Dame figured, 'like man, If he do a whole album, if his raps is wack at least we can throw Cam on every song and save the album, you know, So uh Dame took me into the office, and he's like "yo man, B, B, you don't want a brick, you don't want a brick" "You gotta be under an umbrella, you'll get rained on," I told Hiphop and Hiphop was all, "oh, word," Actually, even with that I was still about to take the deal with Capitol cause it was already on the table and cause of my relationship with 3H, That, you know, cause I told him I was gonna do it, and I'm a man of my word, I was gonna roll with what I said I was gonna do, Then, you know, I'm not gonna name no names, but people told me, "oh he's just a producer rapper, " and told 3H that told the heads of the Capitol, and right-- the day I'm talking about, I planned out everything I was gonna do, Man, I had picked out clothes, I already started booking studio sessions, I started arranging my album, thinking of marketing schemes, man I was ready to go, And they had Mel call me, they said, "yo, Capitol pulled on the deal" And, you know I told them that Roc-A-Fella was interested and I don't know if they thought that was just something I was saying to gas them up to try to push the price up or whatever, I went up, I called G, I said, "man, you think we could still get that deal with Roc-A-Fella," So won't you raise your glass, won't you, So won't you raise your glass, won't you, So won't you raise your glass, won't you, So won't you raise your glass, won't you," and so isn't that kind of like one of those stream of consciousness longest sentence, typed out, it's 1,982 words, which would have beaten Faulkner's 1,288 word sentence back in 1936, and so what else does that say about Kanye, he's a stream of consciousness genius, right, and back to me and so McSweeney's took this piece I'm about to put in here, they fucked with it, as Kanye says, but then didn't take another one, so, yes, I am clearly a mediocre talent, unlike Kanye, and I can only self-publish via Kindle Direct Publishing, me that is, not Kanye, anybody would publish Kanye, and they already did, and "Factography is a type of writing that takes as its topic the structural, socioeconomic, and material conditions of its production, and in some works such factographical showing extends to the socioeconomic conditions of their production, Jean Keller's The Black Book (self published, 2013) is a good example of this type of factography-as-publishing, A gallon of ink used for POD printing costs over four thousand dollars, Keller explains on the Lulu sales page, "However, the price of a book is not calculated according to the amount of ink used in its production, For example, a Lulu book of blank pages costs an artist as much to produce as a book filled with text or large photographs, Furthermore, as the number of pages increases, the price of each page decreases, A book containing the maximum number of pages printed entirely in black ink therefore results in the lowest cost and maximum value for the artist," so maybe I should put the Kanye part in small font, maybe I should put all the book in small font in order to get the most bang for my Amazon buck, and some people can't decide if Kanye is an Enneagram 4 wing 3 or an Enneagram 6 wing 7, there was a podcast partly about this on this podcast called Enneagram for Idiots, and I also can't decide if I am an Enneagram 6 wing 7 or a 4 wing 3, and let's try to figure it out, before I put in the piece that McSweeney's fucked with, OK, cool, and I've read a lot more about my Enneagram type and listened to Enneagram podcasts, and here's what the Enneagram Institute says about my type, or what I believe to be my type, "THE INDIVIDUALIST, Enneagram Type Four, The Sensitive,

Introspective Type: Expressive, Dramatic, Self-Absorbed, and Temperamental, Type Four in Brief, Fours are self-aware, sensitive, and reserved, They are emotionally honest, creative, and personal, but can also be moody and self-conscious, Withholding themselves from others due to feeling vulnerable and defective, they can also feel disdainful and exempt from ordinary ways of living, and David Shields "says," "The process of aggrandizement: relatively ordinary problems are overblown into larger-than-life 'literature,' We, too, can make a myth of our own meager circumstances," and They typically have problems with melancholy, self-indulgence, and self-pity, At their Best: inspired and highly creative, they are able to renew themselves and transform their experiences, Basic Fear: That they have no identity or personal significance, Basic Desire: To find themselves and their significance (to create an identity), Enneagram Four with a Three-Wing: 'The Aristocrat,' Enneagram Four with a Five-Wing: 'The Bohemian,' Key Motivations: Want to express themselves and their individuality, to create and surround themselves with beauty, to maintain certain moods and feelings, to withdraw to protect their self-image, to take care of emotional needs before attending to anything else, to attract a 'rescuer,' When moving in their Direction of Disintegration (stress), aloof Fours suddenly become over-involved and clinging at Two, However, when moving in their Direction of Integration (growth), envious, emotionally turbulent Fours become more objective and principled, like healthy Ones, Type Four Overview, We have named this type The Individualist because Fours maintain their identity by seeing themselves as fundamentally different from others, isn't that true, folks, Fours feel that they are unlike other human beings, and consequently, that no one can understand them or love them adequately, They often see themselves as uniquely talented, possessing special, one-of-a-kind gifts, haha, how much have I talked about that, but also as uniquely disadvantaged or flawed, fatedly so I would say, More than any other type, Fours are acutely aware of and focused on their personal differences and deficiencies, Healthy Fours are honest with themselves: they own all of their feelings and can look at their motives, contradictions, and emotional conflicts without denying or whitewashing them, They may not necessarily like what they discover, but they do not try to rationalize their states, nor do they try to hide them from themselves or others, lol, I am literally putting this embarrassing analysis into this book, They are not afraid to see themselves 'warts and all,' Healthy Fours are willing to reveal highly personal and potentially shameful things about themselves because they are determined to understand the truth of their experience—so that they can discover who they are and come to terms with their emotional history, am I at the truth, Dad, This ability also enables Fours to endure suffering with a quiet strength, Their familiarity with their own darker nature makes it easier for them to process painful experiences that might overwhelm other types, Nevertheless, Fours often report that they feel they are missing something in themselves, although they may have difficulty identifying exactly what that 'something' is, Is it will power, Social ease, Self-confidence, Emotional tranquility—all of which they see in others, seemingly in abundance, Given time and sufficient perspective, Fours generally recognize that they are unsure about aspects of their self-image—their personality or ego-structure itself, They feel that they lack a clear and stable identity, particularly a social persona that they feel comfortable with, While it is true that Fours often feel different from others, they do not really want to be alone, They may feel socially awkward or self-conscious, but they deeply wish to connect with people who understand them and their feelings, The "romantics" of the Enneagram, they long for someone to come into their lives and appreciate the secret self that they have privately nurtured and hidden from the world, is that you dear reader, If, over time, such validation remains out of reach, Fours begin to build their identity around how unlike everyone else they are, The outsider therefore comforts herself by becoming an insistent individualist: everything must be done on her own, in her own way, on her own terms, Fours' mantra becomes 'I am myself, Nobody understands me, I am different and special,' while they secretly wish they could enjoy the easiness and confidence that others seem to enjoy, Fours typically have problems with a negative self-image and chronically low self-esteem, They attempt to compensate for this by cultivating a Fantasy Self—an idealized self-image which is built up primarily in their imaginations, is this whole book that self, A Four we know shared with us that he spent most of his spare time listening to classical music while fantasizing about being a great concert pianist—à la Vladimir Horowitz, Unfortunately, his commitment to practicing fell far short of his fantasized self-image, and he was often embarrassed when people asked him to play for them, haha are you embarrassed for me about this book, His actual abilities, while not poor, became sources of shame, is it poor, this book, the quality, In the course of their lives, Fours may try several different identities on for size, basing them on styles, preferences, or qualities they find attractive in others, But underneath the surface, they still feel uncertain about who they really are, The problem is that they base their identities largely on their feelings, When Fours look inward they see a kaleidoscopic, ever-shifting pattern of emotional reactions, lots of emotions here, and Morrie in the, to me, infamously famous grief memoir, Tuesdays with Morrie, says,

"Ah, You're thinking, Mitch, But detachment doesn't mean you don't let it penetrate you fully, That's how you are able to leave it, [Mitch is] lost, "Take any emotion--love for a woman, or grief for a loved one, or what I'm going through, fear and pain from a deadly illness, By throwing yourself into these emotions, by allowing yourself to dive in, all the way, over your head even, you experience them fully and completely, You know what pain is, You know what love is, You know what grief is, And only then can you say, 'All right, I have experienced that emotion, I recognize that emotion, Now I need to detach from that emotion for a moment,'" Fours accurately perceive a truth about human nature—that it is dynamic and ever changing, But because they want to create a stable, reliable identity from their emotions, they attempt to cultivate only certain feelings while rejecting others, Some feelings are seen as 'me,' while others are 'not me,' as Morrie says, "I know you think this is just about dying, but it's like I keep telling you, When you learn how to die, you learn how to live," By attempting to hold on to specific moods and express others, Fours believe that they are being true to themselves, One of the biggest challenges Fours face is learning to let go of feelings from the past; they tend to nurse wounds and hold onto negative feelings about those who have hurt them, haha lot of old wounds ay, Doc Boner, Indeed, Fours can become so attached to longing and disappointment that they are unable to recognize the many treasures in their lives, oh boy, There is a Sufi story that relates to this about an old dog that had been badly abused and was near starvation, One day, the dog found a bone, carried it to a safe spot, and started gnawing away, The dog was so hungry that it chewed on the bone for a long time and got every last bit of nourishment out of it, After some time, a kind old man noticed the dog and its pathetic scrap and began quietly setting food out for it, But the poor hound was so attached to its bone that it refused to let go of it and soon starved to death, sounds like me and screenwriting doesn't it, Fours are in the same predicament, As long as they believe that there is something fundamentally wrong with them, they cannot allow themselves to experience or enjoy their many good qualities, To acknowledge their good qualities would be to lose their sense of identity (as a suffering victim) and to be without a relatively consistent personal identity (their Basic Fear), Fours grow by learning to see that much of their story is not true—or at least it is not true any more, The old feelings begin to fall away once they stop telling themselves their old tale: it is irrelevant to who they are right now, who am I right now, as I write this, Type Four—Levels of Development, Healthy Levels, Level 1 (At Their Best): Profoundly creative, expressing the personal and the universal, possibly in a work of art, Inspired, self-renewing and regenerating: able to transform all their experiences into something valuable: self-creative, whoa, is this that work of art, is it self-renewing and profoundly creative, Level 2: Self-aware, introspective, on the 'search for self,' aware of feelings and inner impulses, Sensitive and intuitive both to self and others: gentle, tactful, compassionate, and aren't I on the search for self, Level 3: Highly personal, individualistic, 'true to self,' Self-revealing, emotionally honest, humane, Ironic view of self and life: can be serious and funny, vulnerable and emotionally strong, and aren't I serious and funny, vulnerable and strong, Average Levels, Level 4: Take an artistic, romantic orientation to life, creating a beautiful, aesthetic environment to cultivate and prolong personal feelings, Heighten reality through fantasy, passionate feelings, and the imagination, isn't all this beautiful music I am listening to on Spotify that aesthetic environment, and would you believe me if I told you that "Amazing Grace" by the Treme Brass

Band is on, it is, Level 5: To stay in touch with feelings, they interiorize everything, taking everything personally, but become self-absorbed and introverted, moody and hypersensitive, shy and self-conscious, unable to be spontaneous or to 'get out of themselves,' uh-oh here comes the bad stuff, so self-absorbed, Stay withdrawn to protect their self-image and to buy time to sort out feelings, Level 6: Gradually think that they are different from others, and feel that they are exempt from living as everyone else does, They become melancholy dreamers, disdainful, decadent, and sensual, living in a fantasy world, Self-pity and envy of others leads to self-indulgence, and to becoming increasingly impractical, unproductive, effete, and precious, whoa, is that what this book really is self-pity, effete, precious, decadent, and Envy is the passion of 4s and Emerson says, "There is a time in every man's education when he arrives at the conviction that envy is ignorance; that imitation is suicide; that he must take himself for better, for worse, as his portion; that though the wide universe is full of good, no kernel of nourishing corn can come to him but through his toil bestowed on that plot of ground which is given to him to till, The power which resides in him is new in nature, and none but he knows what that is which he can do, nor does he know until he has tried," and Unhealthy Levels, Level 7: When dreams fail, become self-inhibiting and angry at self, depressed and alienated from self and others, blocked and emotionally paralyzed, Ashamed of self, fatigued and unable to function, is this book going to fail, or ruin my life, and alienate me from my loved ones, and I will become ashamed and unable to function, Level 8: Tormented by delusional self-contempt, self-reproaches, self-hatred, and morbid thoughts: everything is a source of torment, Blaming others, they drive away anyone who tries to help them, damn this shit gets dark, Level 9:

Despairing, feel hopeless and become self-destructive, possibly abusing alcohol or drugs to escape, In the extreme: emotional breakdown or suicide is likely, whoa me and my dad, will we have the same end, who knows, and I also compared type 4 with the other type I might be, a 6, and here's that, Misidentifying Fours and Sixes, While there are real similarities between the two types, there are even more differences, The principal difference is that Sixes are usually extremely appealing and relate well to people; they have the ability to unconsciously engage the emotions of others so that others will like them and form secure relationships with them, Fours, in contrast, do not relate primarily to people but to their own inner emotional states, Fours take it for granted that they are alone in life, and find it difficult to form bonds with others—something that comes easily to Sixes, The psychic structures of the two types are also very different: Fours are true introverts, while Sixes are a blend of introversion and extroversion—true ambiverts who possess qualities of both orientations, Confusion arises between these types principally on the part of Sixes who think that they are Fours for two main reasons, First, some Sixes identify with the negative side of the Four (depression, inferiority, self-doubt, and hopelessness, for example) and think they must be Fours because they recognize similar traits in themselves, The difference lies in the motivations for these traits, For example, while all the types can become depressed, Fours do so because they are disappointed with themselves for having lost some opportunity to actualize themselves, They become depressed when they realize that in their search for self, they have gone down a blind alley and now must pay the price, Unhealthy, depressed Fours are essentially angry with themselves for bringing this on themselves or for allowing it to happen, By contrast, Sixes become depressed when they fear that they have done something to make their authority figure mad at them, Their depression is a response to their self-disparagement; it comes from the fear that the authority is angry with them and will punish them, Thus, the depression of Sixes is exogenous (coming from the outside) and can be relieved by a word of reassurance from the authority, This is not the case with Fours whose depression is endogenous (coming from the inside), a response to their self-accusations, Second, we have characterized the Four as The Individualist, and some Sixes who are artistic think that they therefore must be Fours, However, as noted above in the discussion of Fours and Nines, artistic talent is not the sole domain of Fours, so it is entirely possible for Sixes to be artists of one kind or another, Even so, there are important differences in the creative work produced by these two types, In general, Sixes tend to be performing artists, while Fours tend to be original creators, Sixes are more likely to be actors or musicians than poets and playwrights, more likely to perform the words or music of someone else than to create it themselves, Even those Sixes who are creative tend either to be traditionalists, creating within firmly established rules and styles, or they go to an extreme and become rebellious, reacting against traditionalism–such as rock stars and experimental novelists who purposely defy traditional forms, In either case, both tradition and reactions against it are an important aspect of their art, The themes typically found in the art of Sixes have to do with belonging, security, family, politics, country, and common values, Creative Fours, by contrast, are individualists who go their own way to explore their feelings and other subjective personal states, The artistic products of Fours are much less involved either with following a tradition or with reacting against it, Fours are less apt to use political or communal experiences as the subject matter for their work, choosing instead the movements of their own souls, their personal revelations, the darkness and light they discover in themselves as they become immersed in the creative process, By listening to their inner voices, even average Fours may speak to the universal person or fail to communicate to anyone, at least to their contemporaries, They may be ahead of their time not because they are trying to be rebellious or avant-garde, but because they develop their own forms to express their personal point of view, What is important to Fours is not the tradition but personal truth, Tradition is no more than a backdrop against which Fours play out their own personal dramas," and you know what, now I am confused, now I think I am more of a 6, because my art deals with tradition and reaction against it, even though I have narcissistic tendencies, and can be quite self-indulgent, clearly, but I am more of an ambivert than an introvert, though I can be decadent and melancholic, moody and hypersensitive, and wrap myself in music, art, and stay away from others, and isn't this book a process of regeneration, and don't I fear of not having personal significance, and isn't this a book of personal revelation and aren't I self-revealing, ironically serious and humorous at the same time, profoundly creative, but am I just a 6 who wants to romanticize being a 4, but isn't romanticism part of being a 4, and aren't I more concerned with personal truth than tradition or rebelling, but isn't this an experimental book, about breaking tradition of a sentence, but isn't tradition just a backdrop as I play out my personal drama, I dunno, here's what The Enneagram Institute says about 6, THE LOYALIST, Enneagram Type Six, The Committed, Security-Oriented Type: Engaging, Responsible, Anxious, and Suspicious, The committed, security-oriented type, Sixes are reliable, hard-working, responsible, and trustworthy, hm, I think I am hard-working but am I responsible, is this a responsible book to write, and I think I've repeated how untrustworthy I am as a narrator, Excellent "troubleshooters," they foresee problems and foster cooperation, but can also become defensive, evasive, and anxious—running on stress while complaining about it, They can be cautious and indecisive, but also reactive, defiant and rebellious, oh ok so maybe I am counter-phobic, They typically have problems with self-doubt and suspicion, got a lot of that self-doubt and suspicion, I am super worried about those bots, At their Best: internally stable and self-reliant, courageously championing themselves and others, self-publishing is self-reliance, Basic Fear: Of being without support and guidance, Basic Desire: To have security and support, Enneagram Six with a Five-Wing: "The Defender", Enneagram Six with a Seven-Wing: "The Buddy", Key Motivations: Want to have security, to feel supported by others, to have certitude and reassurance, to test the attitudes of others toward them, to fight against anxiety and insecurity, is this book all a test of others, When moving in their Direction of Disintegration (stress), dutiful Sixes suddenly become competitive and arrogant at Three, am I in stress right now, competitive and arrogant about my writing, However, when moving in their Direction of Integration (growth), fearful, pessimistic Sixes become more relaxed and optimistic, like healthy Nine, will there be a future where I am finally relaxed, We have named personality type Six The Loyalist because, of all the personality types, Sixes are the most loyal to their friends and to their beliefs, I am quite loyal to my friends, they are all mentioned in the book, and They will "go down with the ship" that is true about my beliefs, and hang on to relationships of all kinds far longer than most other types, Sixes are also loyal to ideas, systems, and beliefs—even to the belief that all ideas or authorities should be questioned or defied, lol, just said that,

Indeed, not all Sixes go along with the "status quo": their beliefs may be rebellious and anti-authoritarian, even revolutionary, OK, feeling you with that rebel side, In any case, they will typically fight for their beliefs more fiercely than they will fight for themselves, and they will defend their community or family more tenaciously than they will defend themselves, The reason Sixes are so loyal to others is that they do not want to be abandoned and left without support—their Basic Fear, did I mention that my dad tried to kill himself when I was 4, too, was I afraid of abandonment, Thus, the central issue for type Six is a failure of self-confidence, Sixes come to believe that they do not possess the internal resources to handle life's challenges and vagaries alone, and so increasingly rely on structures, allies, beliefs, and supports outside themselves for guidance to survive, If suitable structures do not exist, they will help create and maintain them, Sixes are the primary type in the Thinking Center, meaning that they have the most trouble contacting their own inner guidance, As a result, they do not have confidence in their own minds and judgments, This does not mean that they do not think, On the contrary, they think—and worry—a lot, They also tend to fear making important decisions, although at the same time, they resist having anyone else make decisions for them, They want to avoid being controlled, but are also afraid of taking responsibility in a way that might put them "in the line of fire," (The old Japanese adage that says, "The blade of grass that grows too high gets chopped off" relates to this idea,) Sixes are always aware of their anxieties and are always looking for ways to construct "social security" bulwarks against them, If Sixes feel that they have sufficient back up, they can move forward with some degree of confidence, But if that crumbles, they become anxious and self-doubting, reawakening their Basic Fear, ("I'm on my own, What am I going to do now") A good question for Sixes might therefore be: "When will I know that I have enough security," Or, to get right to the heart of it, "What is security," Without Essential inner guidance and the deep sense of support that it brings, Sixes are constantly struggling to find firm ground, Sixes attempt to build a network of trust over a background of unsteadiness and fear, They are often filled with a nameless anxiety and then try to find or create reasons why, Wanting to feel that there is something solid and clear-cut in their lives, they can become attached to explanations or positions that seem to explain their situation, wait a second, isn't believing in the Enneagram system to explain everything to me an example of this, Because "belief" (trust, faith, convictions, positions) is difficult for Sixes to achieve, and because it is so important to their sense of stability, once they establish a trustworthy belief, they do not easily question it, nor do they want others to do so, oh man, but now I am questioning whether the Enneagram itself is real, too, even though I don't want to question it, The same is true for individuals in a Six's life: once Sixes feel they can trust someone, they go to great lengths to maintain connections with the person who acts as a sounding board, a mentor, or a regulator for the Six's emotional reactions and behavior, They therefore do everything in their power to keep their affiliations going, ("If I don't trust myself, then I have to find something in this world I can trust,") Until they can get in touch with their own inner guidance, Sixes are like a ping-pong ball that is constantly shuttling back and forth between whatever influence is hitting the hardest in any given moment, aren't I ping-ponging between different beliefs in this book, Because of this reactivity, no matter what we say about Sixes, the opposite is often also as true, They are both strong and weak, fearful and courageous, trusting and distrusting, defenders and provokers, sweet and sour, aggressive and passive, bullies and weaklings, on the defensive and on the offensive, thinkers and doers, group people and soloists, believers and doubters, cooperative and obstructionistic, tender and mean, generous and petty—and on and on, It is the contradictory picture that is the characteristic "fingerprint" of Sixes, the fact that they are a bundle of opposites, wow, that also seems like me, but isn't the fact that everyone is a contradiction just a real thing, or is it just my own lack of insight that makes me think that what is true for me is true for everyone else, The biggest problem for Sixes is that they try to build safety in the environment without resolving their own emotional insecurities, When they learn to face their anxieties, however, Sixes understand that although the world is always changing and is, by nature uncertain, they can be serene and courageous in any circumstance, And they can attain the greatest gift of all, a sense of peace with themselves despite the uncertainties of life, Type Six—Levels of Development, Healthy Levels, Level 1 (At Their Best): Become self-affirming, trusting of self and others, independent yet symbiotically interdependent and cooperative as an equal, Belief in self leads to true courage, positive thinking, leadership, and rich self-expression, is this rich self-expression, is this courage, is this positive, I dunno about the last part, Level 2: Able to elicit strong emotional responses from others: very appealing, endearing, lovable, affectionate, am I appealing, endearing, lovable, I've often asked you that, am I, Trust important: bonding with others, forming permanent relationships and alliances, Level 3: Dedicated to individuals and movements in which they deeply believe, I am dedicated to movements, like gun safety, right, Community builders: responsible, reliable, trustworthy, Hard-working and persevering, sacrificing for others, they create stability and security in their world, bringing a cooperative spirit,

Average Levels, Level 4: Start investing their time and energy into whatever they believe will be safe and stable, Organizing and structuring, they look to alliances and authorities for security and continuity, Constantly vigilant, anticipating problems, is part of this writing style, including this part right here, where I vigilantly analyze things like that, and David Shields "says" "An artistic movement, albeit an organic and as-yet-unstated one, is forming, What are its key components, A deliberate unartiness: 'raw' material, seemingly unprocessed, unfiltered, uncensored, and unprofessional, Randomness, openness to accident and serendipity, spontaneity; artistic risk, emotional urgency and intensity, reader/viewer participation; an overly literal tone, as if a reporter were viewing a strange culture; plasticity of form, pointillism; criticism as autobiography; self-reflexivity; self-ethnography, anthropological autobiography; a blurring (to the point of invisibility) of any distinction between fiction and nonfiction: the lure and blur of the real," and so we have finally found out my writing is in a tradition, Level 5: To resist having more demands made on them, they react against others passive-aggressively, Become evasive, indecisive, cautious, procrastinating, and ambivalent, Are highly reactive, anxious, and negative, giving contradictory, "mixed signals," Internal confusion makes them react unpredictably, definitely have a lot of internal confusion, Level 6: To compensate for insecurities, they become sarcastic and belligerent, blaming others for their problems, am I doing that, with my sarcastic tone sometimes, taking a tough stance toward "outsiders," Highly reactive and defensive, dividing people into friends and enemies, while looking for threats to their own security, Authoritarian while fearful of authority, highly suspicious, yet, conspiratorial, and fear-instilling to silence their own fears, is this the same as insistence on authoritarian views of copyright yet counterphobic fear of copyright, Unhealthy Levels Level 7: Fearing that they have ruined their security, they become panicky, volatile, and self-disparaging with acute inferiority feelings, will I ruin myself due to copyright, Seeing themselves as defenseless, they seek out a stronger authority or belief to resolve all problems, is this Enneagram that authority and Numerology, Highly divisive, I am quite polarizing, right, disparaging and berating others, Level 8: Feeling persecuted, that others are "out to get them," they lash-out and act irrationally, bringing about what they fear, Fanaticism, violence, oh man this is getting bad too, Level 9: Hysterical, and seeking to escape punishment, they become self-destructive and suicidal, Alcoholism, drug overdoses, "skid row," self-abasing behavior, Generally corresponds to the Passive-Aggressive and Paranoid personality disorders, yikes, ends in suicide too, guess that makes sense, not many ways to get below unhealthy, maybe we need to consult some other resources, in the Enneagram for Idiots podcast, they say resources pretty funny, like in a British accent, reeesource, not resource, anyway, let's find some other reeesources, but first let's add some stuff from Walter Benjamin, sent over to me by Sandy, "To a true collector the acquisition of an old book is its rebirth, This is the childlike element, which in a collector, mingles with the element of old age," and Benjamin talks about buying a book "To give it its freedom," and he talks about Posthumous Fragments by a Young Physicist by Johann Wilhelm Ritter, "In which the author-editor tells the story of his life in the guise of an obituary for a supposedly deceased unnamed friend, with whom he is really identical, as the most important example of personal prose in German Romanticism," and that he has things that don't belong with his books like "Paste-in pictures which my mother had glued in as a child," and he says that about books, "Not that they come alive in him; it is he who lives in them," and are you living in this book with me, what do you think of this section on Enneagram, will you look up your type and see yourself reflected back at you, like you see characters reflected back at you, and that they make good company even if it's a bit scary to be exposed in that way, and "In his seminal work of Magic Realism, One Hundred Years of Solitude, Gabriel Garcia Marquez documents the tragic genealogy of the Buendia family – a family in which the strengths and flaws of each generation are repeated, magnified, twisted, and reinterpreted by the next," and when my grandma, my dad's mother, was supposed to die of a heart problem four years ago I visited her and read her parts of Marquez's book, but she still lives, literally and otherwise, and I wouldn't be receiving her inheritance someday soonish if she didn't go on to live past my dad, her son, and so what does that mean, that my grandpa who cared so much about money his money is coming to me, not my dad, Marquez says, "Ursula confirmed her impression that time was going in a circle," but what if the circle isn't two dimensional but can elevate up or devolve down, with a third or 5th or more dimension, do you know what I mean, and did you know that Minerva/Athena sprang from Zeus/Apollo's head, and that Gnostics believe in a similar female G-d springing from the head, or as Elaine Pagels says in The Gnostic Gospels, there's a God in depth underneath the old testament God, and Lewis Hyde edited a book about Allen Ginsburg, and here's a parody of Howl called Yelp, I saw the best minds of my generation destroyed by efficiency, data, and productivity, dragging themselves through the gentrified streets at dawn looking for a 5 star Yelp, athleisured millennials searching for lifestyle in the machinery of pelotons, who upper-middle-class and product-buying stand at desks under the LEDs of corporate towers floating across the tops of cities, who bared their brains to Instagram in an iPhone and begrudged the influencers that didn't influence them though, who went overtested and overcharged, underchallenged and underread through universities to Silicon Valleys and Wall Streets, who live in overpriced apartments fed by Postmates, their self-centered self-care cured them of all problems and mysteries, and then there are the comparable blind communities of the shouting emotional, the enraged and bigoted stuck between the poles of New York and California, poisoning social media with hate, who chained themselves to the President for the endless ride from Twitter to Fox until the notifications pushed them into the bleak of heart, who sank all night in their couches and sat through the stale beer afternoon in their couches, swiping through the crack of their screens on the last GB of their data plan, who work endlessly or not enough at all, a lost populace who don't believe they are what they are even when they are, suffering through fast food night-sweats and no health care bone-cancers and opioid-withdrawal, and What sphinx of time and space is needed to open their minds, hearts, and souls, Gnosis, exclamation point, Gnosis, exclamation point, Gnosis Gnosis Gnosis, exclamation point, and Elise Cowen is another American Beat poet who was friends with Ginsberg, she killed herself, and she wrote a poem called Teacher, Your Body My Kabbalah, which begins like this: "Rahamim--Compassion, Tiferete--Beauty, The aroma of Mr Rochesters cigars among the flowers Bursting through I am trying to choke you, Delicate thought, Posed, Frankenstein of delicate grace, posed by my fear, And you Graciously Take me by the throat," and it ends like this, "Fearing making guilt making shame making fantasy & logic & game & elegance of covering splendour emptying memory of the event covering splendour with mere elegance covering sneer between the angels Wouldn't couldn't Fear of the killer dwarf with the bag of tricks & colonels picture To do my killing for me God is hidden And not for picture postcards," and is this alienated Marquez Cowen in my genealogy somewhere, and Lewis Hyde talks a lot about the connection between Greco-Roman mythos and the ego and creativity in Trickster Makes The World, and I believe I am also a Trickster, that this book is a Trickster book, and I hope Lewis reads it and is proud of me, because he's a father figure to me, in the sense that I live with him when I read him, and he talks about Hermes as the archetype Trickster in Western culture, but that "The motif of freeing some needed good from heaven is found all over the world," he says that "We constantly distinguish, right and wrong, sacred and profane, clean and dirty, male and female, young and old, living and dead, and in every case trickster will cross the line and confuse the distinction, Trickster is the creative idiot, therefore, the wise fool, the speaker of sacred profanities," and that "The boundary is where he will be found, sometimes drawing the line, sometimes crossing it, sometimes erasing or moving it, but always there, the god of the threshold," other things he says is that they are shameless, that the liveliness and durability of culture requires their disruption of its very basis, the Trickster is paradoxically sacredly amoral, and that when he lies and steals, it isn't so much to get away with something or get rich but as to disturb the established categories of truth and property, and that he is the archetype who attacks all archetypes and theories of archetypes, and so I think Enneagram is a lens with truth but not Truth, and that a 4 can also be a 6, and not just one or the other, and that it's also not the answer to the Mystery, but happened to be on my path for intimating it, not containing it, and here's something I'd like to add about Lincoln from chapter 10 of

Shenk's Lincoln, that I believe is important to understanding the relationship of the Enneagram to G-d, Lincoln believed "He was not the captain but merely a subject of the divine force, call it fate or God, or the "Almighty Architect" of existence, The determination came from a sense that, however humble his station, Lincoln was no idle passenger but a sailor on deck with a job to do, In his strange mix of deference to divine authority and willful exercise of his own meager power, Lincoln achieved transcendent wisdom, the delicate fruit of a lifetime of pain," and back to Walter Benjamin, he says "Writers are really people who write books not because they are poor, but because they are dissatisfied with the books which they could buy but do not like," and I would like to make a corollary that you can also combine books into a new book that you like more than the other books out there, as of right now, do you like this book still, is anyone reading still, we are still not at Solar Bones so we have to keep going, stay with me, let me say a few more things as well from Lewis Hyde's Trickster book, "Trickster is at once culture hero and fool, clever predator and stupid prey," the Trickster is a Coyote in North American myth, and is a predator who also has a sense of humor that outwits predators bigger than him, such as taking the time to move traps on their back and urinate on them, instead of just avoiding them, and the other Native American Trickster is the raven, who is "born of woundedness," he wanders the road having "the context of no context," right jump cuts, Kanye, and that one of the Trickster's names in Native American stories, is "Imitator," he doesn't only have the ability to copy one instinct, his ability is to copy anything, he is a mimic artist with "the ability to copy many ways," a "cunning reader," with no true, fixed identity, a provoker, a belief that theft is the beginning of meaning, "To put it another way, a prohibition on theft is an attempt to constrain meaning, to stop its multiplication," and also turning essences and Truths into truths that are also falsehoods," and so if it's not clear one of the tenants of the Enneagram is that you are only one type, you can have a wing, but you can't have two types, and I am not the first to say this, but I think I am a 4wing3 an 6wing7 and maybe more things, and I am saying that the Enneagram is both true and falsehood, that these very well may be the 9 sins, a la Dante's 9 circles of hell, and also the Kabbalah's Tree of Life, and that there may be some connection to G-d or the architect like Lincoln might have called him as a Freethinker, but that we don't have just one type, we have all types, and I think that has also been said by others, but I am saying it again here, we have all sins, and all ego fixations, and need to work on them, to remove the ego, and like in the movie The Master, Joaquix Phoenix both realizes that Phil Hoffman doesn't have the Truth but gets enough truth to be a better version of himself, and so I am a believer in the Enneagram and a non-believer in the orthodoxy of the Enneagram, and I wish I could have taught it to my dad, and back to Lewis Hyde, he says the Trickster "Does not seek but finds," which is Picasso's famous dictation, and I literally just found that line by flipping open the book, "Accidental finds are all about us," and "Who's to say what is loss and what is gain," and these are all random book page flips, and I could probably keep going, but I think it's time to back to get back my dad, whose loss is maybe also a gain, who I said was a 9, but also might be a 6, or at times a 2, here's the piece McSweeney's fucked with, and I add it here, because it was subconsciously also about my dad again and his health and my guilt about not giving him a kidney, but in this case I substitute a donated toe for a donated kidney, and a husband and wife for a father and son, and here it is, but don't worry it's funny, punctuation etcetera, A MAN WHO

DONATED HIS BIG TOE TO HIS WIFE ASKS FOR IT BACK NOW THAT THEY'RE GETTING A DIVORCE by Dave Cowen, "You can have the house, Margaret, You can have the apartment in the city, the other house on the boat, and the other apartment in the city, That's right there's another apartment in the city, It's on Houston, right across from the Film Forum, Yes, right where we had our first date, Do you remember, We saw Kramer vs Kramer, We both agreed Meryl Streep should have ended up with the kids, I knew that night I was going to marry you, I'll admit it, I thought we would divorce too, But not until the kids were gone, And not after I gave you my big toe, I didn't want to do it, You know how much I like open-toed shoes, my Tevas; the ones you said weren't actually open-toed, because of how much of the leather covered the foot, Everyone thought I was crazy, The doctors didn't even know if they could graft a big toe onto another foot, But I did it anyway, Not because I felt bad about what happened with the lawnmower, I told you the azaleas didn't need watering, Maybe you didn't hear me, Maybe I should have been using the Weed Whipper, like you said, Sometimes I wonder, When did we stop listening to each other, I remember the party we had the day they took off the casts, You looked so graceful gliding around the houseboat in your polka dot Gucci's, your toes freshly pedicured and polished in that shade of pink you used to wear on the days you signaled for lovemaking, while I hobbled between the cabin and the bathroom, belly-sick from a noxious cocktail of Dramamine, painkillers and anti-depressants, I saw Bill Ruckerson massaging your bunion, The bunion on my big toe, Bill Ruckerson, What does that man have besides an able body, He lives on the South Shore, I didn't know it then, but that was probably when our intimacy began to cool, You always put on a good face when we footsied under the covers, but I could feel you shudder when we touched, your chilly toes betraying your heart, I'll admit it, It does look really good on you, Better than it ever looked next to my big Morton's toe, The hair waxed off, the cuticle free of dirt, the nail re-irrigated with blood, The kids never liked it on me, Alec thought such a small big toe was "effeminate," Little Rachel was simply afraid of the wart, I took Rachel to a birthday party last week, Everything was going great; I was able to crawl around after her on my hands and knees, and the Ruckerson boy ate too much cake and threw up on Bill, but then the parents organized a participatory dance, which to me seemed quite obligatory, So I did the best I could, I put my right hand in, I put my right hand out, I put my right hand in, and I shook it all about, Then I did the same with my left hand, I did all that, knowing what was going to happen next, That I was going to be asked to put my right foot in, But I couldn't, I couldn't put it in, And even if I did, there was no way I was going to be able to pull it out, Little Rachel looked at me, embarrassment coloring her chubby cheeks for the first time, because her father couldn't do the hokey pokey, because he couldn't shake his right foot all about, And that's what this is all about, Margaret, I'm not Daniel Day Lewis, I can't lead a normal life with just my left foot, I'm not Keyser Söze, I can't make up stories about why I have a gimp, or why I'm not another person who I actually am, I can't act like everything's OK, Because even if we were in a lurid Japanese novel, and I grew another penis where my big toe used to be, I wouldn't feel like a complete man, So please, do the right thing and give me back my big toe," and so, yeah, that was 2010, and, yeah, my mom was unable to be a match for medical reasons to be safe to give him a kidney though she wanted to, just saying that, I risk exile, Lewis says, "Such exile is one of the plausible conseqences of shameless speech," but Mom we must not be ashamed of what happened to our family, we must use it to heal ourselves and to heal others, which you are doing, I won't talk too much about it now but you have become even more empathetic, more of an Enneagram 2 but also more of a Numerological 7 which is your destiny point from being a 8, and so you are evolving from powerful to philosophical, this had to happen, it's in our souls, and here's some more from Shenk's Lincoln chapter 10 "Today the connection between spiritual and psychological well-being is often passed over by psychologists and psychiatrists, who consider themselves a branch of secular medicine and science, but For most of Lincoln's lifetime, scientists assumed there was some relationship between mental and spiritual life," William James, for example, gave equal value in The Varieties of Religious Experience to such diverse systems as Christianity, Emersonian transcendentalism, Buddhist mysticism, and civic or personal ideals, "The essence of religious experience, he wrote, is "the belief that there is an unseen order, and that our supreme good lies in harmoniously adjusting ourselves thereto," and sometimes I click on the explore section of Google Docs and it says there's not enough information and I need to create smarter documents, which makes me feel dumb,

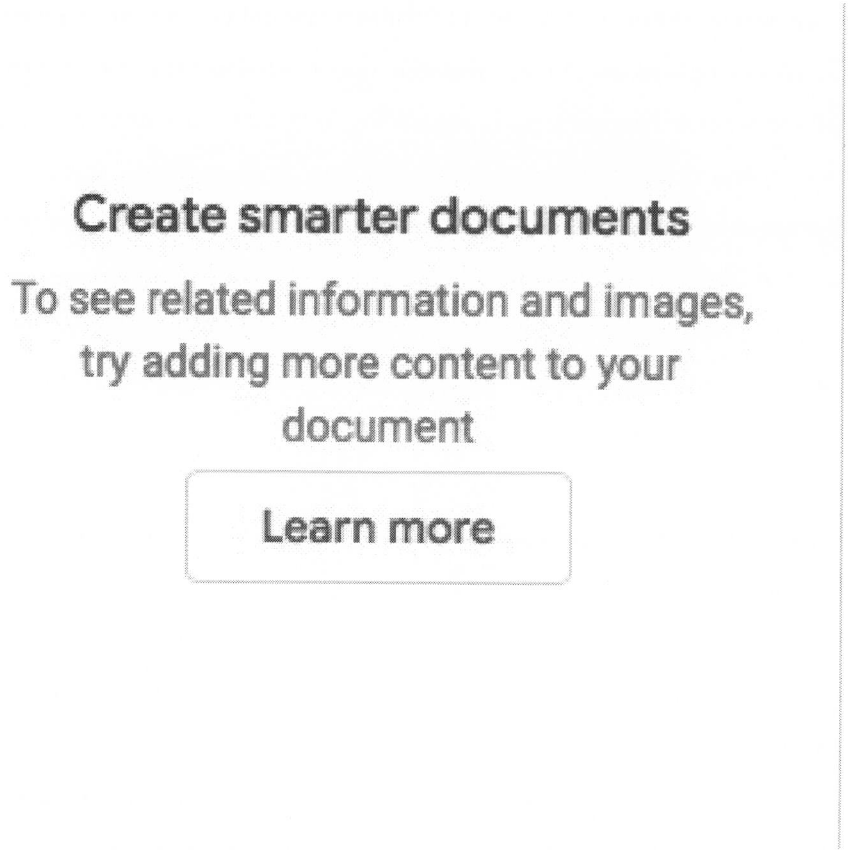

Create smarter documents

To see related information and images, try adding more content to your document

Learn more

like I don't have a rich vocabulary, that's something that a creative writing professor of mine said I need to work on, TC Boyle, do you guys know him, he has a very rich vocabulary and he seems like he's also rich with money as he's been published in The New Yorker many more times than me, which might be due to his richer vocabulary and also just in general the things he writes about are more richly interesting things to people, I dunno, and Joyce has his character Mr Deasy in Ulysses say "You don't know yet what money is, Money is power, When you have lived as long as I have, I know, I know, If youth but knew, But what does Shakespeare say, Put but money in they purse," and Joyce has Stephen Dedalus murmur, "Iago," but TC, he was a good teacher, better than Doc

Boner, much better, and I guess I shouldn't be using his real name either due to defamation, but I can't go back, sorry TC, and maybe I am just not made to write for money, and here's what Lewis says about that in The Gift, "How, if art is essentially a gift, is the artist to survive in a society dominated by the market, Modern artists have resolved this dilemma in several different ways, each of which it seems to me, has two essential features, First the artist allows himself to step outside the gift economy that is the primary commerce of his art and make some peace with the market, Like the Jew of the Old Testament who has a law of the altar at home and a law of the gate for dealing with strangers, the artist who wishes neither to lose his gift nor to starve his belly reserves a protected gift-sphere in which the work is created, but once the work is made he allows himself some contact with the market, And then, the necessary second phase, if he is successful in the marketplace, he converts market wealth into gift wealth: he contributes his earnings to the support of his art, To be more specific, there are three primary ways in which modern artists have resolved the problem of their livelihood: they have taken second jobs, they have found patrons to support them, or they have managed to place the work itself on the market and pay the rent with fees and royalties, The underlying structure that is common to all of these a double economy and the conversion of market wealth to gift wealth may be easiest to see in the case of the artist who has taken a secondary job, some work more or less unrelated to his art, The second job frees his art from the burden of financial responsibility so that when he is creating the work he may turn from questions of market value and labor in the protected gift-sphere, He earns a wage in the marketplace and gives it to his art, The patron's support is not a wage or a fee for service but a gift given in recognition of the artist's own, Someone, somewhere sold his labor in the marketplace, or grew rich in finance, or exploited the abundance of nature, and the patron turns that wealth into a gift to feed the gifted, But the artist who sells his own creations must develop a more subjective feel for the two economies and his own rituals for both keeping them apart and bringing them together, He must on one hand be able to disengage from the work and think of it as a commodity, He must be able to reckon its value in terms of current fashions, know what the market will bear, demand fair value, and part with the work when someone pays the price, And he must, on the other hand, be able to forget all that and turn to serve his gifts on their own terms, If he cannot do the former, he cannot hope to sell his art, and if he cannot do the latter, he may have no art to sell, or only a commercial art, work that has been created in response to the demands of the market, not in response to the demands of the gift, The artist who hopes to market work that is the realization of his gifts cannot begin with the market, He must create for himself that gift-sphere in which the work is made, and only when he knows the work to be the faithful realization of his gift should he turn to see if it has currency in that other economy, Sometimes it does, sometimes it doesn't," and another thing about when I was a graduate student at USC, a screenwriting professor named Scott, I'll hold back his last name because he's more of a regular Joe than TC, and TC is enough of a public figure to be mentioned legally, probably, I don't know, but I think it's OK, hopefully, anyway, Scott, he told me he loved my writing but that it was too weird and political to be movie writing, and that I should stick to more niche writing like books, also here are some other shameful things about my experience at USC, I applied to TC to get into his class, and I fulfilled my assignments and got a decent grade, but I guess I also didn't critique people very nicely, or something, because another USC film student tried to take his class after I did, and was told that they no longer take USC screenwriters, and she implied that it was because of me, and another shameful thing is that when I applied to USC MFA in screenwriting program, I called the admissions office asking if I got in, and I did it like three times, and finally the woman/student worker there said I got in, and I couldn't tell if her exasperation was real or that she just said it, but I took her word for it, and soon enough I did get in, but while I was there on my birthday, a gossipy writer told a story at my birthday party that USC let in a student because a worker just told him he got in, even though he didn't, and I felt so bad, but then now I remember the call from the professor who said she backed my admission, and she told me why, because it was a scene about my parents fighting about whether my dad should go to see his psychiatrist and I was on the roof with my sister looking at the stars and saying that there is a constellation called norma, or normal, can't remember, but the meaning was that we all just want to be normal and we are even though we aren't, that is what's normal, and I also wrote this essay for USC's Most Emotional Moment application essay, The Binary Switch, In college, I learned that film has the power to alter consciousness, At first, I understood this as an abstract or theoretical concept; for example, Luis Bunuel's surrealism awakened bourgeoisie minds, It was not until the end of my third year of college that I personally felt the transformative powers of film, One night, a friend invited me over to his apartment to see the original 1962 The Manchurian Candidate, As I watched, empathy flooded over me, I felt the self-loathing, fear, shame and paranoia of the war hero son, played by Laurence Harvey, I identified so much with him that I actually believed I was he: I believed I had been brainwashed by the US government, This film caused me to completely break away from reality, It was the catalyst that sparked a florid bout of manic psychosis, Stumbling out of my friend's apartment into darkness and pouring rain, I felt a heavy weight pulling me to the ground, Gravity, I thought, was no longer merely a physical force, It had become a Death Force inundating me with absolutes of self-hate and despair, I thought that if I couldn't rise from the ground before I closed my eyes this force would kill me, Metallic pain shot through my mind like currents of electricity, I blinked, Instantly, gravity disappeared and I felt weightless, A black, shadow outline of my body escaped out of me, It hovered in front of me, I rose up and into the figure, yearning to live, And like a binary switch, the self-loathing, fear, shame and paranoia vanished as if it was never present, In its place was epiphanic elation: A transcendent, mystical state of superconsciousness, I was sure I had died and gone to heaven, which was an alternative universe in which everything stayed the same, except my mind aligned with my body, I no longer stuttered or hesitated to act, because every utterance was the Word and every choice was unconflicted by self-consciousness and was the Choice, It's hard to elucidate this ineffable experience, but I think it can be compared to Richard Kelly's use of "vector spears" in his film Donnie Darko, Donnie visually sees characters' behavior linked to a divine purpose, To me behavior was beautiful and perfect, because will was tied to destiny, Everything was in its right place, I sat at my computer and wrote pages and pages of stream of consciousness, Every phrase was a cosmic pun, I wrote about my life as if God had lifted his dramatic irony, and I understood his subtext, Within hours, however, the vicissitudes of bipolar moods took over, My mind was beginning to scramble to keep up with itself, Ideas came too fast, The writing fragmented into nonsensical chaos, as did my mind, I found myself in a parking garage: paranoid, confused and crying, because I couldn't seem to find "Lot 49," It would be days until medication returned me to a normal emotional state, But I don't think I will ever be "normal" again, Bergman's Through a Glass Darkly sums up the postlapsarian state: "Reality (had) burst open, It's like a dream, Anything can happen," Sometimes I feel like Minus and think, "I can't live in this new world," where I have experienced an alternative reality but now live in the normal one, But then I look to another Bergman film, Fanny and Alexander, for strength, In the final scene, the grandmother quotes Strindberg's A Dream Play: "Anything can happen, all is possible and probable, Time and space do not exist, On an insignificant foundation of reality, imagination spins out and weaves new patterns," I do not need the highs of mania to experience other realities or to write, I only need my imagination," and so I think whatever happened I deserved to be in that program, and that I am on this path of being a writer either way, but that professor Scott he said I should focus on prose writing, and not do screenwriting, because I wouldn't be successful in it, but I am very Aries rammy so I didn't listen to him for nearly ten years until I published the Haggadah, which is a long time to spend in the Hollywood desert, very Moses-y and it was a tough time for me and for my dad, who was very worried about me, I think, even though he didn't say so, but he was very happy about the Haggadahs and that I was devoting myself back to prose writing, and was hopeful that between that and my regular job, I would be happy and it would all provide enough of a living to live like I wanted, and I think it might, and I think I am much happier now that I have not been completely ruined by my outsized Hollywood ambitions, sort of like one of my favorite writers, F Scott Fitzgerald had been he claimed, though I think I am more of just a hack, clearly, not a great novelist ruined by the vagaries and randomness and cruelty and bullshittyness of this industry, though is this book a bit like This Side of Paradise, the mixing in of random old things he/I wrote, into the text, how fresh/lazy Scotty/I was/am, or am I crazy, and how it is subtitled or whatever The Romantic Egoist, like my Enneagram, is Scott a 4 too, or is he a 4w3, The Aristocrat, “But more than that, he had formulated his first philosophy, a code to live by, which, as near as it can be named, was a sort of aristocratic egotism,” or is it The Crack-Up, no, The Crack-Up is too bitter, and I have been finding most of these quotes by sheer bibliomancy, which is the use of books in divination, specifically, divination by lines of verse in books taken at hazard, and here’s another one, from Hermann Hesse’s Siddhartha, “One day, when the wound was smarting terribly, Siddhartha rowed across the river, consumed by longing, and got out of the boat with the purpose of going to the town to seek his son, The river flowed softly and gently; it was in the dry season but its voice rang out strangely, It was laughing, it was distinctly laughing, The river was laughing clearly and merrily at the old ferryman, Siddhartha stood still; he bent over the water in order to hear better, He saw his face reflected in the quietly moving water, and there was something in this reflection that reminded him of something he had forgotten and when he reflected on it, he remembered, His face resembled that of another person, whom he had once known and loved and even feared, It resembled the face of his father, the Brahmin, He remembered how once, as a youth, he had compelled his father to let him go and join the ascetics, how he had taken leave of him, how he had gone and never returned, Had not his father also suffered the same pain that that he was now suffering for his son, Was it not a comedy, a strange and stupid thing, this repetition, this course of events in a fateful circle,” and what of this bibliomancy, read on, we find, "Disclosing his wound to his listener," "His wound was healing, his pain was dispersing; his Self had merged into unity," and what of this bibliomancy, Phil K Dick says in VALIS, Mimicry is how God enters the world, invades it, "The true God mimics the universe, the very region he has invaded, he takes on the likeness of sticks and trees and beer cans in gutters, Lurking the true God literally ambushes reality and us as well," and Albert Ayler's "Omega is the Alpha" just came on God's Spotify algorithm, invaded it, and and Emerson says, "God will not have his work made manifest by cowards," and are you following along with the Spotify playlist, I put it above twice, even though I am not sure if it's legal, I'll put it in again here, https(dot)//open(dot)spotify(dot)com/playlist/2xsgUmnOaYdZb34LuMFifR(questionmark)si=67REDpuURBiupvZBNooKg, and do you know Albert Ayler, here's what Pitchfork says about him, "Practicing relentlessly since he started playing as a boy, Ayler had developed a big, rich, honking tone, the kind of sound that could cut through a noisy bar and urge people onto the dance floor, Along with the sheer volume of his attack, Ayler gradually began to favor a sometimes absurdly wavering vibrato, which evoked the pathos of gospel music and brought to mind the mournful sound of an early 20th century New Orleans funeral processional, The final piece of his saxophone sound snapped into place when he found a way to integrate his booming tone and gospel-derived emoting in the context of free jazz, with its flowing and forgiving relationship to pitch and openness to screeching and bellowing at the horn's extreme ranges, Ayler was finding that he could integrate all of these elements into new compositions he was writing, tunes that alternated catchy, sing-song melodies inspired by European folk songs and the propulsive marches he learned in the army band with highly textured and high-energy abstract playing almost completely divorced from form, It was an unusual mix of the cerebral and highly technical and the nakedly emotional," and "Ayler himself described what he was doing as the blues, but a new blues, one that fit with what was going on in the world at this time, He was making music to praise God, He thought of it less as a call to arms and more as a soundtrack to the aftermath, a vision of what the world might become when peace and equality ruled the earth," but "Despite his overtures to the mainstream, Ayler's records sold badly, Some people describe Ayler behaving strangely later that year, including a report of him wearing a fur coat and gloves in the summer heat, his face covered in Vaseline, Others who saw him during these months noted nothing unusual, Mary Parks said that their precarious financial situation, coupled with concerns about Donald and the declining health of his mother, had pushed Albert into a dark place, Following an argument, he left their apartment and disappeared, She notified the police, Three weeks later, his body was found floating in the East River next to the Congress Street pier in Brooklyn, and the coroner said he'd drowned, Suicide seemed likely, but the circumstances of his death remain a mystery," and that was from an article by Mark Richardson on Pitchfork, and On God, "On GOD" by Mustard, Tyga, A$AP Ferg, and A$AP Rocky just came on God's Spotify, and God has invaded the rational, the scientific, the data, the algorithm everyone has the soundtrack now with Spotify that reveals the unconscious, the music reveals the unconscious now, the algorithm reveals the unconscious, God is breaking through the knowledge, the irrational is breaking through the scientific, as Jung would say it would, and Phil K Dick said it did to him, the songs are breaking through, and so what is your last song that has been played on Spotify, and what does it say about you and your life, go ahead look it up, and when you go to davecowendotcom you get:

← → C ⓘ Not Secure | davecowen.com ☆

This page intentionally left blank.

, and I don't own that website, I didn't do this, I didn't do these things, why is it like that, what is this, what is going on, we can't turn away from the unconsciousness, the God being revealed in the technology, the science, Jung, Jung, Jung, Dick, Dick, Dick, and Emerson says, "Trust thyself: every heart vibrates to that iron string, Accept the place the divine providence has found for you, the society of your contemporaries, the connection of events," and Rumi says, "There is no reality but God, says the completely surrendered sheikh, who is an ocean for all beings, The levels of creation are straws in that ocean, The movement of the straws comes from an agitation in the water, When the ocean wants the straws calm, it sends them close to shore, When it wants them back in the deep surge, it does with them as the wind does with the grasses, This never ends," and Spotify's playlist is now playing "Endless" by Portico

Quartet, I am not making this up, and Emerson says, "Whoso would be a man must be a nonconformist, He who would gather immortal palms must not be hindered by the name of goodness, but must explore if it be goodness, Nothing is at last sacred but the integrity of your own mind, Absolve you to yourself, and you shall have the suffrage of the world," and how many writer's consciousnesses are locked up by the Google Library court case that copyright law has stopped, "You were going to get one-click access to the full text of nearly every book that's ever been published, Books still in print you'd have to pay for, but everything else—a collection slated to grow larger than the holdings at the Library of Congress, Harvard, the University of Michigan, at any of the great national libraries of Europe—would have been available for free at terminals that were going to be placed in every local library that wanted one, At the terminal you were going to be able to search tens of millions of books and read every page of any book you found, You'd be able to highlight passages and make annotations and share them; for the first time, you'd be able to pinpoint an idea somewhere inside the vastness of the printed record, and send somebody straight to it with a link, Books would become as instantly available, searchable, copy-pasteable—as alive in the digital world—as web pages, It was to be the realization of a long-held dream, "The universal library has been talked about for millennia," On March 22 of that year, however, the legal agreement that would have unlocked a century's worth of books and peppered the country with access terminals to a universal library was rejected under Rule 23(e)(2) of the Federal Rules of Civil Procedure by the US District Court for the Southern District of New York, and how many of consciousness inside of books are lost in copyright, and how many minds could live again, if they were unlocked, "I asked someone who used to have that job, what would it take to make the books viewable in full to everybody, I wanted to know how hard it would have been to unlock them, What's standing between us and a digital public library of 25 million volumes, You'd get in a lot of trouble, they said, but all you'd have to do, more or less, is write a single database query, You'd flip some access control bits from off to on, It might take a few minutes for the command to propagate," and what if the command was propagated, and what if there was a way to bring people back to life, like, a company like Google came up with a way to bring everyone back to life who was dead, but there was a lawsuit, and, like, it was class action like the book authors' case, and people were, like, we don't know if people want to be brought back to life, as they were like we don't know if authors want their work brought into public again, so they can't be brought back, so then you couldn't have Google bring back your loved one, and Google couldn't bring back my dad, and would my dad even want to be brought back, he chose to leave this world, he didn't want to stay, I don't know, and does this writer James Somers who wrote that Google books article want his words in my book, I don't know, and like David Shields, "I'm finding it harder to just "write," The seeking and sculpting of found text or sound have become my primary 'artistic' function," and "In our work, we have the right to quote what pleases us," and Flann O'Brien in At Swim Two Birds says, "The entire corpus of existing literature should be regarded as a limbo from which discerning authors could draw their characters as required, creating only when they failed to find a suitable existing puppet, The modern novel should be largely a work of reference, Most authors spend their time saying what has been said before, usually said much better," and I think that we need or do you want more proof that the Enneagram is Trickster Truth/truth, here's Donny Quixote's, from

The Enneagram Institute, aka Trump, we're saying his name now, we're not afraid, 8 THE CHALLENGER, Enneagram Type Eight, The Powerful, Dominating Type: Self-Confident, Decisive, Willful, and Confrontational, Eights are self-confident, strong, and assertive, Protective, resourceful, straight-talking, and decisive, but can also be ego-centric and domineering, Eights feel they must control their environment, especially people, sometimes becoming confrontational and intimidating, Eights typically have problems with their tempers and with allowing themselves to be vulnerable, At their Best: self- mastering, they use their strength to improve others' lives, becoming heroic, magnanimous, and inspiring, Basic Fear: Of being harmed or controlled by others, Basic Desire: To protect themselves (to be in control of their own life and destiny), Enneagram Eight with a Seven-Wing: "The Maverick", Enneagram Eight with a Nine-Wing: "The Bear", Key Motivations: Want to be self-reliant, to prove their strength and resist weakness, to be important in their world, to dominate the environment, and to stay in control of their situation, When moving in their Direction of Disintegration (stress), self-confident Eights suddenly become secretive and fearful at Five, However, when moving in their Direction of Integration (growth), lustful, controlling Eights become more open-hearted and caring, like healthy Twos, Type Eight Overview, We have named personality type Eight The Challenger because, of all the types, Eights enjoy taking on challenges themselves as well as giving others opportunities that challenge them to exceed themselves in some way, Eights are charismatic and have the physical and psychological capacities to persuade others to follow them into all kinds of endeavors—from starting a company, to rebuilding a city, to running a household, to waging war, to making peace, Eights have enormous willpower and vitality, and they feel most alive when they are exercising these capacities in the world, They use their abundant energy to effect changes in their environment—to "leave their mark" on it—but also to keep the environment, and especially other people, from hurting them and those they care about, At an early age, Eights understand that this requires strength, will, persistence, and endurance—qualities that they develop in themselves and which they look for in others, Thayer is a stockbroker who has worked intensively on understanding her type Eight personality, She recounts a childhood incident in which she could clearly see the development of this pattern, "Much of my tenacity and toughness comes from my Dad, He always told me not to 'let anybody push you around,' It was not okay to cry, I learned to master my weaker side early on, At the tender age of eight, a huge horse ran away with me, When an adult caught the horse, I resolutely dismounted without a tear, I could tell my father was proud," Eights do not want to be controlled or to allow others to have power over them (their Basic Fear), whether the power is psychological, sexual, social, or financial, Much of their behavior is involved with making sure that they retain and increase whatever power they have for as long as possible, An Eight may be a general or a gardener, a small businessman or a mogul, the mother of a family or the superior of a religious community, No matter: being "in charge" and leaving their imprint on their sphere is uniquely characteristic of them, Eights are the true "rugged individualists" of the Enneagram, More than any other type, they stand alone, They want to be independent, and resist being indebted to anyone, They often refuse to "give in" to social convention, and they can defy fear, shame, and concern about the consequences of their actions, Although they are usually aware of what people think of them, they do not let the opinions of others sway them, They go about their business with a steely determination that can be awe inspiring, even intimidating to others, Although, to some extent, Eights fear physical harm, far more important is their fear of being disempowered or controlled in some way, Eights are extraordinarily tough and can absorb a great deal of physical punishment without complaint—a double-edged blessing since they often take their health and stamina for granted and overlook the health and well-being of others as well, Yet they are desperately afraid of being hurt emotionally and will use their physical strength to protect their feelings and keep others at a safe emotional distance, Beneath the tough façade is vulnerability, although it has been covered over by layer of emotional armor, Thus, Eights are often extremely industrious, but at the price of losing emotional contact with many of the people in their lives, Those close to them may become increasingly dissatisfied with this state of affairs, which confounds Eights, ("I don't understand what my family is complaining about, I bust my hump to provide for them, Why are they disappointed with me,") When this happens, Eights feel misunderstood and may distance themselves further, In fact, beneath their imposing exterior, Eights often feel hurt and rejected, although this is something they seldom talk about because they have trouble admitting their vulnerability to themselves, let alone to anyone else, Because they fear that they will be rejected (divorced, humiliated, criticized, fired, or harmed in some way), Eights attempt to defend themselves by rejecting others first, The result is that average Eights become blocked in their ability to connect with people or to love since love gives the other power over them, reawakening their Basic Fear, The more Eights build up their egos in order to protect themselves, the more sensitive they become to any real or imaginary slight to their self-respect, authority, or preeminence, The more they attempt to make themselves impervious to hurt or pain (whether physical or emotional), the more they "shut down" emotionally to become hardened and rock-like, When Eights are emotionally healthy, however, they have a resourceful, "can-do" attitude as well as a steady inner drive, They take the initiative and make things happen with a great passion for life, They are honorable and authoritative—natural leaders who have a solid, commanding presence, Their groundedness gives them abundant "common sense" as well as the ability to be decisive, Eights are willing to "take the heat," knowing that any decision cannot please everyone, But as much as possible, they want to look after the interests of the people in their charge without playing favorites, They use their talents and fortitude to construct a better world for everyone in their lives, Type Eight—Levels of Development, Healthy Levels, Level 1 (At Their Best): Become self-restrained and magnanimous, merciful and forbearing, mastering self through their self-surrender to a higher authority, Courageous, willing to put self in serious jeopardy to achieve their vision and have a lasting influence, May achieve true heroism and historical greatness, Level 2: Self-assertive, self-confident, and strong: have learned to stand up for what they need and want, A resourceful, "can do" attitude and passionate inner drive, Level 3: Decisive, authoritative, and commanding: the natural leader others look up to, Take initiative, make things happen: champion people, provider, protective, and honorable, carrying others with their strength, Average Levels Level 4: Self-sufficiency, financial independence, and having enough resources are important concerns: become enterprising, pragmatic, "rugged individualists," wheeler-dealers, Risk-taking, hardworking, denying own emotional needs, Level 5: Begin to dominate their environment, including others: want to feel that others are behind them, supporting their efforts, Swaggering, boastful, forceful, and expansive: the "boss" whose word is law, Proud, egocentric, want to impose their will and vision on everything, not seeing others as equals or treating them with respect, Level 6: Become highly combative and intimidating to get their way: confrontational, belligerent, creating adversarial relationships, Everything a test of wills, and they will not back down, Use threats and reprisals to get obedience from others, to keep others off balance and insecure, However, unjust treatment makes others fear and resent them, possibly also band together against them, Unhealthy Levels, Level 7: Defying any attempt to control them, become completely ruthless, dictatorial, "might makes right," The criminal and outlaw, renegade, and con-artist, Hard-hearted, immoral and potentially violent, Level 8: Develop delusional ideas about their power, invincibility, and ability to prevail: megalomania, feeling omnipotent, invulnerable, Recklessly over-extending self, Level 9: If they get in danger, they may brutally destroy everything that has not conformed to their will rather than surrender to anyone else, Vengeful, barbaric, murderous, Sociopathic tendencies, Generally corresponds to the Antisocial Personality Disorder, Addictions, Ignore physical needs and problems: avoid medical visits and check-ups, Indulging in rich foods, alcohol, tobacco while pushing self too hard leads to high stress, strokes, and heart conditions," and did you know Miguel de Cervantes tried to be a playwright for most of his life, he wrote like thirty plays, and failed to get any of them put on, because it was expensive to put on plays back then, it was like financing a movie today, so that's why he wrote the firstish novel, some people say, just so he could do something with his writing after so many years of struggling and failure, and my pursuit of screenwriting is sort of like that and also it's like often been a way to sublimate my guilt about being away, that it will all be worth it, one day when I make him proud with a movie, and sometimes I even turned good ideas for movies into things about my dad, like this idea I had sorta about LeBron James, this outline I wrote was when my dad was losing his memory and having Parkinson's-like reactions with his body due to not doing dialysis when he needed to do it, which we didn't know that was the problem at the time, we thought it might be lewy body dementia, and so since I am crazy I ended up trying to pitch to LeBron's creative executive, this guy S-, this crazy pitch, this is the pitch without punctuation, etcetera, this was the crazy version I almost emailed him, titled STAY IN SACRAMENTO OR ELSE, LOGLINE: "A comedy-drama about a basketball fanatic, Jason, who instead of moving to Los Angeles with his girlfriend after college, has to move back home to Sacramento to care for his depressed father, who claims to only want to continue living in order to see their favorite NBA team win a championship, Though Jason finds a job in the GM's office, he's faced with the fact that their hometown superstar can leave in free agency, As his father becomes more incapacitated, his college girlfriend more distant, and his life more isolated, Jason's desperation to keep the player, whom he has come to know, and who also desires to escape home, spirals out of control into a manic kidnapping as Jason learns he's also bipolar, too, SILVER LININGS PLAYBOOK meets THE KING OF COMEDY," and so that was the version of a LeBron free agency "comedy" I was going to pitch before my friends, Matt, Alec, and Al interceded, and helped me from sending that long document to turn the email into this, "S-, I should now say GO LAKERS, So cool LeBron's making his home here now, Must be really fun for you all at SpringHill, Made my 4th, too, The idea is actually pretty in sync with recent events, The logline's below, Happy to hop on a call if you have interest in it, FREE AGENCY In this LeBron James free agency inspired comedy in the vein of GET HIM TO THE GREEK and BLOCKERS, Jason and his two best friends are basketball fanatics who are dying to witness their beloved Kings finally win an NBA championship in Sacramento, However, they're faced with the fact that their hometown MVP superstar can leave in free agency after the end of the playoffs, When the enterprising Jason, who has access as a team blogger, and his two best friends (including a longtime female friend he's had an unspoken love for since their Sactown middle school days), discover that the superstar wants to leave home and try to win his first championship with his two best Team USA free agent friends in LA, they become desperate to keep him, So desperate, in fact, that they attempt to mobilize an eclectic mass of community members to influence their favored son, orchestrate a half-baked rumor-mill/burner-phone scheme to poison the superstar's perception of his free agent friends and the LA team, and pull off an ill-advised "DeAndre Jordaning" over the July 4th holiday weekend, all of which spirals way out of control," of course, S- didn't call me in for a longer pitch and the idea died like they always do, like all the good ideas of mine, sickly vines, but what was I doing spending a month turning this fun summer basketball comedy into a dark and depressing father dying mental illness story, who the hell would pay money to see that, and why would the NBA or LeBron or anyone sign off on that, and I almost pitched that to LeBron's creative executive, how insane, but also kind of beautiful, and here's what Lewis Hyde says about grief in his book A Primer For Forgetting Getting Past The Past, "The unforgettable, Some emotions grip us, then fall away, a great happiness can bring sleepless nights when first it blooms, but the possession eventually fades, Two years out, no one says, 'I cannot shake my joy' is this true, Lewis, father figure, I disagree with that part, I believe in happiness, it can go on, but I will continue, "Grief and rage, however, these can go on and on, Decades go by and still a loss or wound from childhood colors our days, In Sophocles's play that bears her name, Electra speaks of her father's murder as a sorrow (or evil) that cannot be forgotten and describes her own passion (or anger) that cannot be forgotten and describes her own passion (or anger) in similar terms, though in this case the Greek for "not forgetting" might better be translated from its root meaning, 'it does not escape notice,' 'it is not hidden,' The image is of anger as a thing that the mind cannot bury, cannot help being aware of, Electra's passion won't let her alone, It's intrusive, It bugs her, We do not control the unforgettable; it controls us, The spirits of such unforgetting are called the Furies, the Erinyes, They cling to the memory of hurt and harm, injury and insult, Their names are Grievance, Ceaseless, and Bloodlust, Their names are Grudge, Relentless, and Payback, They bloat the present with the undigested past," but how do we deal with this, I look back to Shenk's Lincoln, "Lincoln saw how man's reason could discern purpose even in the movement of a vast machine that grinds and cuts and mashes all who interfere with it, Just as a child learns to pull his hand from a fire when it is hot, people can learn when they are doing something that is not in accord with the wider, unseen order, suffering was medicinal & educational," in other words, it could be an agent of growth, and Jungian writer James Hollis also says, "If we are fortunate to suffer enough, we are stunned into a reluctant consciousness, If we are courageous enough, care enough about our lives, we may, through that suffering, get our lives back," and so here is the third piece I ever submitted to The New Yorker that was rejected, and after it was rejected I pretty much lost my outlet there, it seemed that things soured, or maybe I was just being a 6 who is suspicious even though the piece is about a 4's search for significance, and so here is some more unpublished struggle, Wikipedia Deletion Page, By Dave Cowen, I am Philip Roth, I had reason recently to read for the first time the Wikipedia entry discussing my novel "The Human Stain," The entry contains a serious misstatement that I would like to ask to have removed, This item entered Wikipedia not from the world of truthfulness but from the babble of literary gossip—there is no truth in it at all, Yet when, through an official interlocutor, I recently petitioned Wikipedia to delete this misstatement, along with two others, my interlocutor was told by the "English Wikipedia Administrator"—in a letter dated August 25th and addressed to my interlocutor—that I, Roth, was not a credible source: "I understand your point that the author is the greatest authority on their own work," writes the Wikipedia Administrator—"but we require secondary sources," -The New Yorker, September 7, Wikipedia Deletion Page, 12 September 2012, Dave Cowen, AFDs for this article: Articles for deletion/Dave Cowen Articles for deletion/Dave Cowen (3rd nomination) Articles for deletion/Dave Cowen (4th nomination) Articles for deletion/Dave Cowen (5th nomination) Articles for deletion/Dave Cowen (second nomination) Dave Cowen (edit|talk|history|links|watch|logs) – (View AfD) (Find sources: "Dave Cowen" — search, news, books, scholar, images) Roughly five versions of this article have been created and brought to Articles For Deletion, with an overwhelmingly consistent opinion in favor of deletion per the inadequate notability clause, I'd encourage editors to review the past discussions, but I would summarize the dominant view as being that while Dave Cowen may have collaborated with the notable writer Bill Ruckerson, neither his personal role in the collaboration nor the collaboration itself has ever been corroborated by a significant secondary source, Socrates21 (talk) 12:42, 12 September 2012 (UTC), I would like to direct editors to the secondary source Authorhousedotcom/ComingSoon/DaveCowen, which clearly outlines Dave Cowen's extensive involvement with notable writer Bill Ruckerson in their book: Dave Cowen Interviews Bill Ruckerson, Cowman5 (talk) 12:57, 12 September 2012 (UTC), In common with preceding source claims, this is merely a link to a website for self-published books, The contents of the page are in fact the subject's own writing, a promotional foreword to his ostensibly forthcoming, but still unpublished, and, therefore, not yet notable book, The only apparent development to the biographical article Dave Cowen since it was last deleted (25 August 2012) is a link to an op-ed piece authored by Mr, Cowen in a newspaper called, The Democrat and Chronicle, in which he calls for more governmental funding for struggling writers in Western New York -- which cannot yet have had much impact, if it is going to -- before immaterially detailing issues pertaining to the profitability of a failed collaborative project with Bill Ruckerson, Given the lack of change from its earlier incarnations, my suggestion is to delete this article, However, I admit that my view may be colored by my irritation at how this situation has reoccurred over five times, and I'd like to see what editors with fresh eyes think of the article, Socrates21 (talk) 13:16, 12 September 2012 (UTC) The previous post contains numerous egregious errors that other editors should be aware of before making their own informed decisions, Firstly, the promotional foreword was written by Mr, Cowen's brother, Woody Cowen, another frequent collaborator of Bill Ruckerson, and not by the subject Dave Cowen, Secondly, The Democrat and Chronicle is one of the widest read newspapers in Rochester, New York, which is one of the five biggest cities in population in New York State, which is the third biggest state in population in the United States, which is the most powerful country in the world, Any piece of writing published in such a publication should be categorized as nothing other than notable, Thirdly, the article, Dave Cowen, has been reposted exactly and not over five times, It would be much less if it was approved as it rightfully should be, and will be much more if it is not, Finally, and most importantly, the "immaterial" discussion of a collaborative project with Bill Ruckerson was actually a discussion of a second, discrete project, which itself is now moving forward to completion as sourced here: Authorhouse(dot)com/AlsoComingSoon/DaveCowen, DC555 (talk) 13:22, 12 September 2012 (UTC), What remains unsaid is the fact that Dave Cowen's claim to notability rests in the claim that a collaboration with the notable writer Bill Ruckerson is notable, However, this editor wonders if even Bill Ruckerson himself properly demonstrates claims to notability as established in Wikipedia:BIO#/Any_Biography, Socrates21 (talk) 13:49, 12 September 2012 (UTC), Now hold on one second, To review the notability of Dave Cowen is one thing, but to besmirch the reputation of Bill Ruckerson, a writer of two notable self-published and one notable regularly published books, an influential, tenured professor at a first-tier SUNY, and a kind, decent human being and friend is an utter and abhorrent abuse of editorial power, DC21 (talk) 13:51, 12 September 2012 (UTC), OK, I may have went too far, but I don't think I am alone in speculating that the incessant recreation of the article seems to have been provoked by Dave Cowen himself, Socrates21 (talk) 13:54, 12 September 2012 (UTC) What are you trying to say, Plato22 (talk) 13:54, 12 September 2012 (UTC) I'm saying Dave Cowen complains constantly about the deletions on his moderately trafficked blog, canvasses for support on Wikipedia, and has even tried to change the No

Original Research policy to allow himself to be used as a source in this article, Discussion here, His has been the most belligerent campaign to have his own Wikipedia page that I can recall in the six years I've been editing, And I would not be surprised if he has resorted to creating multiple, fake editorial personas in order to drum up a defense against deletion, Socrates21 (talk) 14:00, 12 September 2012 (UTC) You calling me a sockpuppet, Socrates, I have your IP address, I'm outside your house motherfucker, If you don't write an apology and a correction notice in the next three minutes, I'm going to come in there, tie you up, cut off every last one of your chubby, Orwellian pig fingers and type it myself, TheRealDaveCowen (talk) 14:02, 12 September 2012 (UTC) Yeah right you are, I'm not scared of you, Cowen, Socrates21 (talk) 14:04, 12 September 2012 (UTC) Time's up, TheRealDaveCowen (talk) 14:05, 12 September 2012 (UTC) Oh god, hes he rheplpll pleabnm,/, Socrates21 (talk) 14:05, 12 September 2012 (UTC) REINSTATE article Dave Cowen, Socrates21 (talk) 14:10, 12 September 2012 (UTC)," and that piece of course was rejected by The New Yorker, and it must have reeked of undigested furies, un-self-aware ones, perhaps, and maybe that is the larger lesson, to be self-aware and Higher Power aware at all times, Holy Origin and Holy Faith, 4 and 6, the Enneagram would say, and so today is June 7th, and I am leaving the document to go have the meal with the person who reached out from Imagine Impact for We Bought a Gun, as "Body and Soul" by the Benny Goodman Trio plays, as I write this, and I'll be back in a few, and, and, and, and, and, and, and, and I am back, but I am not back, something magical happened to me, something transcendent, I will try to explain, as best I can, knowing that words are ineffable but hopefully the effable is contained within, I was reading Steven Zultanski's book On The Literary Means Of Representing The

Powerful and Powerless or something like that, given to me by Aaron and I was shopping/browsing the bookstore Family on Fairfax and found a book about the stuff that Danny Snelson had been showing me, and the Zultanski book was about how un-powerful power really is, and was saying basically saying that some powerless people believe that even if the powerful kill them they will come back to life in another form, and I was thinking of my dad and reincarnation, and I was thinking how nice it would be not to be afraid all the time, to have Holy Faith that you'd be OK no matter what happens to you in life, as I've always had a fear of death, and of not making money, and of security, and success not having it, and it started to lift, that fear, just as I walked over to Jon & Vinny's to meet this Imagine Impact person, and I was calm, in a way I hadn't been in many years, if ever, and this person was running late, and the old Dave would have been anxious about that, and pushy in his heart, a pusher, as Lincoln's contemporaries would have wanted me to be, but this Dave had genuine concern for him because he said he was in a car accident, except he meant only a car accident near him, and so he came to the lunch not that soon after, and he was tall and kind and we sat down for lunch, and he had been to Italy recently, and I was going to Italy, and we compared notes, and we ordered Roman pie like the Roman Catholic stuff in Lewis Hyde's The Gift I had been reading, and we started talking about the script and his work and his life, and I connected to him as a person, not as an object to help me, and that had been rare for me in my career, to be honest, and as we connected I learned about his acting, and his own writing, and he described wanting to write a script about The Legend of Sleepy Hollow, and if you haven't read the book here's the Wikipedia summary, Washington Irving, "The Legend of Sleepy Hollow", The story is set in 1790 in the countryside around the Dutch settlement of Tarry Town (historical Tarrytown, New York), in a secluded glen known as Sleepy Hollow, Sleepy Hollow is renowned for its ghosts and the haunting atmosphere that pervades the imaginations of its inhabitants and visitors, Some residents say this town was bewitched during the early days of the Dutch settlement, while others claim that the mysterious atmosphere was caused by an old Native American chief, the "wizard of his tribe, before the country was discovered by Master Hendrik Hudson," The most infamous spectre in the Hollow is the Headless Horseman, supposedly the ghost of a Hessian trooper whose head had been shot off by a stray cannonball during "some nameless battle" of the Revolution, and who "rides forth to the scene of battle in nightly quest of his head", The "Legend" relates the tale of Ichabod Crane, a lean, lanky and extremely superstitious schoolmaster from Connecticut, who competes with Abraham "Brom Bones" Van Brunt, the town rowdy, for the hand of 18-year-old Katrina Van Tassel, the daughter and sole child of wealthy farmer Baltus Van Tassel, Ichabod Crane, a Yankee and an outsider, sees marriage to Katrina as a means of procuring Van Tassel's extravagant wealth, Bones, the local hero, unable to force Ichabod into a physical showdown to settle things, plays a series of pranks on the superstitious schoolmaster, Ichabod mysteriously disappears, leaving Katrina to later marry Brom Bones, who was said "to look exceedingly knowing whenever the story of Ichabod was related", Although the true nature of both the Headless Horseman and Ichabod's disappearance that night are left open to interpretation, the story implies that the ghost was really Brom (an extremely agile rider) in disguise, and suggests that Crane survived the fall from his horse and immediately fled Sleepy Hollow, never to return but to prosper elsewhere, Irving's narrator concludes the story, however, by stating that the old Dutch wives continue to promote the belief that Ichabod was "spirited away by supernatural means", and while he was telling me about his version I thought of The Gift again, and how creativity for the sake of money leads to bad art and how relationships for the sake of money lead to bad feeling, and my heart felt pure, for the first time maybe ever in terms of movie business talk, and so our conversation became this pre-destined but willed for thing, that Lincoln paradox, and we talked about We Bought a Gun, and here's some more about it from the Imagine Impact application, "We Bought a Gun is a political romantic comedy set in Austin, Texas, about a progressive married couple: Adam (a New York transplant, guidance counselor, lover-not-a-fighter), and Maggie (a native Texan, NPR journalist, lover-AND-a-fighter), Their plans to start a family are upended after they're mugged at gunpoint and Maggie thinks Adam didn't do enough to protect her, so, much to both of their surprise, she responds by bringing home a gun, Maggie makes Adam a deal: learn to use the gun to protect their family, and they can start trying for a baby again, so Adam agrees, But the more he trains with the gun, the more obsessed he becomes (he feels like Dirty Harry and Rambo and James Bond all wrapped up into one); meanwhile, Maggie is confronted by the ugly truths of gun violence in America and the world, and she dislikes the macho changes she sees in her gentle partner, When their lives are threatened by an alienated high school student whom Adam has been trying to mentor, Maggie and Adam must come back together and figure out their best form of protection: Is it the gun, or is it something else," and I didn't conceal anything like a 3 wing in my 4, I guess, or I had a Christian heart as Ezra a Jew would say, do you get the Trickster paradox I am talking about, and so I told him that it had been around in different drafts, some quite bad, and that I had often alienated people by pursuing the project around times of gun deaths, and how I had learned that this problem, this ideal we were fighting for, shouldn't be connected to real events at the same time as it should, that you can't exploit even though you must try to make the movie, and he was relieved by that, I think, and he told me that he truly believed in the comedy and message and that, honestly, he sees award nominations if it gets made the right way, and I had never told anyone I felt that same way, and I had never had it told to me by anyone else, and to hear that from him, to be seen, to be understood, for my art, after really never getting that for so many years, and maybe never again, who knows, who knows what will come of this, all the way seen though by someone, it gave me such faith in what I was doing as a reborn person in that moment, being nice, and kind, and open, and giving, and trusting, and so who knows what will come of this, probably nothing, but I told him if we couldn't get the actors he hoped to get, he should just star in the low budget version and I honestly meant it, it wasn't the usual stuff I don't mean sometimes when I'm grasping for success, I really wanted him to have as much ownership over the project as possible, I truly wanted to share it with him, because at that moment, I realized it wasn't mine, none of these things that I own or say or make or do, none of it is mine, it is God's or Nature's or the Universe's, or whatever the mystery is, and it is the people's, because it is not me who writes, it is a Gift, The Gift, from somewhere, something else, the muse, and I think that is God, a Higher Power, the Holy Spirit, or maybe Aliens sometimes, ha, but no, I did think it was God, and I do now, and as we parted, I got in my car, and I drove home listening to Vampire Weekend, a song sampled from one of my favorite African artists SE Rogie, "When I was young, I was told I'd find, One rich man in ten has a satisfied mind, And I'm the one, A hundred to one says I wouldn't react, But I'm the one in a hundred who will swing right back, Yes I'm the one, Thousands of steps and staircases to climb, Thousands of men you'd most likely decline, And yet I'm the one, 10, 000 to 1, could I possibly bet, I'm compelled by your love and I haven't lost yet, Clearly you're the one, One in a million don't mean what it meant, And these millions of gold coins won't gleam when they're spent, And you're left with none, Ten million dollars could win the whole lot, But if ten million dollars is all that you got, You won't be the one, Hundreds of millions of papers to sign, Hundreds of millions of souls left behind, And yet we're the ones, A billion to one, don't the odds make you sick, To be one in a billion's a terrible trick, You're the wretched one, When I was young, I was told I'd find, One rich man in ten has a satisfied mind, And I'm the one," and I thought about the old lessons of money and power versus love and kindness, and they rang in my ears and in my soul so True that I cried, and then that night, I went to dinner at my old writing partner's house, J-, and for the first time since we split and he had gone on to make two movies without me, I felt no envy in my heart, I felt only pure love, and then I went home, and went to bed, but I couldn't sleep, and I started to face it, I started to really face what it meant that my dad was gone, and what it was that was done, and I felt like even though it wasn't my fault, it was my fault, that even though he died when he should, he also didn't, that even though I was a good son, I also wasn't, these Trickster, Jungian paradoxes, but the thing is, I felt him forgive me, I felt my dad and God forgive me, even as they judged me, they forgave me, and I wept, and I felt the angel of death heal me, I felt it, I felt the "Just a Closer Walk with Thee," and I felt my dad in my eyes, like he was looking at what I was looking at, looking through my eyes, and so were all the fathers before him, in my eyes, looking through them with me, and I felt like a Father, like all the Fathers, after Thich Nhat Hanh lost his mother he suffered for a year until he realized “I knew this body was not mine alone but a living continuation of my mother and my father and my grandparents and great-grandparents, Of all my ancestors,” and I saw that the Fathers saw everything that I had done in my life, including the shameful things, but that they weren’t ashamed of me, they only had love for me, that once you’re dead judgment is there but gone, that judgment day is really no judgment day at all, it is forgiveness day, and my friends Satbhajan and Alice did my Tarot during this time and I got Judgment/Forgiveness, and it said “The word ‘judgment’ conjures up fear & guilt in many people, This card, however, concerns itself with another aspect of this word, it’s about seeking truth, No more blaming yourself or others, no more excuses, Now is the time for forgiveness & personal freedom, This card asks you to rise up, let pettiness & fear fall below you, Expand your wings & be reborn, What a relief it will be,” and CS Lewis says the dead might “See, in some measure, like God, His love and His knowledge are not distinct from one another, nor from Him, We could almost say He sees because He loves, and therefore loves although He sees,” and I realized that in this world, our ego feels pain and strives for pleasure, but that there’s nothing to fear or hope for, even as there is, that Buddhism and Judeo-Christianity go together, that predestination and free will do, too, that we’re on a path, you have to keep your will going in sync with the path, you fall off, but you can get back in sync, and it feels Holy when you do, and Elaine Pagels in The Gnostic Gospels says, “When the disciple attains enlightenment, Jesus no longer serves as his spiritual master: the two have become equal, even identical,” and Van Morrison says, “Enlightenment, Don't you know what it is

It's up to you," I felt like Jesus and also knew that I was not Jesus, that old Trickster paradox, that it's not a bipolar delusion to say that you Gnostically live the myth of Jesus, as long as you don't think you are literally him, and don't believe that no one else can become the myth, that we all can live the myth in the transcendent experience, and should do so to reach self-knowledge, Gnosis, so, yes, writing this book, it lead to a bipolar manic episode but also an ecstatic spiritual experience, and that's a Jungian, Trickster paradox, those things are Transpersonal Psychology, they are not just Abnormal Psychology, and you should know it's now November, November 2019, and that experience of oneness and the synchronicity of seeing signs everywhere, literal signs on the road, that spoke to what was happening in my mind at that moment, and also signs in what people were saying to me, the underlying meaning that they are not aware of maybe, but that there is God's dramatic irony underneath the words illuminating their personality or essences or something about the world, and the feeling of the unification of intention and destiny, and the way pursuing kindness in all interactions, it opens doors to Holy Moments, the perpetual Holy Moment, it has put me on a spiritual path, that gives me peace and serenity even now, after it's over, the mania, and I am integrating this, I am integrating still, but I believe in God now, and I speak to God now, or a Higher Power, or the Holy Spirit, even now when I am "normal," and I guess I don't know if it's God for sure, but what I think I know and what I believe is that I have a voice in my head now, that sounds bad, I know, that sounds bad, to say I have a voice in my head, that sounds Abnormal, but it's more of a Conscience, maybe The Holy Spirit, instead of a "What is so wrong with me," voice, a voice that tells me how bad I am doing all the time, a critical superego voice that needed cognitive behavioral therapy, it's a: "Dave, you should be proud of this book, it's healing you, and will heal others," and for the first time my voice in my head is speaking to me in the third person it's not saying, "What is wrong with me, I'm such a fucking idiot, I fucking hate myself, what the fuck is wrong with me," that's all gone, or if it comes up briefly, it's given a talking to by this new third person Conscience, it's not me me me, it's you you you, from the first person only to a first and third person shared, and I can ask it questions, the Conscience, the voice of the Higher Power, and it speaks to me, and it might be The Holy Spirit, because it knows things, it knows what to do about things, and what to think about things, things that I couldn't know on my own, and it knows what other people are needing from me, when before I would guess wrong, or force wrong things, and when I ask it for advice, it's there for me, and I believe it's a Higher Power and it's in me, but outside of me, and even though the manic episode is gone, it's still here, it's staying, so what does that say, so what does that say, it says, "Dave, that's good, Dave, I love you, I'm here for you, I'm your inner voice," and I never knew what an inner voice meant, it was always talked about sorta in the New Age things, but now I know what having an inner voice means, and I think it's a Higher Power, that it's me and God together, and my dad, and all the Fathers before him, and James Hollis says, the act of speech and generative power of images resonate with the power of divine creativity, and that even though we shouldn't "fall in love with our own constructs and believe they contain the mystery, [which] is blasphemous, for such reification seeks to colonize the mystery on behalf of ego's dominion," meaning-making intimates the Mystery, which is universal to all people, for instance, "When inner and outer are one is the experience of the daimon (in Greek) a most personal encounter with the divine, The daimon may be seen as both transpersonal and intrapersonal, The daimon is the intermediary agency, as in the Christian mythologem of the Holy Spirit," and so I say Spotify is still being used by God, I believe the outer and inner are one, as Bob Dylan's "Pressing On" just came on, it's on right now, it really is, and Bob's singing, "Well I'm pressing on, Yes, I'm pressing on, Well I'm pressing on, To the higher calling of my Lord, Many try to stop me, shake me up in my mind, Say, 'Prove to me that He is Lord, show me a sign,' What kind of sign they need when it all come from within, When what's lost has been found, what's to come has already been, Well I'm pressing on, Yes, I'm pressing on, Well I'm pressing on, To the higher calling of my Lord, Shake the dust off of your feet, don't look back, Nothing now can hold you down, nothing that you lack, Temptation's not an easy thing, Adam given the devil reign, Because he sinned I got no choice, it run in my vein, Well I'm pressing on, Yes, I'm pressing on, Well I'm pressing on, To the higher calling of my Lord," and this is a 7,000 song shuffle, so what does that say, and I'm still in sync with Kanye, he dropped his Gospel album at the end of October, "God Is" has been blasting in my car all the time, and here are its lyrics, "My light in darkness, oh, God, God is, He, He is my all and all (And I'll never turn back), God is, Everything that I felt, praise the Lord, Worship Christ with the best of your portions, I know I won't forget all He's done, He's the strength in this race that I run, Every time I look up, I see God's faithfulness, And it shows just how much He is miraculous, I can't keep it to myself, I can't sit here and be still, Everybody, I will tell 'til the whole world is healed, King of Kings, Lord of Lords, all the things He has in store, From the rich to the poor, all are welcome through the door, You won't ever be the same when you call on Jesus' name, Listen to the words I'm sayin', Jesus saved me, now I'm sane, And I know, I know God is the force that picked me up, I know

Christ is the fountain that filled my cup, I know God is alive, yeah, He has opened up my vision, Giving me a revelation, This ain't 'bout a damn religion, Jesus brought a revolution, All the captives are forgiven, Time to break down all the prisons, Every man, every woman, There is freedom from addiction, Jesus, You have my soul, Sunday Service on a roll, All my idols, let 'em go, All the demons, let 'em know, This a mission, not a show, This is my eternal soul, This my kids, this the crib, This my wife, this my life, This my God-given right, Thank you, Jesus, won the fight, That's what God is, That's what God is, That's what God is," and I discovered that Bob Dylan had a spiritual reckoning, too, in the late 1970s, I read a book about it in October, I kinda knew a little, but know more now, and I finally listened to those albums, Slow Train Coming, Saved, and Shot of Love, and I guess as a Jew I had a reaction against listening to them before, and whatever I am now, just spiritual, I am open to experience, and Saved is really sticking with me, and it opens with A Satisfied Man, and Ezra literally references, "A Satisfied Man," in "Rich Man" the song I listened to before having the breakthrough, and Bob sang, "How many times have you heard someone say, If I had his money I'd do things my way, Hmm, but little they know, Hmm, it's so hard to find, One man in ten with a satisfied mind," and Ezra sings, "When I was young, I was told I'd find, One rich man in ten has a satisfied mind, And I'm the one," and then Bob sings, "Hmm, once I was wading in fortune and fame, Everything that I dreamed of to get a start in life's game, But suddenly it happened, Hmm, I lost every dime, But I'm richer by far with a satisfied mind, Hmm, when my life is over and my time has run out, My friends and my loved ones I'll leave there ain't no doubt, But one things for certain, When it comes my time, I'll leave this old world with a satisfied mind," and Ezra sings, "And these millions of gold coins won't gleam when they're spent, And you're left with none," and in Jesus is King, Kanye sings "Use this gospel for protection, It's a hard road to Heaven, We call on your blessings, In the Father, we put our faith, King of the kingdom, Our demons are tremblin', Holy angels defendin', In the Father, we put our faith," and in "Saving Grace," Bob sings, "If You find it in Your heart, can I be forgiven, Guess I owe You some kind of apology, I've escaped death so many times, I know I'm only living, By the saving grace that's over me, By this time I'd-a thought I would be sleeping, In a pine box for all eternity, My faith keeps me alive, but I still be weeping, For the saving grace that's over me, Well, the death of life, then come the resurrection, Wherever I am welcome is where I'll be, I put all my confidence in Him, my sole protection, Is the saving grace that's over me, Well, the devil's shining light, it can be most blinding, But to search for love, that ain't no more than vanity, As I look around this world all that I'm finding, Is the saving grace that's over me, The wicked know no peace and you just can't fake it, There's only one road and it leads to Calvary, It gets discouraging at times, but I know I'll make it, By the saving grace that's over me," and Dad I think you helped me get this satisfied mind, you've lead me through the angel of death to a satisfied mind, and you should know that I am aware of Ducks, Newburyport, which is the 1,000 page book that is mostly one sentence, ha, don't worry, everyone, I am not going for the record anymore, that's part of the satisfied mind, I feel satisfied with just sharing my experience, I'm not going to make you read ~600 more pages of this, can you imagine, but here's what I wrote before I found out about it, how I ended the sentence, or was planning to end the book after I beat Mike McCormack, and by beat, I mean "beat," because I don't think that way anymore, I don't, not after writing this book that's turned into a book about my dad and myself, because after that meal with the Imagine Impact person, that manic episode/spiritual awakening that lasted for 7 days, my first since my first when I was 21, it was very different than the manic episode that came before, because after that one when I was 21, I had a severe depression, before and after, and the episode itself was mixed with some severe paranoia, so it was a breakdown, and this, it wasn't a breakdown but a breakthrough, and it didn't result in a depression after, and so it's Truth and not truth that it was a manic episode, and I dug deeper into a Pitchfork review of Kanye's Gospel album, and I found a link that lead me to the writer Kiana Fitzgerald's piece on Jesus Is King and how Kanye's spiritualism is related to his unspoken bipolarism which was linked in the Pitchfork review and so I will put it here without the periods, etcetera, except I won't because I sent Kiana an email, "Hi Kiana, I am a bipolar writer who is a recent reader and follower of your work, I feel so fortunate to have found you and I am resonating with your piece on Kanye for Vibe, your Twitter feed, and your podcast with Bernie Beitman in ways synchronous and spiritual, but also sensitive to the medical realities of bipolar disorder, I understand that just because I resonate with you and your writing doesn't mean you have time to interact with me right away or ever, But I am very interested in conducting an exchange with you about our paths, our spiritualities, our experiences of mania, our experiences with medicine/psychology, our synchronicities with following signs and performing acts of kindness, and our relationship to Kanye and music, A bit about me, I wrote a humor piece sparked by Kanye for The New Yorker and have since self-published some spiritual/political satire and parody humor books, I'm working on a book that is a memoir about my bipolar dad's recent suicide, my own recent manic episodes afterward, their relationship with my recent spiritual awakening also after that, its connection to psychologists and psychology that integrate the medical with the spiritual, like Carl Jung and the Enneagram, also its connection to other New Age modalities like Numerology, and also its connection to writing, music, and in particular Kanye, Your piece resonated with me profoundly, especially: "Since the day my religious epiphany was explained to me as a symptom of my condition, I've been trying to draw a line from point A to point Z, and drag people from the medical side and others from the spiritual side and have them meet somewhere in the middle for a discussion, As of now, the chasm between the two communities couldn't be more wide," I'm very interested in this discussion and want to hear more about where you are at in integrating the different sides as well as help us both find resources and ways to bridge the chasm with others in our lives, the country, and the world, Thanks for reading this email and for putting yourself out there, You're not only an inspiration but also a genius writer, Hope to hear from you, Doesn't need to be soon, Sending you thoughts and prayers for health and meaning in your pursuit, Dave Cowen," and so there are other Thomas Pynchon Crying of Lot 49 Sensitives out there who don't believe in the only either/or but wonder about the paradox/both, "Communication is the key, The Demon passes his data on to the sensitive, and the sensitive must reply in kind, At some deep psychic level he must get through, The sensitive must receive that staggering set of energies, and feed back something like the same quantity of information," and so we'll see what happens there, and what happened is that we emailed back and forth a number of times and talked on the phone and she is going to read the book and add a 250 word commentary of her own, because Vibe wouldn't let me just put in her article without consulting with their legal team, and so we are learning to respect copyright, I guess, and we are also going to add 250 word commentaries from other friends who we are going to pass the baton so that one author equals many authors equals all the authors equals one sentence equals all sentences equals all humanity equals all, and if you are reading this far, add your 250 words in an Amazon comment, and I will add it to the ebook, which can go on pretty much infinitely, but for now read this Katy Waldman New Yorker review of the book with the real longest sentence ever written and then published, Ducks, Newburyport, which, it is really funny how similar it is in certain ways, she has a much bigger vocabulary, like orders of magnitude bigger vocabulary, and she uses "the fact that" to connect her thoughts instead of "and" but it has a similar deranged quality to it, and surprising jumps, and I'll put in a quick quote before Katy's review, and so the similarity in the projects, it feels like there is a Jungian synchronicity collective unconscious thing happening with me and Lucy Ellmann, as I was writing this unaware of her book, and yet we both had similar ideas, and methods, and yet I failed to get mine to market fast enough like usual, ha, but who cares, and here's a quote to give you an idea, "The fact that the racoons are now banging an empty yogurt carton around on the driveway, the fact that in the early morning stillness it sounds like gunshots, the fact that, even in fog, with ice on the road and snow banks blocking their vision, people are already zooming around our corner, the site of many a minor accident, the fact that a guy in a pickup once accidentally skidded into our garage, and next time it could be our house, or a child, Wake Up Picture Day, Dicamba, Kleenex," and so it has that ranty rhythm, but it's more traditionally literary, and more dictiony, and it's being listed as the best book of the year, and if you want me to take it out Lucy, or this upcoming review Katy or The New Yorker, I will, like I took out Kiana's Vibe piece, I'll just put a note, please buy this book and read these pages or please go to these pages of this site and imagine there are no periods, and same with anybody else whose work is in this book, I am going to put your stuff in, but if you want it out, just let me know, and I'll take it out of the PDF that will be on Amazon in the ebook and also POD, so it won't be printed in it again, or downloaded with it again, and I understand not everyone feels the way I felt about copyright before Lewis Hyde taught me, by the end of Common as Air, to respect it somewhat, even though I didn't want to hear it, and also Erich Fromm in The Art of Loving taught me that I may have not learned enough discipline and consequences, how society we are born into will treat me based on my behaviors, how the ways of the world work, so I don't fail in it, because my father practiced unconditional love as well as my mom, instead of conditional love like fathers are supposed to, according to Fromm, so I believe that everyone will love this book enough not to sue me, that it deserves unconditional love, like me, even though that's not how society works, I guess, but I also wonder if conditional love is good, if it's good for society, and if Fromm not applying the ethic of unconditional love to society would be beneficial, even though he believes in paradox and the need for both in the world, which makes sense, and I also wonder how I am supposed to show the paradox that I've learned this lesson without leaving my mistakes above, am I supposed to have the discipline to go back and cut out or paraphrase the things I quoted from without permission, if the reader is to experience my arc, what to do, I dunno, anyway here's Katy Waldman's review of Ducks, Newburyport, or maybe not, we'll see, "Can One Sentence Capture All of Life, The soaring ambition of "Ducks, Newburyport," By

Katy Waldman, September 6, 2019, In Lucy Ellmann's new novel, "Ducks, Newburyport," the narrator lives in a country whose mythic propositions hang in the same limbo as her thousand-page run-on sentence, Where does one start with "Ducks, Newburyport," the new novel by Lucy Ellmann, with its single, sinuous sentence tracking a middle-aged Ohio woman's perambulations of thought, It seems vacuous to dwell on the look of the thing, but, well, look at it: thick as a phonebook, red and blue, with an upside-down duck on the cover, Open the book, which has been short-listed for the Booker Prize, and you are greeted by block upon block of forbidding text, (There are no paragraph breaks,) Each section of the sentence, which runs for about a thousand pages, starts with the phrase "the fact that": "the fact that I think Frances Borshun likes her new dog better than she likes her first grandchild, the fact that she's nutty about that dog," Wordplay, snippets of music, and loopy associations multiply, Every so often, the story of a female mountain lion breaks in, told in crystal-clear, pared-down prose, In 1976, the critic Edward Mendelson described the "encyclopedic narrative," his term for a fiction, like "Don Quixote," that attempts "to render the full range of knowledge and beliefs of a national culture," Ellmann, the daughter of the Joyce scholar Richard Ellmann, marries this impulse to an experimental, stream-of-consciousness style, much as "Ulysses" did, This means gathering up ephemera alongside abiding truths, in the personal and also the sociopolitical spheres, Here are some of the types of things that the unnamed narrator thinks about: her husband; her ex-husband; her four children; her dreams; a bout of cancer that she survived; school shootings; the collapsing climate; Flint, Michigan; types of cakes; types of sandwiches; taxes; necrotizing fasciitis; "the fact that velvet's created by warp, and velveteen by weft"; "the fact that Emily

Dickinson didn't know how to tell the time"; the plots of Harrison Ford movies; "the fact that Daddy died before I really got to know him"; rape; the word "hydrangea"; novels she read in college; the massacre of Indians by American settlers; and "the fact that there's maybe too much emphasis on facts these days, or maybe there are just too many facts," What emerges is almost a joking definition of consciousness: the facts of life exist, in a jumble, and this book is content to perform awareness of them, (Ellmann to Karl Ove Knausgaard: "Hold my beer,") Verisimilitude is not the goal here: real people don't verbalize their emotional weather so relentlessly or spin off into constant rhymes and puns, The narrator occasionally corrects herself for clarity, which implies that she realizes that we can hear her, Instead of evoking the felt experience of inner life, Ellmann seems to be creating a stylized braid of conscious and unconscious thought—an artifice that's aware of its own construction, Maximalism drives home Ellmann's social critique—maybe there are "just too many facts," "Ducks, Newburyport" proceeds as if the deadliest narrative sin were that of omission, Yet there are (I thought to myself, wrestling the tome into my purse) other ways to be a book, There is the time-honored method of drawing a charged circle around a handful of topics and then studying them with care, Indeed, a vein of fear runs through Ellmann's collector's lust—that, even if one puts the world in a book, the story might remain incomplete, This fear stands in contrast to Ellmann's mountain lion, with her single-minded focus, her stark and queenly solitude, It's tempting to conclude that the book upholds her as a moral alternative to the self-delusions, compromises, and empty trivia of contemporary life, But that takeaway feels too simple, Anyone can lament our hellscape of constant distraction, The harder, and more rewarding, work is to sift through the debris, to surrender to it, and to wait for insight to emerge, Ellmann's commitment to compilation and description suggests a resistance to hierarchies, It also flickers with tenderness, The time and care that she lavishes on her narrator seem like their own form of political speculation—that every individual is owed an unending devotion, and that such devotion, applied universally, might change the fate of the world," and I tried to limit what I took of Waldman's essay to 10% or so, and I really like Waldman's conclusion there, that the devotion of universal kindness might change the fate of the world, and that's what I felt when I was having my manic episode/spiritual breakthrough in June after my meeting with the guy from Imagine Impact, after my identity imploded, I started to talk to everyone with universal and unconditional and unlimited kindness, and as a result I felt a Holy Love for everyone I met, that felt like we were all in Heaven together, and here's what Jack Kerouac said about that moment, "I have a lot of things to teach you now, in case we ever meet, concerning the message that was transmitted to me under a pine tree in North Carolina on a cold winter moonlit night, It said that Nothing Ever Happened, so don't worry, It's all like a dream, Everything is ecstasy, inside, We just don't know it because of our thinking-minds, But in our true blissful essence of mind is known that everything is alright forever and forever and forever," and "Practice kindness all day to everybody and you will realize you're already in heaven now, That's the story, That's the message," and Kerouac said, "Beat doesn't mean tired, or bushed, so much as it means beato, the Italian for beatific: to be in a state of beatitude, like St Francis, trying to love all life, trying to be utterly sincere with everyone, practicing endurance, kindness, cultivating joy of heart," and Kerouac said, "I want to work in revelations not just spin silly tales for money, I want to fish as deep down as possible into my own subconscious in the belief that once that far down, everyone will understand because they are the same that far down," and it's December 11th, 11 remember, and two things happened today, Kiana Fitzgerald responded to my email from November, and through her I found out about the DSM's categories of "Spiritual Emergencies" via her Youtube posts, and I read a book by one of the videomakers Sean Blackwell, who is now a shamanic guide and advocate that helps bipolar people through manic episodes, which is a diagnosis that rose 4,000% between 1994 and 2003, because he believes "The vast majority of the symptoms of bipolar mania were identical to the symptoms of a spiritual emergency," such as "a feeling of oneness with everything; timelessness; thinking that you are a type of messiah, like Jesus; that you are on a mission from God; outpourings of love to almost anyone you feel good with; a confrontation with death; and rage when this experience is controlled or suppressed by parents, doctors or the police," he reaches a hypothesis that "bipolar mania is like a psycho-spiritual vomiting - a process that needs to continue until its completion or it will return again," and for the vast majority, their manic process is 'blocked' and that 'block' is solidified with the medication," he believes "God is crazy, Crazy like a fox, operating on a whole other level," and "As scary, frustrating and confusing as life can be sometimes, I've learned that it's best to simply surrender to God's will and forget about your own plans, Because while life may look like utter madness, there is always a sublime love hidden beneath all the drama - a love which brings tears to my eyes, Living in the light of a God like that, how can we not have faith," his goal is to "'pave the road' to take back and validate what once had the potential to be the most sacred experience of their lives; one that our entire society has violently stripped away from them out of fear and ignorance," and "a natural mechanism which is intended to heal through a form of spiritual awakening," and like a latter-day Jungian he says, "The notion that God is a factual entity which can be experienced directly by anyone through what has been commonly referred to as a 'manic episode' calls into question the fundamental tenets of both modern science and its historical rival, religion" and "One of the joys of being in touch with people from around the world has been to verify that this divine encounter has been experienced by Christians of many denominations, Jews, Muslims, those who follow Buddhist practices and even atheists, Of course, there are no atheists afterward," and right now Glass Candy's "Warm in the Winter" is playing, and it's lyrics are: "Love is in the air love is in the air, We're warm in the winter, Sunny on the inside, Love is in the air, I'm crazy like a monkey, eee-oooh Happy like a new year, Yeah yeah / Woo hoo, That's right everybody, This is Glass Candy, Making our way around the world, Searching out a face-to-face with you, One more time, Looking for a heart-to-heart, Whenever you're ready, We want you to know, If ever you should look in the mirror, And wonder who it is that you are, And wonder what it is that you came for, Well I know the answer, You're beautiful, You came from heaven, You came down to this place, To fill out the dark corners, With your everlasting light, And that's why I love you, We love you, C'mon shout Hey shout, Shout, Yeah you, I love you, We love you," and as I write this book I am letting go of having to have the career I always wanted, divinely surrendering, and I am interested in becoming a librarian or a therapist or something else I don't know yet and yet today is also the day I got an email from Imagine Impact today, "Dear Dave, We're excited to invite you to join the Impact App, As you may know, we've just wrapped up our third content accelerator, Impact 3, Over the course of the last year, we've developed 61 projects - 23 of which have been setup or sold to major studios and production companies, We've also had a lot of demand from showrunners, producers, and studios for our writers - they've been staffed on shows at Marvel, Netflix, Amazon, Disney+, and have been hired to collaborate with leading producers across the industry, As one of the top applicants we've had since we launched Imagine Impact in 2018, we'd like to invite you to start using the Impact App as a tool to connect you to Impact's growing network of executives across Hollywood, We now have active users from over 250 organizations across town, including all of the major studios, networks, platforms, production companies, agencies, and management companies, On the Impact app, you will be able to create a profile for yourself, upload samples, and showcase what makes you special, If you do not currently have representation, we will help you find it by making your profiles and materials available to representatives, And with staffing season just around the corner, the Impact App can also facilitate the distribution of your materials to the showrunners and executives from the production companies, studios and networks on our platform, Please use the link below to join our waitlist and be among the first writers outside of our alumni on the Impact App," and so I loaded We Bought a Gun's logline and also another script I wrote called Sex Change which is a gender body swap comedy, and the first song that came up on my 7,000 song shuffle when I turned it back on was Lil Dicky's "Freaky Friday" where he switches bodies with Chris Brown and Kendall Jenner among others, no joke, you might wish I were lying to you, except you don't, you want to believe too, and it's true, don't worry, it's true, that just happened, on God, and so we'll see what happens, and the quest continues, and Juice Wrld just died, and I have been listening to "Ring

Ring" and thinking of my dad and how I used to call his phone and it going to voice mail, and "Ring Ring, I don't feel like coming to the phone today, Everyone should just leave me alone, I don't feel like coming to the phone today, But I don't feel like being alone," and I found on Amazon Customers who viewed Sean Blackwell's book also like The Spiritual Gift of Madness: The Failure of Psychiatry and the Rise of The Mad Pride Movement, by Seth Farber, and how he and the Mad Pride movement and the Icarus Project believe that madness might be a sociobiological response to the insanity of the normal way of living, ie war, capitalism, climate destruction, materialism, superficiality, etc, and that the spiritual growth of a manic episode can actually when guided and understood, as in RD Laing's The Politics of Experience, provide a higher level of sanity, and a higher consciousness along the lines of Ekhart Tolle's The Power of Now and A New Earth, "dangerous gifts" that are commonly misdiagnosed and labelled as mental illness, the cooperative, nonrational, communal and spiritual or religious dimensions of existence not being recognized by our individualistic, competitive, materialistic, rationalistic, conformist mental health professional society, if society is insane, adjustment to society is not a sign of mental health or of spiritual well-being, the metanoia theory of madness, a transformation of consciousness, the recognition that we are in fact spiritual beings who are cast into a material form, but budding prophets of today are captured, cured and transformed into chronic mental patients, before they have the opportunity to complete the death and rebirth process, and become creatively maladjusted, as Martin Luther King says, who will endeavor to bring the world closer to the visions they have had, Farber is saying this, the ascent of man into heaven is ascent here into spirit, heaven on Earth, not one Messiah, but all of us messiahs, an evolutionary bid for the transformation of consciousness, John Weir Perry wrote that "almost universally" within "acute psychosis" lies a messianic vision of a new world order based on "equality and harmony, tolerance and love," and as Laing presciently wrote, "if the human race survives, future men will look back on our enlightened epoch as a veritable Age of Darkness, The laugh's on us, They will see that what we call schizophrenia was one of the forms in which, often through quite ordinary people, the light began to break in the cracks in our all-too-closed minds," and Joseph Campbell asks what's the difference between 'psychosis' and mysticism, he stated that the mad person and the mystic are immersed in the same ocean of beatitude, but the mystic is swimming while the mad person is drowning, and I drowned when I was 21 but I am starting to swim now at 35, and this book is a signpost for others, as Tolle says in A New Earth, "In the service of the Truth, religious teachings represent signposts or maps left behind by awakened humans to assist you in spiritual awakening, There is only one absolute Truth, and all other truths emanate from it, When you find that Truth, your actions will be in alignment with it, Can the Truth be put into words, Yes, but the words are, of course, not it, They only point to it," and this is a signpost for the 80s and 90s and 00s kids born into the secular, scientific left, and the future 10s and 20s kids, and for everyone, and Benji Hughes' I Am You, You Are Me, We Are One," is on as I look through this part of the book again, in January of 2020, and there's only 6 weeks until the anniversary of my father's death when I plan to publish this book, six weeks left in the mourner's kaddish, and so I think I will add here what I wrote on my quest, before knowing all that, right before I had the manic episode/breakthrough in June, and I will add interjections as I read through it, these next six weeks, read through it again and again, and add interjections again and again, and it will end the book, a combo of what I wrote right before having the breakdown with interjections about how I feel now that I've broken-through, and settled, for now, I will continue to add interjections in parenthesis, and it would be so much easier if there were chapters to read this, maybe broken up by date, is what I was told by a friend who read this far, but I don't think I can do that, even if she is right, I won't break the conceit in that way, or at least I don't think I will as of today, January 16th, but I might change my mind, or I might not, and so I wrote, before the breakdown/breakthrough, He's gone now, my dad, (but it's OK, [these are the interjections in parenthesis]), but what it feels like to never talk to him again now, it is rough, (it's actually OK, to me at least, right now, he's a Father, and one of the Fathers in my Higher Power/Conscience) and a lot of people know what that's like, and we would have made sure to talk to that person or people every day, many times a day, (I do now still, it's true) and keep up our relationship(s) and not let you avoid talking to me, Dad, because you hated to share how sad you felt all the time, and burden people with your emotions, and so you often avoided talking to your family and friends, but when you did talk to us, you would be so happy, because your favorite thing in life was having a conversation with people, including perfect strangers, and that is what is ironic about depression is that it makes you do the exact opposite of what you want to do with your life, it's truly the darkest irony, and so sometimes I wonder if I had just never stopped talking to you, if I never left your side, and just endlessly talked to you, and we had an endless conversation about everything in our lives and the world, maybe your life would have gone on endlessly and you wouldn't have died, and maybe I would know you better, because now that you're gone I can't have any conversations with you, and that's the hardest part, (but death doesn't have to be an interruption it can be an awakening to a different connection, in my experience at least), and it's impossible in real life to not interrupt a conversation, as we have to go to work, and write emails, Sure thing, Steve, will send by EOD, and we have responsibilities, and we get selfish temporarily, and need our alone time, or we just need to sleep, and of course we will all die someday, but a conversation between two people, in real life, or in a book between the writer and the reader, that is a sacred thing, (and the thing is though I know you are reading this, you are still alive in the spiritual world, we are connected, [and during the edit I dove into Joan Didion's The Year of Magical Thinking, the ultimate grief memoir of our time, and it says, "Nor can we know ahead of the fact, and here lies the heart of the difference between grief as we imagine it and grief as it is, the unending absence that follows, the void, the very opposite of meaning, the relentless succession of moments during which we will confront the experience of meaninglessness itself," and I apologize to Joan, but I say, my ego I guess, or my essence, or both, we say, with the utmost respect, you might be wrong, or in my experience, at least, there is not meaninglessness, that's vain to say, me to say, and maybe you, too, Joan, to say without qualification, and you say it "reinforces my awareness of the final silence that separated us," But again no, I disagree, in my experience, sorry, and she says, "I also know that if we are to live ourselves there comes a point at which we must relinquish the dead, let them go, keep them dead," and yet I disagree again, the dead live among us, and so does Laura Lynne Jackson who says, "Each of us has a Team of Light--a group of unseen helpers who work together to guide us to our highest path, This team is made up of our loved ones who have crossed, our spirit guides {also commonly known as guardian angels} a higher angelic realm, and God energy, which is based in the strongest force there is or ever will be: love, If you open your mind and heart to the secret language your Team of Light uses, the very way you live your life will change, Your relationship with the world and with the universe will be different: better, brighter, more powerful, When we learn to recognize and trust the many ways in which the universe communicates with us, we experience what I call a Great Shift, This change in perspective leads us to heightened engagement, connectivity, vibrancy, and passion, It makes it easier for us to grasp the true meaning of our existence, Once you learn to see these signs and messages, you will never be able to unsee them, They will forever have the power to infuse your past, present, and future with new and profound meaning, and in this way transform your life,")] and so I hope you as a reader are not disliking this conversation that I am having with my dad and with you, (and taking shots at Joan, sorry, Joan) even if it is a monologue, or a soliloquy, is what they call Joyce's Molly Bloom sentences and do you know that the writer who may have invented stream of consciousness before Joyce was Dorothy Richardson, with her book Pilgrimage, and what does that say about literary history that I just learned that today, is it a male thing, but why did Virginia Woolf also get major credit with Faulkner and Proust, and back to me, as this is still mostly for me, the writer, do you maybe like it enough that you like the idea that a sentence and a book and a writing and a thought and a consciousness can never end as long as you live in it, or go back to it, it will always be there for you, the printed words, the sentence, the consciousness, and why aren't there more stream of consciousness memoirs, records of flow, and some people say that movies put viewers in a state of flow, that's why they are so popular, and also I want to bring up Martin Seligman, and how I read Learned Optimism and Authentic Happiness and Flourish and tried to get my dad into Positive Psychology, and I bring up Marty because he is big on flow as part of happiness and well-being, and I brought up Positive Psychology to my dad the week before he killed himself, and he said it wouldn't work, but then he left that note "Think Positive" and so what does that mean, ("It means, THINK POSITIVE," says my Conscience, and yes, Dad, that is what I am doing, [and Laura Lynn Jackson says "Here are many of the most common default signs sent by the Other Side: Birds and butterflies, deer, electrical events, often with cellphones, coins appearing in our path, rainbows, pictures, slogans, billboards, magazines, license plates, street signs, music/songs, feathers, ladybugs, and numerical sequences," and before I read her book Signs I had noticed many of these without knowing about their use as signs by the Other Side and she says "It's very easy for us to get stuck in our grief, to feel overwhelmingly sad and empty and lonely, But our loved ones on the Other Side do not want us to feel that way, so they send us signs that can transform our grief into something quite profound, the feeling that we continue to be, and will always be, connected to those we love, even after they cross to the Other Side, That's not all, I have seen how individuals who had a hard time communicating with their loved ones here on earth become much better communicators after they cross, Which means that our relationships not only continue, but can also improve, Think of that, We can find new levels of closeness and contentment with our loved ones after they have crossed, We may even feel their love more purely than we did when they were here"]) and all I know is what I am doing is I am living in this sentence, right now, too, and not closing it, and dad you are here in the sentence, and he is throwing me a baseball in our side yard, and I have a big red bat maybe a blue one and it's swollen in the sweet spot, the bat, and I hit the ball and it crashes into the window and it breaks it, and my dad and I look at each other, then laugh, and I am with my dad when we swam in the pool in Florida together, and he is swimming laps, and I am jumping on his back and he is laughing, and I am helping him trim the hedges, and we are having lemonade afterwards, and his eyes, man, the softest eyes, the sweetest blues, would never hurt a fly, and he's cooking up ribs with a recipe he got from a random stranger at the supermarket because he believed everyone is equal, and we're digging out snow in the driveway, and we're skiing, and we're picking out my first stereo, and we're laughing like hyenas with my uncle, and his eyes, man, like Clapton says, look into, and the soft hair, baby fine, and the tucked in shirt, and the way he crossed his leg when he sat, his memory, and his soft hands, cold but soft, and his smile, crooked but warm and wide, and I wish I could remember more, and I hope it is tolerable to you, too, this book about that all of a sudden, and it hasn't been all of a sudden, you've seen it become that, with me, and him, we've all lived it together, and isn't that great, and I hope you are getting something out of it, too, because I am still not ready to end the sentence, not ready to end it, no, I don't want to let it go yet, (and this feels like a denouement with the interjections doesn't it, and it feels more anticlimactic, but more peaceful I think, and that's OK,) I don't want to let this sentence end, and I have just checked the word count, and we are at exactly whoa we are way over 80,000 words, we already have the record, we have over 224 pages, too, and I didn't even realize it, (we don't have the record) and I'm not even sure how I feel about having the record yet, (we don't have it [instead we didn't miss life, we got healed, it's like listening to James Blake's "Don't Miss It" and not being mad anymore that you are still "missing it"]) I was going to let James Joyce put us over the top with his previous longest sentence record holder of 3,687 words, which if you add it to the words so far you get a number that, well, it's not poetic, dang, but even though I beat McCormack, the robot, dang, is it coming for me, I better add Joyce's sentence anyway, here it is (intercut with the people/friends I am having add to the sentence [and even intercut with anyone who writes an Amazon review, if you write an Amazon review I will add it/intercut it into this Ulysses monologue, I will, whatever you say as a comment, as long as you are a verified purchaser, of course, ha, I will take out the periods and add your comment to this part of the sentence, this Ulysses monologue, so you can be part of having written the longest sentence, you, too, all of us, one voice, one author, one oneness, right]): "no thats no way for him has he no manners nor no refinement nor no nothing in his nature slapping us behind like that on my bottom because I didnt call him Hugh the ignoramus that doesnt know poetry from a cabbage thats what you get for not keeping them in their proper place pulling off his shoes and trousers there on the chair before me so barefaced without even asking permission and standing out that vulgar way in the half of a shirt they wear to be admired like a priest or a butcher or those old hypocrites in the time of Julius Caesar of course hes right enough in his way to pass the time as a joke sure you might as well be in bed with what with a lion God Im sure hed have something better to say for himself an old Lion would O well I suppose its because they were so plump and tempting in my short petticoat he couldnt resist they excite myself sometimes its well for men all the amount of pleasure they get off a womans body were so round and white for them always I wished I was one myself for a change just to try with that thing they have swelling up on you so hard and at the same time so soft when you touch it my uncle

John has a thing long I heard those cornerboys saying passing the comer of Marrowbone lane my aunt Mary has a thing hairy because it was dark and they knew a girl was passing it didnt make me blush why should it either its only nature and he puts his thing long into my aunt Marys hairy etcetera and turns out to be you put the handle in a sweepingbrush men again all over they can pick and choose what they please a married woman or a fast widow or a girl for their different tastes like those houses round behind Irish street no but were to be always chained up theyre not going to be chaining me up no damn fear once I start I tell you for their stupid husbands jealousy why cant we all remain friends over it instead of quarrelling her husband found it out what they did together well naturally and if he did can he undo it hes coronado anyway whatever he does and then he going to the other mad extreme about the wife in Fair Tyrants of course the man never even casts a 2nd thought on the husband or wife either its the woman he wants and he gets her what else were we given all those desires for Id like to know I cant help it if Im young still can I its a wonder Im not an old shrivelled hag before my time living with him so cold never embracing me except sometimes when hes asleep the wrong end of me not knowing I suppose who he has any man thatd kiss a womans bottom Id throw my hat at him after that hed kiss anything unnatural where we havent I atom of any kind of expression in us all of us the same 2 lumps of lard before ever Id do that to a man pfooh the dirty brutes the mere thought is enough I kiss the feet of you senorita theres some sense in that didnt he kiss our halldoor yes he did what a madman nobody understands his cracked ideas but me still of course a woman wants to be embraced 20 times a day almost to make her look young no matter by who so long as to be in love or loved by somebody if the fellow you want isnt there sometimes by the Lord God (, and here's Kiana Fitzgerald's addition, it's from 1/28/2019, Dave Cowen, writer of the longest sentence ever written and then published, reached out to me because of an article I wrote about Kanye West; I'm guessing either immediately before or after this insertion, Dave will tell you more about it, anywho, I'm writing pretty freely because I know Dave is going to take out the periods after I send this anyway, I hope I'm doing this right, let's talk about the book, when I first started reading this book, I was highly anxious, I kept looking for an end, an end, WHERE IS THE END, or the period, the favorite word of Florida rappers the City Girls but eventually I got into the rhythm of things, and I began to see slivers of Dave peeking through: honesty and wit interwoven, side note, I just used a period and had to backtrack and delete, I don't know how you pulled this off, Dave, end side note, this book is an undulating, never-conforming vacillation between broken-open vulnerability and smart-alecky humor: the moments in which Dave literally asks his readers if we love him, if we love his book, transition seamlessly into raw emotions about his father, and then they veer into the territory of he-who-must-not-be-named, and his friend Kanye West, who brought Dave and me together in the first place, I have to take a moment here to acknowledge that Dave dug into every element of Kanye that I've been thinking about on my own, but in particular the bipolar diagnosis we share and the things that characterize it, like being so manic — so energetically heightened — that you feel motivated enough to write the longest sentence ever published, or, dare I admit, motivated enough to write the piece inspired by Kanye that brought Dave and me together, I'm not saying I was manic, but I was getting there, and it's moments like that that make me wonder why bipolar is seen as such a bad thing, I'm getting distracted, back to the book, well actually, to stay on topic, it felt reassuring to read in someone else's words the things I've been thinking about for years, but with such specificity that it gives me hope that one day many of us bipolar people will assemble our voices and be loud enough to be heard by all; that's the gist of how I feel about Dave's book, it's cerebral at times and nutty at others, self-aware at times and comically self-aggrandizing at others — but altogether, it explores the gamut of things that won't leave my brain: Jung's teachings, and Life Path Numbers (I'm a 22, like his dad) and spiritual breakthroughs and connectivity and God and Kanye freakin' West, subjects that I furiously research and attempt to explain on my own, then it turns around and deals with the death of a parent who had mental health issues, which I myself am dealing with and have been for 10 years now, it's powerful to read the real-time reverberations of such a significant loss, to feel someone parse through the end of that life and the beginning of a life with absence, I've written too much (literally, I've gone over the word count Dave recommended) so I'll try to wrap this up: this book is equal parts remembrance, exploration, and explication; it grapples with the notions of success and pain, and the crux of those points is the idea that we're mortals, capable of being deeply affected by just about everything life throws at us — how could you not relate to that," and back to Joyce,) I was thinking would I go around by the quays there some dark evening where nobodyd know me and pick up a sailor off the sea thatd be hot on for it and not care a pin whose I was only do it off up in a gate somewhere or one of those wildlooking gipsies in Rathfarnham had their camp pitched near the Bloomfield laundry to try and steal our things if they could I only sent mine there a few times for the name model laundry sending me back over and over some old ones odd stockings that blackguardlooking fellow with the fine eyes peeling a switch attack me in the dark and ride me up against the wall without a word or a murderer anybody what they do themselves the fine gentlemen in their silk hats that K C lives up somewhere this way coming out of Hardwicke lane the night he gave us the fish supper on account of winning over the boxing match of course it was for me he gave it I knew him by his gaiters and the walk and when I turned round a minute after just to see there was a woman after coming out of it too some filthy prostitute then he goes home to his wife after that only I suppose the half of those sailors are rotten again with disease O move over your big carcass out of that for the love of Mike listen to him the winds that waft my sighs to thee so well he may sleep and sigh the great Suggester Don Poldo de la Flora if he knew how he came out on the cards this morning hed have something to sigh for a dark man in some perplexity between 2 7s too in prison for Lord knows what he does that I dont know and Im to be slooching around down in the kitchen to get his lordship his breakfast while hes rolled up like a mummy will I indeed did you ever see me running Id just like to see myself at it show them attention and they treat you like dirt I dont care what anybody says itd be much better for the world to be governed by the women in it you wouldnt see women going and killing one another and slaughtering when do you ever see women rolling around drunk like they do or gambling every penny they have and losing it on horses yes because a woman whatever she does she knows where to stop sure they wouldnt be in the world at all only for us they dont know what it is to be a woman and a mother how could they where would they all of them be if they hadnt all a mother to look after them what I never had thats why I suppose hes running wild now out at night away from his books and studies and not living at home on account of the usual rowy house I suppose well its a poor case that those that have a fine son like that theyre not satisfied and I none was he not able to make one it wasnt my fault we came together when I was watching the two dogs up in her behind in the middle of the naked street that disheartened me altogether I suppose I oughtnt to have buried him in that little woolly jacket I knitted crying as I was but give it to some poor child but I knew well Id never have another our 1st death too it was we were never the same since O Im not going to think myself into the glooms about that any more I wonder why he wouldnt stay the night I felt all the time it was somebody strange he brought in instead of roving around the city meeting God knows who nightwalkers and pickpockets his poor mother wouldnt like that if she was alive ruining himself for life perhaps still its a lovely hour so silent I used to love coming home after dances the air of the night they have friends they can talk to weve none (and my friend, Mike Heller, who I have known for twenty years now, 18 years now, he wrote a beautiful piece for Medium about parenting/pregnancy/healthcare, me an email, "In the spirit of your book, I was very honest, Hope this is ok, I remember reading Dave's first piece of writing, or at least the first piece of writing I read, which was a screenplay about a lunatic on a diet, which was called, I'm looking back now, THE DIET OF WORMS, and I remember thinking it was so weird, but good weird, like how Dave is weird, but also raw, and that it had a Charlie Kaufman type vibe to it, but then Dave started writing really big, broad comedies, and I was always confused by that, because the first thing I read, that DIET OF WORMS script, felt more like him than a broad comedy ever did, and I realize now that I never said anything to him about that, and I feel bad about that, too, because I know that I could and should be able to say anything to Dave because of how far back we go and how close we are, but ever since I've been waiting to read something by him that really FEELS like him, and the Haggadahs were the on-ramp, so impressive and fun and felt like he was really onto something, but then he wrote this thing, this longest sentence book, and DAMN this is Dave Cowen, like this is the thing, and I couldn't help but feel, really, everything about it, because it was equal parts vulnerable and frustrating and amazing and didactic and inspiring and, let's be honest, way over-populated with massive block quotes, and I had this realization: that any imperfection about this book actually lends to its perfection, that Dave actually opened up his head and let us in, and at times it was intense and beautiful and at times it was slow and too in the weeds, but that's how people are, that's how people think, that's how DAVE thinks, and because of that, it's perfect, even the general concept of this book, the longest sentence, where I went from, "this seems like too much of thing," like it's trying too hard, to realizing this form is exactly what was necessary to fully open Dave up and open his writing up, and I'm going to say something here, and my fear is that it's going to sound condescending, but I really, truly don't mean it that way, and it's that I am so proud of Dave for writing this and sharing himself, and at least for me, really sharing his voice in a way that I have not seen before, not hiding behind broad comedy or parodies but really truly writing in HIS voice which should be what Dave writes in forever now, Dave, write this way forever, and JESUS, I just checked the word count and I went VERY over, sorry, I had a lot of feelings about this, and honestly, writing this way is incredibly freeing, I feel free, baby, I'm ALIVE," and the script Mike was talking about was this weird comedy where a yes a lunatic mean angry leader of a no carb diet company gets into hot water with the Catholic church when he rules that communion wafers are no longer food of minimal nutritional value and must not be eaten as they are carbs, but along the way meets an obese living in her bed mother Theresa figure who teaches him to love himself again and accept himself no matter what weight he is so he can be nice to his wife and have a baby, lol, and so about ten years later in 2018 I think, Mike and I tried to write a big, broad comedy together, called The Best Man Competition but I turned it into a Buddhist ending where the competitive groomsmen have to learn to be peaceful Buddhists so spirituality is in everything I do I guess sometimes, and this writer new friend Tom Comitta who also plays quite heavily with the conceptual aspects of using other people's writing in his own writing, and he even published a book that took the first sentences from The New Yorker's fiction short stories to construct his own book and it's called First Impressions, and he says about it, "'First Impressions'" consists entirely of first sentences from 268 short stories published in The New Yorker over the past 20 years, from 1997 to 2017, all of which are cited below, After collecting every first sentence, I found they fell into a number of patterns, some surprising, others obvious: points of view, different tenses, genre fiction like western and military, stories set in smalltown America, stories set in Montana (oddly there were a lot), etc, I then arranged these patterns into a sequence of vignettes, a short story in its own right, In writing this piece I wanted to examine the production of prestige fiction as well as the editorial character of The New Yorker fiction section, its idiosyncrasies, biases and imaginative limits, As with any fully sampled text, the source material directed the kind of stories I could tell, Some sections almost wrote themselves given the abundance of a particular pattern, Some sections blended two or more related patterns into one narrative, Some came together under the constraint of scarcity (eg a majority of these sentences were written from a male point of view; I could tell the story of a man's life, but only a fragment of a woman's), In these ways each vignette of "First Impressions" doubles as narrative and archive, microfiction and data analysis, —TC, and so Tom is also pretty critical of The New Yorker or at least aware of its limitations in what it will accept and promote as part of the literary canon at this time in history, and he's in the document now at 12:19 PM and I am supposed to talk to him at 12:30 PM today, so I will let you guys know whether he wants to add to the sentence, and he does, we just got off the phone and he does want to add to the sentence and so does the person from Imagine Impact who sent me that email and who I met with that fateful day, and he's a musical improv actor and writer and he's really genius, he's a real genius, and I hope one day he plays my character in We Bought a Gun, and his name is Ryan DeNardo, and I love this dude, he's so talented and kind and brave, and people are stepping out into public with me, and now so does another friend writer Leryl who wrote a book called The Table, and she included bookmarks of a playlist to listen to at her book party that I helped throw for her which partly gave me the idea to make a Spotify playlist, and it's all coming together, everyone is contributing, and my friend Alec who I mentioned above a few times is going to contribute now, too, and my Vice horoscope today says, "Partners who can stand in the spotlight with you are important to you right now--connect with the people you're in relationship about whether they're ready to step out in public with you exclamation point," how funny is that, and there are some people who don't but that's OK, that's OK, too, and we're still flowing, the flow goes until the 25th, anniversary of my dad's death, that's the project, flowing and manifesting, manifesting destiny, and my buddy Dan Marshall who wrote Home Is Burning, which is a memoir about how he went home to take care of his dying dad, while his mother had cancer, too, and when I read that book, it was one of the things that truly opened me up to the possibility of what books could be for our generation I mean it is so full of filthy insane humor yet so full of heart and meaning, and I remember I sent the book to a literary agent friend of mine saying it was like Dave Eggers meets South Park or whatever and he liked it and I think even worked with Dan for a minute, but was ultimately like this is too nuts for publishing, and now years later what's too nuts for publishing that standard is even crazier both in protecting the establishment and what is just being done anyway outside of that industry, and so Dan's book is really good, you should really read that one, Home Is Burning, and he's going to add to the book too, and what's cool about this is it's like a rap song where people just spit some bars, 250 words, they just spit them on whatever they want, doesn't have to be about me, Amazon reviewers, you too, you can literally put anything you want into the review and I will put it into the book, be creative, be crazy, be free, we're trying to turn books into Instagram and back again and then back again and then back again and some which way so we don't even know what we have anymore, and back to Joyce) either he wants what he wont get or its some woman ready to stick her knife in you I hate that in women no wonder they treat us the way they do we are a dreadful lot of bitches I suppose its all the troubles we have makes us so snappy Im not like that he could easy have slept in there on the sofa in the other room I suppose he was as shy as a boy he being so young hardly 20 of me in the next room hed have heard me on the chamber arrah what harm Dedalus I wonder its like those names in Gibraltar Delapaz Delagracia they had the devils queer names there father Vilaplana of Santa Maria that gave me the rosary Rosales y OReilly in the Calle las Siete Revueltas and Pisimbo and Mrs Opisso in Governor street O what a name Id go and drown myself in the first river if I had a name like her O my and all the bits of streets Paradise ramp and Bedlam ramp and Rodgers ramp and Crutchetts ramp and the devils gap steps well small blame to me if I am a harumscarum I know I am a bit I declare to God I dont feel a day older than then I wonder could I get my tongue round any of the Spanish como esta usted muy bien gracias y usted see I havent forgotten it all I thought I had only for the grammar a noun is the name of any person place or thing pity I never tried to read that novel cantankerous Mrs Rubio lent me by Valera with the questions in it all upside down the two ways I always knew wed go away in the end I can tell him the Spanish and he tell me the Italian then hell see Im not so ignorant what a pity he didnt stay Im sure the poor fellow was dead tired and wanted a good sleep badly I could have brought him in his breakfast in bed with a bit of toast so long as I didnt do it on the knife for bad luck or if the woman was going her rounds with the watercress and something nice and tasty there are a few olives in the kitchen he might like I never could bear the look of them in Abrines I could do the criada the room looks all right since I changed it the other way you see something was telling me all the time Id have to introduce myself not knowing me from Adam (and Leryl Joseph just emailed me and here's what she wrote, "end of the world if I don't write the longest sentence in the world, and that's not a question, that's a fact because it's not, actually, the end of the world if i don't write the longest sentence, and that's what i've been reminding myself of—that it's okay to not be record-breaking because the only thing God wants me to do is love and everything else is stuff that i've made up because i know that God put something in me to desire to be great, so I'm constantly trying to be great by doing record-breaking things, but if I don't achieve any of those record-breaking things and I just love always and with my whole heart, I've actually lived the life I was destined to live, and that might be better than breaking records, but it might not be, I don't know yet and I'm not actually sure if I'll ever find out and I guess that's the real point—that I shouldn't be focused on what I'm getting out of living but just on the living part, however that's hard to do when life feels average, relationships are unpredictable, trouble always comes, and all the while I'm telling myself that I'm meant to be great because there's another voice inside of me that told me that first, and then I'm exhausted because life becomes one conflicting, constant, inescapable thought, and then i realize I'm not actually living, I'm just thinking about living, and then the mental hamster wheel restarts," and that was from Leryl Joseph, who is a friend from my day job, or was, now she's just a friend from real life, and buy her book The Table on Amazon, and thank you Leryl the hamster wheel does restart sometimes even now but now I am aware I can slow or stop it, I have control over the hamster wheel now most of the time, and I believe others do too, if you feel you don't right now, you can do it, I know you can, I believe in you, and back to Joyce) very funny wouldnt it Im his wife or pretend we were in Spain with him half awake without a Gods notion where he is dos huevos estrellados senor Lord the cracked things come into my head sometimes itd be great fun supposing he stayed with us why not theres the room upstairs empty and Millys bed in the back room he could do his writing and studies at the table in there for all the scribbling he does at it and if he wants to read in bed in the morning like me as hes making the breakfast for I he can make it for 2 Im sure Im not going to take in lodgers off the street for him if he takes a gesabo of a house like this Id love to have a long talk with an intelligent welleducated person Id have to get a nice pair of red slippers like those Turks with the fez used to sell or yellow and a nice semitransparent morning gown that I badly want or a peachblossom dressing jacket like the one long ago in Walpoles only 8/6 or 18/6 (and Tom Comitta just added his words and they are beautiful and poignant and smart and here they are enjoy, "when Dave asked me to contribute 250 words, I was surprised for a few reasons, especially because his book is so personal and I did not know his father, but the more I thought about his project, the more I realized that Dave is doing something similar to what I'd love to do some day if I have the time and guts to do so: to create a book as a kind of historical record of someone who is gone, the person for whom I'd most like to write a book, particularly a biography, is my uncle who shares Dave's name -- his name was David Turner -- I never knew him, he took his life in San Diego around New Years Day in 1997, when I was 11, and while there are pictures of us meeting when I was a baby, I have no memory of him, and not knowing him has haunted me for years, partially because he is the only other openly queer person in my family and I would have loved to have felt less alone when I was younger, and also because he was the first artist on my mothers' side of the family, and also because in my early adult life my mother regularly compared my artistic sensibilities and former drug use to him, both of us moving from the East Coast to California being the most superficial of our connections, so he has felt like some combination of a shadow self, an echo, an omen, and when I went to San Diego for the first time last November I made a point to do some detective work and try to go to as many places that I was certain that he had been to -- his old house, the dirt alley behind his house, the park that the alley leads to, the place where he shot himself, the hospital where he died two hours later, San Diego's gay neighborhood that was also there in the 90s -- the only place I could not find was the place where he shot himself, and so my detective work continues, but one of the reasons I would bring this up in Dave

Cowen's book is one of my main takeaways from this detective work is that 22 years is long enough for someone to be almost completely erased; few people talk about David Turner in my family anymore and I was unable to find any real traces of him in San Diego, and this was frustrating, while I was there I wanted to find some concrete mark that he had left behind, a monument of sorts that I could touch and feel some direct connection to him, but could find none, I even went to thrift stores in the gay neighborhood thinking that some of those objects might have been his at some point, but of course this was futile, and so my grief for this man I did not know feels unfinished, 22 years later where David Turner lives is in the few documents and photos that I have gathered and in people's memories, so one day soon I plan to interview people who knew him and compile the fragments of information that are available into a biography that shows the gaps in the story (aka there will be a lot of white/negative space because memory is flawed and at least at the moment I don't have access to anyone who really knew him in the 90s apart from one family friend -- he had become estranged from my family because of his substance use disorder) and so the reason I bring this up here is on one hand, there's resonance between me writing a book about someone I never knew, David Turner, and contributing to Dave Cowen's book about his father, whom I also never knew, and on the other hand to provide some outside context about how important it is to write things down as Dave is doing here, because the marks, the traces of life, can be easily erased, in our digital age it is important that books still exist; they are mark-keepers, and however flimsy and inadequate the written word can be, paper and ink are more durable than digital files, which can become obsolete as new programs supersede others or computers crash or hundred-year solar flares erase all hard drives on earth, paper and ink stored well are more durable than footprints, which wind and rain quickly wash away, or house paint, which can easily be painted over by the next occupant, or names carved into trees, which become submerged as the tree grows or are simply lost because only those present knew about them, it is so easy for marks to disappear, and writing is one way that marks, memories, people can endure, even live a bit longer, or find a new life," and it's 2:22 and that's a good time right ha and it was 22 years ago when Tom's Uncle died, when he was 11, ha not and so let's mark this moment, let's mark this moment for Tom's Uncle David Turner, and for anyone else who has died by their own hand, and back to Joyce) Ill just give him one more chance Ill get up early in the morning Im sick of Cohens old bed in any case I might go over to the markets to see all the vegetables and cabbages and tomatoes and carrots and all kinds of splendid fruits all coming in lovely and fresh who knows whod be the 1st man Id meet theyre out looking for it in the morning Mamy Dillon used to say they are and the night too that was her massgoing Id love a big juicy pear now to melt in your mouth like when I used to be in the longing way then Ill throw him up his eggs and tea in the moustachecup she gave him to make his mouth bigger I suppose hed like my nice cream too I know what Ill do Ill go about rather gay not too much singing a bit now and then mi fa pieta Masetto then Ill start dressing myself to go out presto non son piu forte Ill put on my best shift and drawers let him have a good eyeful out of that to make his micky stand for him Ill let him know if thats what he wanted that his wife is fucked yes and damn well fucked too up to my neck nearly not by him 5 or 6 times handrunning theres the mark of his spunk on the clean sheet I wouldnt bother to even iron it out that ought to satisfy him if you dont believe me feel my belly unless I made him stand there and put him into me Ive a mind to tell him every scrap and make him do it out in front of me serve him right its all his own fault if I am an adulteress as the thing in the gallery said O much about it if thats all the harm ever we did in this vale of tears God knows its not much doesnt everybody only they hide it I suppose thats what a woman is supposed to be there for or He wouldnt have made us the way He did so attractive to men then if he wants to kiss my bottom Ill drag open my drawers and bulge it right out in his face as large as life he can stick his tongue 7 miles up my hole as hes there my brown part then Ill tell him I want £1 or perhaps 30 /- Ill tell him I want to buy underclothes then if he gives me that well he wont be too bad I dont want to soak it all out of him like other women do I could often have written out a fine cheque for myself and write his name on it for a couple of pounds a few times he forgot to lock it up besides he wont spend it Ill let him do it off on me behind provided he doesnt smear all my good drawers O I suppose that cant be helped Ill do the indifferent l or 2 questions Ill know by the answers when hes like that he cant keep a thing back I know every turn in him Ill tighten my bottom well and let out a few smutty words smellrump or lick my shit or the first mad thing comes into my head [and Dan Marshall, who knows smutty smellrump, just sent in his words, here they are, "Here you go dude, below and attached, Let me know if that works and all that, See you soon exclamation point, Dave told me I could write anything I fucking wanted to for his amazing book, well he didn't say it that way, he was much nicer about it and tossed a few "mans" in there to make sure we're cool, but I warned him that giving me free range was a bad idea because I'd be liable to write about something stupid like the Utah Jazz, since they are my favorite basketball team, but he still said to write about anything I wanted to write about, and I thought about this some, and I think what I want to write about is Dave and how he's a really great dude, despite getting down on himself at times, I mean, he's helped me in more ways than I can imagine or that he probably even knows, starting at USC Film School, where he passed an internship at Gary Sanchez Productions off to my friend Matteo, who then passed it along to me, and that internship was cool because I got to see how a successful Hollywood production office worked, and one of the perks of the internship was that all the interns eventually got to have lunch with Will Ferrell, and then through that internship, I got to write every Will Ferrell movie over the next ten years,,, just joking, I didn't get to write any Will Ferrell movies at all, but I did get to have that lunch with him once, and get him lunch a bunch of times, so some of the shit that Will Ferrell has shat is because of food I've either gotten for him or eaten with him, not to brag, and none of this would've happened without Dave, then, after all this Will Ferrell business, Dave continued being a good pal by reading this really long and crass and not fully developed memoir about my dad dying of Lou Gehrig's disease called Home is Burning, becoming one of the first people to read it and say nice things about it, and Dave was so encouraging and supportive of my writing and I wasn't even super duper close with him at the time that it made me think that he's probably really great to everyone in his life, that he sees life as a sort of game where you need to choose your teammates and once you choose those teammates you then have to support them and champion them and love them no matter what, so when he started to tell me about what was going on with his dad's kidney over lunches of our own, which didn't include Will Ferrell, I could see the pain on his face, that he wasn't sure what to do about any of it, that his heart was breaking in real-time because one of his most important teammates and loved ones was hurting, his dad's pain becoming his pain, and then when his dad passed away, and Dave told me over another meal—this one a dinner if you can believe it—that he was writing about his father, I immediately felt very proud of Dave for having the strength, for having the determination, for having the courage to dig into the sad and yucky parts of life so that he could honor and champion his dad, the same dad who had championed him and taught Dave to champion people like me, and then I thought, if I'm proud of him, then I can't even imagine the pride his dad would feel for this great accomplishment, because the truth is that he'd be very, very, very, very proud and I'm sure Dave and I will continue to be pals, and maybe we'll be even closer teammates now because those of us without dads have to look out for one another in order to replace some of what we've lost, and I'm sure we'll get more dinners and lunches and, fuck, maybe even some breakfasts together, and maybe one day we'll be lucky enough to watch Will Ferrell eat together, and fuck I'm way over my 250 words, but I just asked Dave if I could go over and he said, "Definitely, No limit", proving once again how supportive a dude he is, a true champion," and I had dinner with Dan last night, the 20th, and with Mike Heller the night before that, and I thank you my dudes for accepting my truth and being there for me and reading and adding] then Ill suggest about yes O wait now sonny my turn is coming Ill be quite gay and friendly over it O but I was forgetting this bloody pest of a thing pfooh you wouldnt know which to laugh or cry were such a mixture of plum and apple no Ill have to wear the old things so much the better itll be more pointed hell never know whether he did it or not there thats good enough for you any old thing at all then Ill wipe him off me just like a business his omission then Ill go out Ill have him eying up at the ceiling where is she gone now make him want me thats the only way a quarter after what an unearthly hour I suppose theyre just getting up in China now combing out their pigtails for the day well soon have the nuns ringing the angelus theyve nobody coming in to spoil their sleep except an odd priest or two for his night office or the alarmclock next door at cockshout clattering the brains out of itself let me see if I can doze off 1 2 3 4 5 what kind of flowers are those they invented like the stars the wallpaper in Lombard street was much nicer the apron he gave me was like that something only I only wore it twice better lower this lamp and try again so as I can get up early Ill go to Lambes there beside Findlaters and get them to send us some flowers to put about the place in case he brings him home tomorrow today I mean no no Fridays an unlucky day first I want to do the place up someway the dust grows in it I think while Im asleep then we can have music and cigarettes I can accompany him first I must clean the keys of the piano withmilk whatll I wear shall I wear a white rose or those fairy cakes in Liptons I love the smell of a rich big shop at 7 1/2d a lb or the other ones with the cherries in them and the pinky sugar 11d a couple of lbs of those a nice plant for the middle of the table Id get that cheaper in wait wheres this I saw them not long ago I love flowers Id love to have the whole place swimming in roses God of heaven theres nothing like nature the wild mountains then the sea and the waves rushing then the beautiful country with the fields of oats and wheat and all kinds of things and all the fine cattle going about that would do your heart good to see rivers and lakes and flowers all sorts of shapes and smells and colours springing up even out of the ditches primroses and violets nature it is as for them saying theres no God I wouldnt give a snap of my two fingers for all their learning why dont they go and create something I often asked him atheists or whatever they call themselves go and wash the cobbles off themselves first then they go howling for the priest and they dying and why why because theyre afraid of hell on account of their bad conscience ah yes I know them well who was the first person in the universe before there was anybody that made it all who (and Ryan DeNardo just sent his contribution and it's a song/poem and he's a lyrical dude with his musical improv where he comes up with songs and rhymes right on the spot, and this is kind of like that, improv writing, and here's what he wrote, "It was years before I realized this sentence had begun, it appears to run on as if somebody meant it to be fun, then infinity was labeled with a looming expiration, is the fable doomed or capable in gloomy exploration (question mark), and the questions start in both the heart and the head, will I ever achieve what I hope to be before I drop dead, did I fly right past a different path, not notice since I'm reckless, I should check this, no let's skip the math, just focus the perspective; if I wreck this, you should know that the rules of the game apply, the school of the frame abides by an absence of deletion, there's no edit, so regret is jettisoned to seek completion, this consciousness streams from a pool of insane supply, explains to you why there was no buoyant point of exclamation, a flagrant ploy to sell my hollow act of braggadocio, word play a la Kanye with a nose to match Pinocchio, the prose continues, so there is no final punctuation; for sentence is a long game with an ending to be earned, commas shape the journey leaving stones still yet unturned, regrets I've had a myriad but know they do not matter, as I've fully built the pyramid and now descend the ladder, is there penance in the end, that remains to be seen, it's painful being honest, but say what you mean, remembrance is our friend, but what stays when we leave, did you get what you were promised, that's hard to believe, I wish I'd been less cynical, I'm nearing it; I no longer see the pinnacle, I'm fearing it; the piper's call is lyrical, I'm hearing it; my life was all a miracle but now I've met the period," and man that has gems in it, dense nuggets of gold and thank you Ryan for letting me put this and our Imagine Impact escapades into the book and back to Joyce), ah that they dont know neither do I so there you are they might as well try to stop the sun from rising tomorrow the sun shines for you he said the day we were lying among the rhododendrons on Howth head in the grey tweed suit and his straw hat the day I got him to propose to me yes first I gave him the bit of seedcake out of my mouth and it was leapyear like now yes 16 years ago my God after that long kiss I near lost my breath yes he said I was a flower of the mountain yes so we are flowers all a womans body yes that was one true thing he said in his life and the sun shines for you today yes that was why I liked him because I saw he understood or felt what a woman is and I knew I could always get round him and I gave him all the pleasure I could leading him on till he asked me to say yes and I wouldnt answer first only looked out over the sea and the sky I was thinking of so many things he didnt know of Mulvey and Mr Stanhope and Hester and father and old captain Groves and the sailors playing all birds fly and I say stoop and washing up dishes they called it on the pier and the sentry in front of the governors house with the thing round his white helmet poor devil half roasted and the Spanish girls laughing in their shawls and their tall combs and the auctions in the morning the Greeks and the jews and the Arabs and the devil knows who else from all the ends of Europe and Duke street and the fowl market all clucking outside Larby Sharons and the poor donkeys slipping half asleep and the vague fellows in the cloaks asleep in the shade on the steps and the big wheels of the carts of the bulls and the old castle thousands of years old yes and those handsome Moors all in white and turbans like kings asking you to sit down in their little bit of a shop and

Ronda with the old windows of the posadas 2 glancing eyes a lattice hid for her lover to kiss the iron and the wineshops half open at night and the castanets and the night we missed the boat at Algeciras the watchman going about serene with his lamp and O that awful deepdown torrent O and the sea the sea crimson sometimes like fire and the glorious sunsets and the figtrees in the Alameda gardens yes and all the queer little streets and the pink and blue and yellow houses and the rosegardens and the jessamine and geraniums and cactuses and Gibraltar as a girl where I was a Flower of the mountain yes when I put the rose in my hair like the Andalusian girls used or shall I wear a red yes and how he kissed me under the Moorish wall and I thought well as well him as another and then I asked him with my eyes to ask again yes and then he asked me would I yes to say yes my mountain flower and first I put my arms around him yes and drew him down to me so he could feel my breasts all perfume yes and his heart was going like mad and yes I said yes I will Yes," and so we are well over the record, officially, and so we have written the longest sentence in the English language, (we don't, just thought we would back then when I wrote this, who cares now) though I guess it's possible that some people will say that since we didn't write 3,687 words of the sentence, then we should be disqualified, and that I didn't write the longest sentence in the English language that has ever been published, even though I only added the Joyce sentence after I set the record, (and I intercut it) but they might still say that because the sentence is not all our original words, that we didn't author every word in the sentence, like the Lou Reed, and etcetera, and so maybe we should cut those parts of the sentence, but I can't due to my rules, vis-a-vis the real time, via, due to George Saunders, (ha, not anymore but listen to all this fear, ha) and oh, here's another email, too bad it's another short response, Confirmed, did receive, thanks, Victoria, and we really don't want to pad more, we have already barely won this record in so many ways and so maybe that was a mistake to have done that with Joyce's words adding them to my own, but as I keep saying, I can't go back, to delete all those words, (ha, we are going back now, I guess I could delete Joyce and if I have to I will) and also I am happy about putting Joyce's sentence into our sentence because I guess as I was typing out Joyce's sentence it is clear that he is a genius and a great writer, but back to me, I also think after reading his sentence again that we share some things in common, he's also a provocateur, and a prankster, and there's an energy and abandon and madness to his writing, and the pace of the words and the flow is similar to mine here, am I crazy to think that, too, in its exuberance, and passion, and also frankly its broken syntax and grammar, and it's fiery, furious, recklessness on a content level like I always am, and like this sentence and book is, and I guess I like living on the edge while writing, because it makes you feel alive, and Joyce's writing always makes me feel alive, too, so maybe I am not as bad of a writer as I always think of myself as, as a big time hack I am not, maybe, and maybe even though this isn't the best sentence in the English language it is a pretty decent one, and my dad would be proud of me for writing it, and for publishing another book, via Kindle Direct Publishing, this will be the fourth in two years, even though KDP is not a real publisher, and that's OK that it's not a real publisher like real writers, because what does that even mean anyway these days, as Florian Cramer says, "In the 21st century, even the primal criterion of literature has become obsolete: that of being published, In the age of homepages, blogs and social networks, the classical distinction between non-published personal writing and published writing is moot, and with it the distinction between everyday communication and publishing, If there ever has been a clear divide between amateur and professional writers at all, now it has collapsed completely," and so it has probably always been like it is now, and the other thing about Joyce is that I also read Alison Bechdel's Fun Home, and I believe she said that Joyce kind of took back publishing rights from Sylvia Beach, or didn't just kind of, he did, take them, he did, and that she just had to be chill about it, and say stuff like she was just the midwife, and the book should grow and profit without her, what a Giving Tree, and I also read from Lewis Hyde that James Joyce's estate would refuse to let editors publish his short stories in their collections of 20th century literature without steep costs, and that they were very litigious, and even though most of his work has since fallen into the public domain now that we're deeper into the 21st century, I am now also realizing there is a chance though that Amazon and Kindle Direct Publishing itself will not print the sentence and the book due to its bot content rules as I have used a significant part of Joyce's Ulysses, which is in the public domain, so it should be cool to do that in terms of copyright infringement, right, the bots can't get me there, right, wrong, because something that Amazon's Kindle Direct Publishing rules also say is that, "Some types of content, such as public domain content, may be free to use by anyone, or may be licensed for use by more than one party," however, "we will not accept content that is freely available on the web unless you are the copyright owner of that content," and for example, "if you received your book content from a source that allows you and others to re-distribute it, and the content is freely available on the web, we will not accept it for sale on the Kindle store," and I guess this Joyce stuff is web content because I got the quote from Ulysses for free, and of course there is all the other flotsam I've stolen from the

Internet, and from Kanye, and from all those other writers and their books, like a vampire, and put into this book, (and also now I will add a contemporary review of Ulysses by 20th Century philosopher Carl Jung, "Ulysses is a book which pours along for seven hundred and thirty-five pages, a stream of time of seven hundred and thirty-five days which all consist in one single and senseless every day of Everyman, the completely irrelevant 16th day of June 1904, in Dublin – a day on which, in all truth, nothing happens, The stream beings in the void and ends in the void, Is all of this perhaps one single, immensely long and excessively complicated Strindbergian pronouncement upon the essence of human life, and one which, to the reader's dismay, is never finished, Perhaps it does touch upon the essence of life; but quite certainly it touches upon life's ten thousand surfaces and their hundred thousand color gradations, As far as my glance reaches, there are in those seven hundred and thirty-five pages no obvious repetitions and not a single hallowed island where the long-suffering reader may come to rest, There is not a single place where he can seat himself, drunk with memories, and from which he can happily consider the stretch of the road he has covered, be it one hundred pages or even less, But no, The pitiless and uninterrupted stream rolls by, and its velocity or precipitation grows in the last forty pages till it sweeps away even the marks of punctuation, It thus gives cruelest expressions to that emptiness which is both breath taking and stifling, which is under such tension, or is so filled to bursting, as to grow unbearable, This thoroughly hopeless emptiness is the dominant note of the whole book, It not only begins and ends in nothingness, but it consists of nothing but nothingness, It is all infernally nugatory," and "I had an uncle whose thinking was always to the point, One day he stopped me on the street and asked, "Do you know how the devil tortures the souls in hell," When I said no, he declared, "He keeps them waiting," And with that he walked away, This remark occurred to me when I was ploughing through Ulysses for the first time, Every sentence raises an expectation which is not fulfilled; finally, out of sheer resignation, you come to expect nothing any longer, Then, bit by bit, again to your horror, it dawns upon you that in all truth you have hit the nail on the head, It is actual fact that nothing happens and nothing comes of it, and yet a secret expectation at war with hopeless resignation drags the reader from page to page, You read and read and read and you pretend to understand what you read, Occasionally you drop through an air pocket into another sentence, but when once the proper degree of resignation has been reached you accustom yourself to anything, So I, too, read to page one hundred and thirty-five with despair in my heart, falling asleep twice on the way, Nothing comes to meet the reader, everything turns away from him, leaving him gaping after it, The book is always up and away, dissatisfied with itself, ironic, sardonic, virulent, contemptuous, sad, despairing, and bitter," and Jung also wrote to Joyce directly and said, "Dear Sir, Your Ulysses has presented the world such an upsetting psychological problem that repeatedly I have been called in as a supposed authority on psychological matters, Ulysses proved to be an exceedingly hard nut and it has forced my mind not only to most unusual efforts, but also to rather extravagant peregrinations (speaking from the standpoint of a scientist), Your book as a whole has given me no end of trouble and I was brooding over it for about three years until I succeeded to put myself into it, But I must tell you that I'm profoundly grateful to yourself as well as to your gigantic opus, because I learned a great deal from it, I shall probably never be quite sure whether I did enjoy it, because it meant too much grinding of nerves and of grey matter, I also don't know whether you will enjoy what I have written about Ulysses because I couldn't help telling the world how much I was bored, how I grumbled, how I cursed and how I admired, The 40 pages of non stop run at the end is a string of veritable psychological peaches, I suppose the devil's grandmother knows so much about the real psychology of a woman, I didn't, Well, I just try to recommend my little essay to you, as an amusing attempt of a perfect stranger that went astray in the labyrinth of your Ulysses and happened to get out of it again by sheer good luck, At all events you may gather from my article what Ulysses has done to a supposedly balanced psychologist, With the expression of my deepest appreciation, I remain, dear Sir, Yours faithfully, CG Jung," and this comes from Brainpickings(dot)org as a lot of stuff does, but 21st Century philosopher Eckhart Tolle says James Joyce and the other modernists of the twentieth century such as Kafka, Camus, and Eliot, they "Recognized alienation as the universal dilemma of human existence, probably felt it deeply within themselves and so were able to express it brilliantly in their works, They don't offer a solution, Their contribution is to show us a reflection of the human predicament so that we can see it more clearly, To see one's predicament clearly is a first step toward going beyond it," but that in the 21st century "Partly as a result of the spiritual teachings that have arisen outside the established religions, but also due to an influx of the ancient Eastern wisdom teachings, a growing number of followers of traditional religions are able to let go of identification with form, dogma, and rigid belief systems and discover the original depth that is hidden within their own spiritual tradition at the same time as they discover the depth within themselves," and so this book is both a sequel to Ulysses as well as a step forward, perhaps, [and Kanye wrote a self help book on Twitter, "With something like 13 tweets in 15 minutes, he announced he was writing a 'book,' 'Oh by the way this is my book that I'm writing in real time, No publisher or publicist will tell me what to put where or how many pages to write, This is not a financial opportunity this is an innate need to be expressive," he wrote, adding in another tweet, "I will work on this 'book' when I feel it, When We sit still in the mornings We get hit with so many ideas and so many things We want to express, When I read this tweet to myself I didn't like how much I used the word I so I changed the I's to We's,'" and some more of that 'book' is "Be here now, Be in the moment, The now is the greatest moment of our lives and it just keeps getting better, The bad parts the boring parts the parts with high anxiety, Embrace every moment for its greatness, This is life, This is the greatest movie we will ever see," and so Kanye believes in the real time book and the power of now] and back to what I wrote before) Kindle Direct Publishing says that Kindle Direct Publishing "does accept public domain content but may choose not to sell a public domain book if its content is undifferentiated or barely differentiated from one or more other books," and so I guess parts of my sentence are undifferentiated, and you could argue this whole book is barely differentiated perhaps, depending on what type of math the bots are using to determine differentiation, (this is real, what to do, ha, who cares all words are the same, everything is all, have you read The Four Agreements, "This realization changed his life, Once he knew what he really was, he looked around at other humans and the rest of nature, and he was amazed at what he saw, He saw himself in everything - in every human, in every animal, in every tree, in the water, in the rain, in the clouds, in the earth, And he saw that Life tonal and the nagual in different ways to create billions of manifestations of Life, In those few moments he comprehended everything, He was very excited, and his heart was filled with peace, He could hardly wait to tell his people what he had discovered, But there were no words to explain it, He tried to tell the others, but they could not understand, They could see that he had changed, that something beautiful was radiating from his eyes and his voice, They noticed that he no longer had judgment about anything or anyone, He was no longer like anyone else, He could understand everyone very well, but no one could understand him, They believed that he was an incarnation of God, and he smiled when he heard this and he said, 'It is true, I am God, But you are also God, We are the same, you and I, We are images of light, We are God," [and James Hollis says, "Our ego tendency to seize upon the image and hold it captive to our agenda for security leads to the oldest of religious sins, the sin of idolatry, The living mystery is hardened into a concept, a belief rather than an experience, and loses the vigor of the mystery, Then one is left only with the artifacts of belief but not the living experience," and so I hope and want this experience of reading this book to give you the experience of the numinous, to be a shamanic voyage for yourself just as much as it has been for me, do you feel anything, maybe try following Spiritual Instagram, I started following Spiritual Instagram, it's like saying NBA Twitter, it's not just one account, it's tons, and and here's what some of Spiritual Instagram looks like:

AT&T LTE 10:15 AM 73%

Instagram

spiritual_god

and:

AT&T LTE 10:28 AM 65%

Instagram

astral.dimension ...

How it feels living in a society who thinks being busy means being productive when really it's not about reaching the destination but enjoying the journey

Liked by **spiritual_god** and **others**

astral.dimension Follow 👉 @Astral.Dimension •Tag someone who needs to see this •Turn on post... more

View all 23 comments

 Add a comment...   

4 hours ago

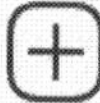

and:

AT&T LTE 10:18 AM 70%

 Instagram 

 **a.course.in.miracles** •••

LESSON 41

God goes with me wherever I go.

Liked by **katfowler** and **others**

a.course.in.miracles LESSON 41
God goes with me wherever I go... more

View all 6 comments

  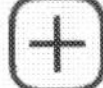  

and:

ha, that last one wasn't Spiritual Instagram, that's a joke, see I can still be funny, and

I've been unfollowing most Hollywood people in my Instagram, because most of them only post pictures of themselves or advertise their upcoming work, and a general rule of thumb has been if you are putting your face in your Instagram you are doing it wrong for me, but then I see our old friend, Caroline Calloway, provocateur, and I think there is something sacred in this profanity and maybe something beautifully sad about the promotions that Hollywood people have to do to continue to be famous, like so:

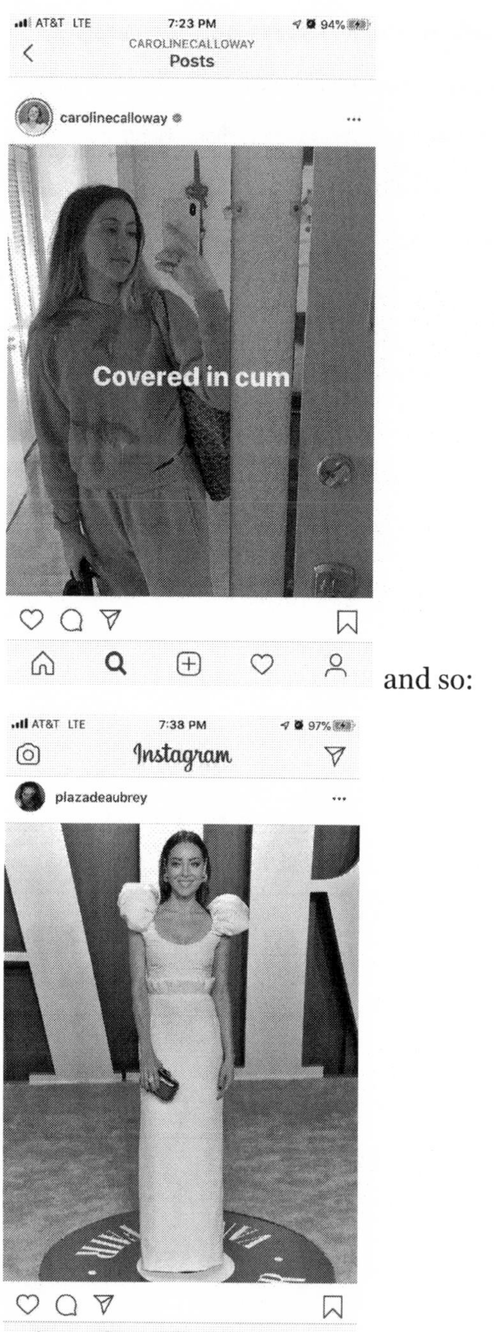

and so:

and that post of Aubrey Plaza was the first Instagram post that was from a celebrity that came up on my feed after I wrote what I wrote above, and that's crazy because I wrote a screenplay when I was somewhat hypomanic back in 2009, when I published the piece in The New Yorker, called Laughing With You which was about a comedian who went crazy, who was now having a comeback show and revealing all of his demons on stage, and it was all about suicide, almost every joke was somehow related to suicide, and I named the love interest character Aubrey because I had a thing for Aubrey Plaza back then, and the jokes about suicide really grate on me now, and yet I understand the sadness of my genealogy and our teological end normally and so I must heal myself to heal that lineage of suiciders or depressives or both, and here is more from spiritiual instagram:

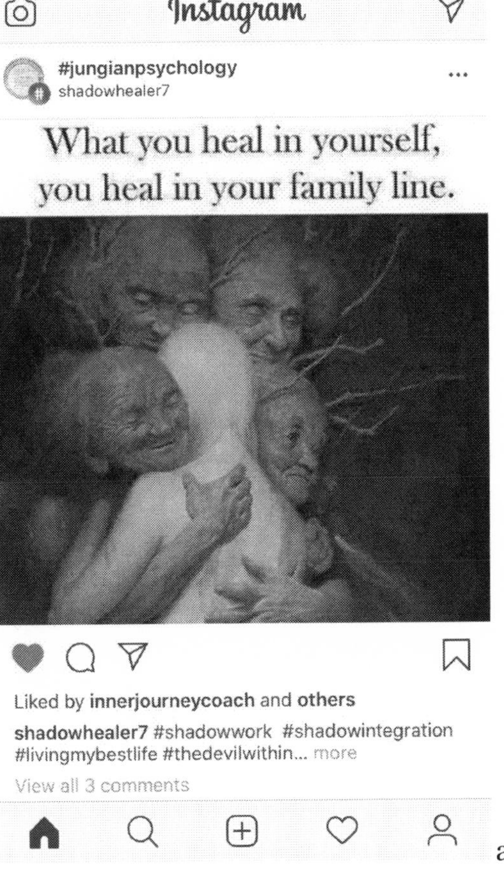

and it must be said that the

family line thing is real, when I was manic/enlightened I was obsessed with figuring out what had happened in our family line, and learning about the pain that was caused or felt or passed down or healed or repaired and the good that was also passed down, and so even as the world seems to crumble, the family lines are being healed, and there is now pointilism in this book, and cubism, time is being refracted, time is

being refracted, and "Wow" by Beck with Guau Mexican Institute of Sound remix is playing and put it on and dance, dance between the two worlds, the spiritual and the material, just dance baby, with the luminous moves, like, wow, it's like right now, it's like, right now, it's like wow, do you feel it, it's just a big party this life, it's like, wow, it's like right now, it's just another perfect night, and my dad was a great dancer, he once held a dance contest on top of his classroom's physics tables dancing to Michael

Jackson with gloves on and everything against the kids, and which the kids still remembered years later when they saw him, and do you know what "Wow" spun into, Jonsi's "Animal Arithmetic" from his album Go in which he sings "We should all be alive," and it's just such a fun song, check it out, and now Dion & The Wanderers just came on with "Now," and here's the lyrics, "Now you taste the sunlight, Now you feel the colors, And you know it my friend, That you don't have to hide anymore, Now you hear the silence, Now you see its beauty, And you know it my friend, That you don't have to hide anymore, Now it's real, No one knows better than I, How you feel, Now you hear the music, Now you have the moment, And you know it my friend, That you don't have to hide anymore, Now it's real, No one knows better than I, How you feel, Now you hear the music, Now you have the moment, And you know it my friend, That you don't have to hide, No, you don't have to hide, No, you don't have to hide anymore," and I feel that the spiritual world is real now, I feel the beauty and it doesn't need to be hid from me anymore, I feel the colors, and the sunlight, I feel the spiritual world now, now, in the now, and from Spiritual Instagram

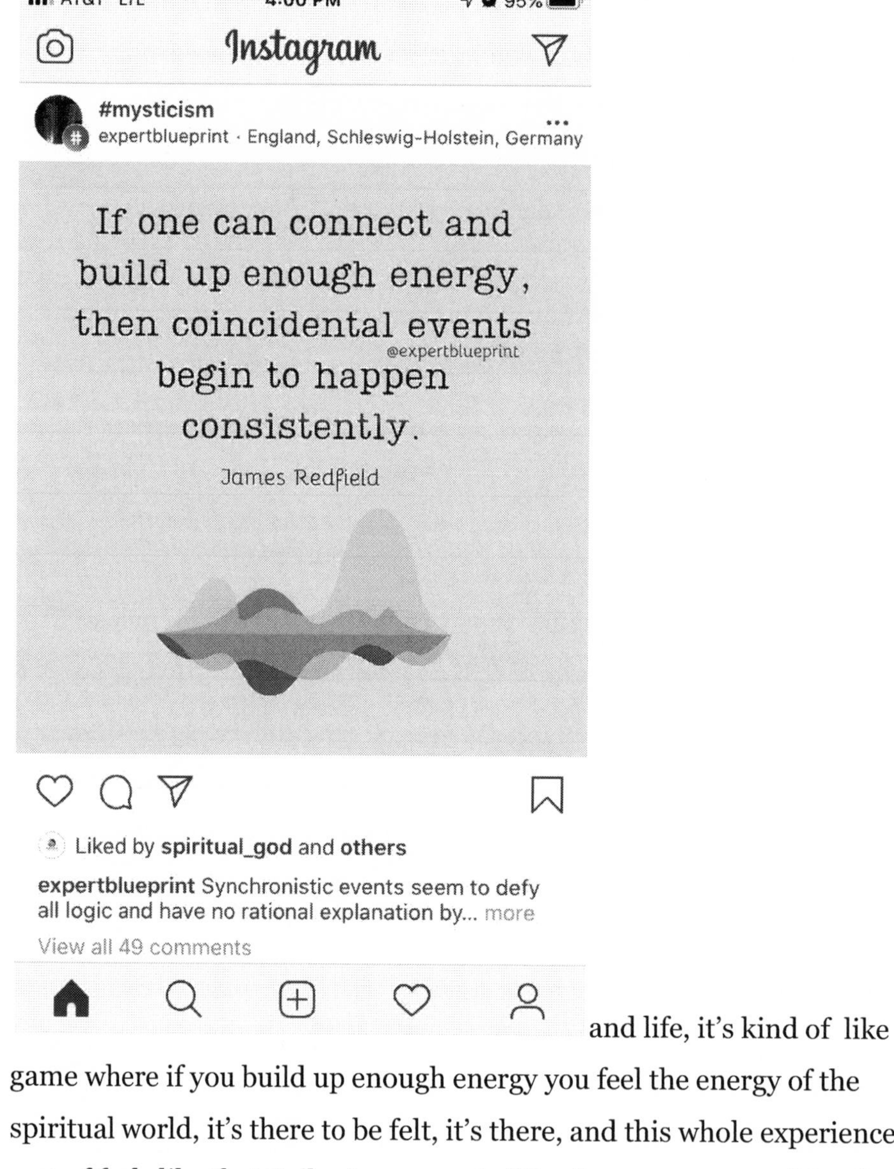

and life, it's kind of like a game where if you build up enough energy you feel the energy of the spiritual world, it's there to be felt, it's there, and this whole experience sort of feels like that Spike Jonze movie "Her," except we can all be the AI, the ScarJo voice, when you learn to love everyone and everything as much as you love your romantic partner, you love all and you rise up into the Instagram ether with fellow like-mindeds, except it's not just the Instagram ether, there's so many people ready to mirror you back on the earth, "I'll Be Your Mirror," is what Lou Reed wrote, and it's true the mirror thing as Don Ruiz says in The Four Agreements, and it's the truth and not the Truth, or maybe it is The Truth too) and so I guess my record due to all these quotes, this record for writing the longest sentence in the English language, it's fate, it's up to the bots after all, those dang Amazon bots, dang, or perhaps the real Kindle Direct Publishing people, (even if we don't care anymore) and I know there are some real Kindle Direct Publishing people, I've talked to them before, they are very nice, and exceedingly helpful, I almost feel bad potentially causing them a problem with my content, but I guess there's a chance I have provoked them, which is something I am wont to do, and I am realizing now that I have only emailed with them, and never talked in person to them, so the KDP so-called real people, maybe they are chat bots, oh my, and due to my provocations there is a chance, a real chance, that this sentence and this content will never be published, and also that I may have provoked Jeff Bezos who will never let it be read, and never set the record, and all this will have been for nothing, like I had feared above, but I actually love you Jeff Bezos, dear publisher, as you enabled me to be a semi-legitimate writer, but maybe you will not love me back, so maybe I will not have left this mark of myself and my work and my dad on the world, but to be honest, I am OK with that, I truly am, as it is sort of a perfect balance of my dad's modest, measured way of living and my ambitious, unbalanced one, as I am still proud of this sentence even if it never gets published and never sets the record or is not read by anyone besides my family and friends, if that's what happens to the content, that's OK, I'm at peace with that, (I still am [and it's January 31st and Imagine Impact just invited me to input my profile and script into their app, see: "Create Your Account Log-in now to input your credits, upload your best samples, and create a bio, highlighting the major life experiences or keywords that make you stand out from the crowd, Please ensure that you upload your scripts as samples (not projects) for visibility, The Writer Search portal is your opportunity to present yourself and your writing abilities to the top producers and showrunners in the industry, Check-your inbox for your invitation email now, {and so I wouldn't be mad if someone wanted my script either, I wouldn't be not at peace with that either

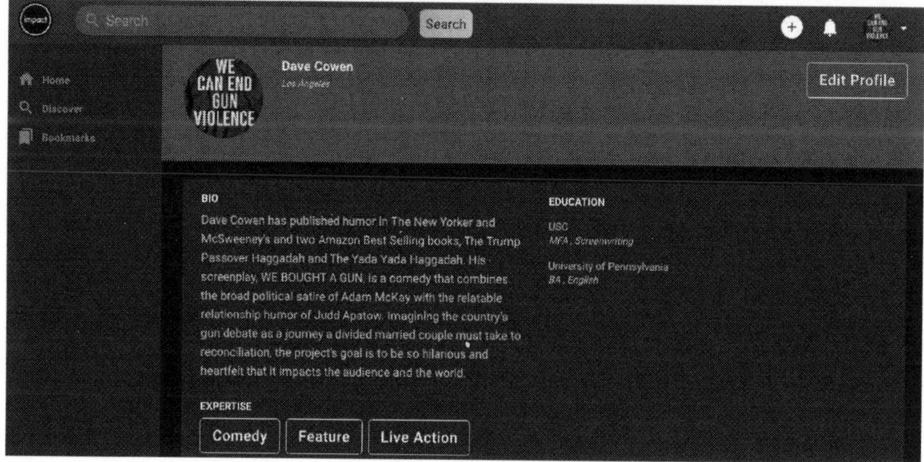

and one of the essays I wrote for Imagine Impact was about Groundhog Day, and here it is, "If you could have written any television show or movie in history, which would you choose and why, I've mentioned in this application that a goal of mine is to synthesize romantic comedy and politics with WE BOUGHT A GUN, Thinking about this question, I realized that the movie I'm most jealous of, that is to say, ha, the one I wish I would've written the most, is GROUNDHOG DAY, GROUNDHOG DAY marries the philosophy of the ethics of how to be happy and a good person with the tone and story of a romantic comedy, It does this with an extraordinarily unique yet simple high concept, a hilarious protagonist, a beautiful romance, and a rigorous, OK pretty much flawless, screenplay structure, Bill Murray's external goal, to escape from repeating the same day in the Pennsylvanian town, is only achieved by fulfilling his internal character arc, of letting go of his ego, accepting life as it comes, being good to people, and not doing so expecting anything in return, As someone who looks to art and movies to not only entertain but also to instruct, I admire the progression of Phil's character from sarcastic and self-absorbed to opportunistic and manipulative to depressed and nihilistic and then finally to peaceful self-actualization, As much as I want to make commercially successful movies, I also want to make influential, long-lasting films, What's particularly special about GROUNDHOG DAY is that its philosophy applies to all audiences, when it came out, now, and forever," and so we've lived that together, in this book, we've lived Groundhog Day, the arc of my character, we've lived it,

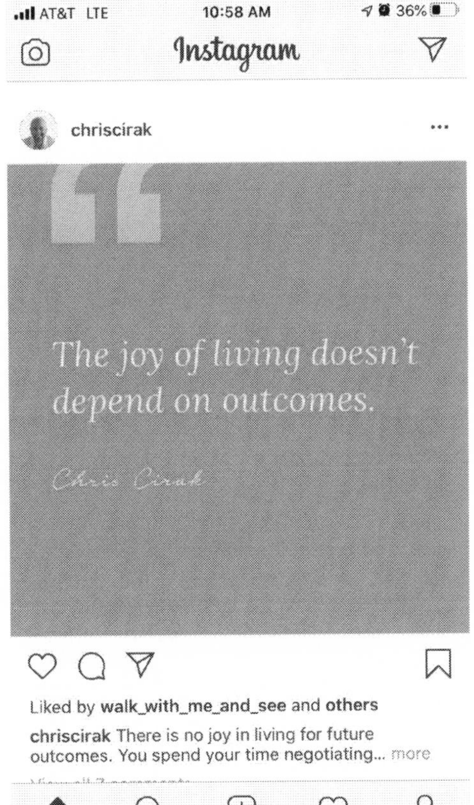

do you believe that and there is pointillism and cubism to time now in this book, time isn't real even as it is real, it's folding back on itself, and I already said it but this bears repeating, <and Ryan DeNardo just told me he shared the script with an actress friend who has like 47K Instagram followers and I've seen them perform together live and they have great chemistry, so maybe they will star in it together, and he's drafting something to add to the book, and who do we think will help more Ryan my buddy now or Imagine Impact, ha, I think I could guess, and David Shields "says" "An artistic movement, albeit an organic and as-yet-unstated one, is forming, What are its key components, A deliberate unartiness: 'raw' material, seemingly unprocessed, unfiltered, uncensored, and unprofessional, Randomness, openness to accident and serendipity, spontaneity; artistic risk, emotional urgency and intensity, reader/viewer participation; an overly literal tone, as if a reporter were viewing a strange culture; plasticity of form, pointillism; criticism as autobiography; self-reflexivity; self-ethnography, anthropological autobiography; a blurring (to the point of invisibility) of any distinction between fiction and nonfiction: the lure and blur of the real," and I just opened up Harold Bloom's The Anxiety of Influence which Sandy gave me and it says, a quote from Kierkkegaad, "If the young man had believed in repetition, of what might he not have been capable, What inwardness he might have attained," another page says, "the hero's purgation is an askesis, a road through to freedom that is significant act," and Wikipedia says that Bloom's askesis is a "movement of self-purgation which intends the attainment of a state of solitude" The author curtails the impression of his/her own "human and imaginative endowment" in order to separate themselves from others and stress his/her own individuality," and that after that comes Apophrades the "return of the dead" The poet, toward the end of his/her life, opens up his poem - this time deliberately

rather than naturally - to the precursor's influence, But this deliberateness creates the uncanny effect that the precursor's work seems to be derivative of the later poet, and Bloom took the word apophrades from the Athenian concept of the days on which the dead return to reinhabit the houses in which they once lived," and 10,000 whispering and nobody listening, the song of poet who died in the gutter, the sound of a clown who died in the alley and that is Bob Dylan's A Hard Rain's A-Gonna Fall playing right now, and influence Bloom says means inflow, and so we let it all inflow, we introject, which is what Enneagram 4s do, introjection is the unconscious adoption of the ideas or attitudes of others and so now I must consciously choose what to adopt and what not to, and I choose to believe that it's important to accept the dead into our work but not that that means I am close to death I reject that thought, and there is pointillism and cubism in the time of this book the time, the time is being cut and pasted forward and backward, and pointillism is "Instead of a visual work of art with paints defining each point that makes up the whole, words are arranged in such a manner that, while seemingly incongruous, they fit together to form a text with depth and richness, That is, the text contains a series of moments or experiences that do not necessarily relate directly to the preceding or following "moment," but are woven together in such a way that vibrancy of text is being developed through the used of these interrelated textual moments, Each moment can stand on its own and has impact, Further, each moment, however contradictory to the rest of the text, contributes to the total effect of the entire text and Atlas Sound's "Walkabout" was on as I am writing this and is on, and it's lyrics are "What did you want to see, What did you want to be when you grew up, What did you want to see, What did you want to be when you grew up,

To go away and not look back, And think of what the others say, To go ahead and change your life, Without regard to what is said, And everyone must do the same, You find yourself lost again, Forget the things you've left behind, Through looking back you may go blind," and so I won't go back to a life without inner peace or the awareness that it is possible at or most of the times you are alive, it's available, and I guess this book makes me an evangelical or a lightworker or a vibetribe or whatever and yet how can you not be, it's like winning a million dollars, you'd want anyone to win a million dollars, even your "worst enemy" I hope everyone wins this million dollars, how can you not testify to that, and I just opened up Anthony de Mello's Sadhana: A Way To God Christian Exercises in Eastern Form, and bibliomancy reveals to me, and to us, "Formerly, I would accept the statement of retreatants who said to me, 'I cannot pray with my imagination,,,I have a very poor imagination,' And I would advise them to use some other form of prayer, Today I have become convinced that with a little practice everyone can develop his power to fantasize and thus acquire untold emotional and spiritual riches," and I just did another bibliomancy of this book and it says, "You may have misgivings, as many do, about imagining you hear Christ say things to you, In some of the fantasy exercises, I recommended that you talk to Christ and imagine him talking to you, You may ask, 'How am I to know whether it is really Christ, who is saying these words to me or whether I am just inventing them, Is it Christ who is talking to me or is it I who am talking to myself through this image of Christ that I have conjured up, The answer to that question is that, in all likelihood, it is you who are talking to yourself through this image of Christ that your fantasy has produced, However, beneath the surface of this dialogue that you have with this imaginary Christ, the Lord will begin to work on your heart, It won't be long before you experience this imaginary Christ say something to you, and the effect of his words will be such (in the way of consolation, of light and inspiration, of a fresh infusion of joy and strength) that you will know in your heart that those words either came directly from the Lord or they were your own invention and were used by the Lord to communicate to you what he wanted to," and in Astro Poets a book by Alex Dimitrov and Dorothea Lasky they say that Aries people think they have discovered everything for the first time, and that's clearly true with this stuff, it's clearly everywhere, these truths that I am just finding and putting into this book, and yet my friend Ashley showed me this thing called Primal Signs which combines Chinese Zodiac with the more Westernish one so years and months, east west right baby, and so I am what's called a Piranha, and here's what they say about Piranhas, and why maybe this book is needed to get this stuff out there, you gotta get this stuff out there in new forms, that's what new forms are for, so everyone can experience it in their own time, and here's what it says about Piranhas "In nature, the Piranha is a small but powerful with razor sharp teeth and a hunger to consume whatever is foolish enough to get in its way, In human society, members of the Piranha Primal Zodiac sign aren't all that different, They are fearless, aggressive, and get what they want every time, They are highly career-oriented and use their charm and high energy levels to push forward consistently, Piranhas have an over-sized appetite for success that is never satisfied, They have the smarts and the will to do whatever it takes to get ahead, and they often do, This is not to say that Piranhas are unlikable, In truth, they usually have many friends and are fiercely loyal to their families, Members of this sign are as popular as they choose to be, but they also make many enemies, While they are mostly in control of every situation, they can sometimes lash out at others unnecessarily and can be excessively mean spirited, After they have cooled down, though, don't expect a Piranha to apologize for their behavior, Instead they will walk away blaming you for the whole event, As with the fish, the only ones safe from the wrath of the Piranha are those they consider one of their own, Very close lifelong friends are like family to them, and members of this sign never turn their back on family (unless they are betrayed, then look out), Piranhas have little affection for anyone outside of their family, though they will often ignore those who are smart enough to get out of their way, This makes the Piranha very polarizing, They are charming and sly, able to manipulate people without them noticing, Piranhas don't make very good co-workers or employees, They need to be in charge, so they may find it best to work in a job where they rely on others as little as possible, Many Piranhas are entrepreneurs for this very reason, They have a vision and want to see it through, They also have the charm and enthusiasm to draw people into that vision and make them want to be a part of it, Not surprisingly, Piranhas also make good directors, Business, catering, finance, film, or stage - they work through any situation as long as they are calling the shots, and I had a friend tell me that he liked the WBAG script but that since I didn't have a direct connection to gun violence it didn't matter enough to get me noticed, can you believe that, I need to have a gun violence incident in my life in order to be real enough for it to be a true story, and that kind of cynicism is it real, and when I was really manic or whatever in June, I was asking my mom about our ancestors and I asked about her father and his father, my great-grandfather, because I never met him or heard much about him, and listen to this story, my mom told me that my great-grandfather was shot by a gun and killed, but wait for it, by his own brother, and it was accidental, but my grandfather's uncle who shot his brother, my great-grandfather, he married my great-grandmother, and my mom said, my grandfather never talked about him once to her, but think of that genetic trauma, genealogical trauma, is that why I feel this type of way about guns, is that enough to get me a true story credibility, and here's some more genealogical trauma, my mom and grandma were robbed when she was 13 and they were tied up at gunpoint in their house so how much 2nd-hand, 3rd-hand, 4th-hand, 5th-hand gun trauma do you need to add up to first degree trauma, Hollywood, Lord shine your light on us, lord shine your light on us, set us free, and I checked Instagram for inspiration, and here's the first post, no joke,

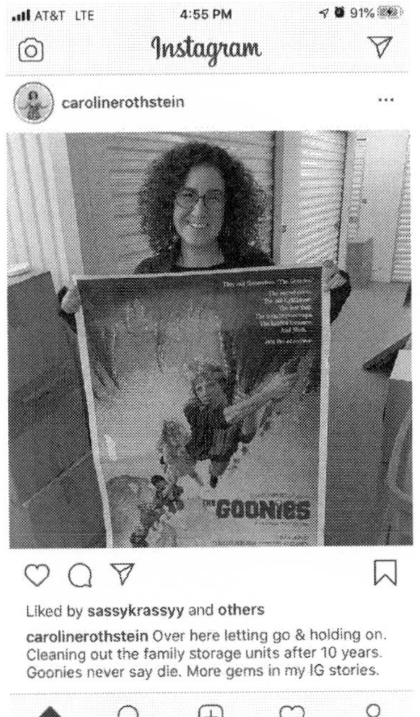

and this is Caroline Rothstein who is a friend and a journalist and a spoken word poet who wrote about her Dad sort of losing it when her brother died and his deal with an airline for unlimited travel was taken away because he liked to share it with random strangers and such, out of the kindness of his heart, and it was a really touching piece to me as I read it last year, right after my dad passed it seemed, and it showed a way to write about something dark about your family but with respect and we talked on the phone about the ethics of non-fiction writing, both in truth to the reader, and respect of the subject, and though we feel differently on both, I respect her approach, and sometimes wish I could be more principled in how I write, and so maybe she will talk about that or maybe she won't because she's also a spoken word poet who emotes like crazy in that medium so she mixes reason with emotion too, just in a different way, and look at her caption, "Over here letting go & holding on, Cleaning out the family storage units after 10 years, Goonies never say die," cleaning out the family's skeletons in the closet I am and it's relationship to movies and our ancestors never die, and letting go of trauma but holding onto the memory, Piranhas are cunning enough to charm their way up the corporate ladder, but they are sometimes too aggressive and impatient to put up with a boss that makes them wait for their promotion or partnership in the firm, Piranhas should remember that a patient fish will feed more in the long run," hah I think that's what I could have turned into without spirituality maybe, or maybe this book is also a bit of that, in the ruthlessness of quoting others to get the right words down, and the ruthlessness of putting in every tidbit of reality without concern for others, but I do honestly feel the words need to be quoted, God doesn't believe in copyright the way it's constructed right now, and reality needs to be shown, and I am talking to my Christ in my head and it's saying you better watch out for what you wish for, just being real, that's what it's saying, so maybe that will be a future cross to bear, hopefully not, and no joke Martin Rev's "Salve Dominus" just started playing, which means "Hello God," in Latin, hah, and then it went into "Professional Rapper," by Lil Dicky featuring

Snoop Dogg, “Literally I can reinvent myself, I got a forum to project myself,” and “I wanna do this whole thing different, What the fuck you mean you wanna do the whole thing different, Uh, you know, I-I think, like, you know, Traditionally people have been doing the job the same kind of way for a long time, But traditionally speaking, this shit works, right, Nah, like, I get that, but I-I just think that, you know, You don't know if it could be working even better, And I think you should look at me as an opportunity to find that out, I don't mean any disrespect by that, I'm just saying I have a different background, Like a different perspective way of looking at things than your typical applicant” and Charles Bukowski said, “Some people never go crazy, What truly horrible lives they must lead,” and “An intellectual says a simple thing in a hard way, An artist says a hard thing in a simple way,” and “If you're going to try, go all the way, Otherwise, don't even start, This could mean losing girlfriends, wives, relatives and maybe even your mind, It could mean not eating for three or four days, It could mean freezing on a park bench, It could mean jail, It could mean derision, It could mean mockery--isolation, Isolation is the gift, All the others are a test of your endurance, of how much you really want to do it, And, you'll do it, despite rejection and the worst odds, And it will be better than anything else you can imagine, If you're going to try, go all the way, There is no other feeling like that, You will be alone with the gods,” and “God’s Plan” by Drake just came on, no joke, and I used to not like Drake I took Kanye’s side over Drake but I’ve grown to like Drake now, I like everyone now and I love everything now, and here’s the preface to A Course In Miracles, A Course In Miracles began with the sudden decision of two people to join in a common goal, Their names were Helen Shucman and William Thetford, Professors of Medical Psychology at Columbia

University's College of Physicians and Surgeons in New York City, It does not matter who they were, except that the story shows that with God all things are possible, They were anything but spiritual, Their relationship with each other was difficult and often strained, and they were concerned with personal and professional acceptance and status, In general, they had considerable investment in the values of the world, Their lives were hardly in accord with anything that the Course advocates, Helen, the one who received the material, describes herself: Psychologist, educator, conservative in theory and atheistic in belief, I was working in a prestigious and highly academic setting, And then something happened that triggered a chain of events I could never have predicted, The head of my department unexpectedly announced that he was tired of the angry and aggressive feelings our attitudes reflected, and concluded that 'there must be another way,' As if on cue, I agreed to help him find it, Apparently this Course is the other way, Although their intention was serious, they had great difficulty in starting out on their joint venture, But they had given the Holy Spirit the 'little willingness,' that, as the Course itself was to emphasize again and again, is sufficient to enable Him to use any situation for His purposes and provide it with His power, To continue Helen's first-person account: Three startling months preceded the actual writing, during which time Bill suggested that I write down the highly symbolic dreams and descriptions of the strange images that were coming to me, Although I had grown more accustomed to the unexpected by that time, I was still very surprised when I wrote, 'This is a course in miracles,' That was my introduction to the Voice, It made no sound, but seemed to be giving me a kind of rapid, inner dictation which I took down in a shorthand notebook, The writing was never automatic, It could be interrupted at any time and later picked up again, It made me very uncomfortable, but it never seriously occured to me to stop, It seemed to be a special assignment I had somehow, somewhere agreed to complete," and Harold Bloom says that Emerson said, "It is by yourself without ambassador that God speaks to you," and Bloom also says that, "To live, the poet must misinterpret the father, by the crucial act of misprision, which is the re-writing of the father," and all stories are the same stories just being rewritten for the present, and that's something that Joseph Campbell is saying with The Hero With A Thousand Faces, let's do some bibliomancy and see what we find "When the envelopment of consciousness has been annihilated, then he becomes free of all fear, beyond the reach of change, This is the release potential within us all, and which anyone can attain--through herohood" and "Furthermore, we have not even to risk the adventure alone; for the heroes of all time have gone before us; the labyrinth is thoroughly known; we have only to follow the thread of the heropath, And where we had thought to find an abomination, we shall find a god; where we had thought to slay another, we shall slay ourselves; where we had thought to travel outward, we shall come to the center of our own existence; where we had thought to be alone, we shall be with all the world," and "Freedom to pass back and forth across the world division, from the perspective of the apparitions of time to that of the casual deep and back-not contaminating the principles of the one with those of the other, yet permitting the mind to know the one by virtue of the other-is the talent of the master," and

and I just flipped to the next Kanye song in the shuffle that's not already in the book and it's "Roses" about Kanye's grandmother dying and the chorus is "I smile when roses come to see me, And I, can't wait for a sunny day (seeing it through your eyes) Can't wait for the clouds to break," and it's like the Pixar movie Coco mixed with the movie Inside Out up in here, do you feel me, and I ain't mad at movies anymore, I ain't mad at movies anymore, I ain't mad anymore I'm "mad" now,>}]) and I wouldn't be disappointed that the content ended up unpublished, blocked, or whatever, this book and its content, because I don't necessarily have to make a mark on the world to talk about the mark my dad made on my life and the lives of many others, and so I think I will push the envelope one more time with the public domain content rule for Kindle Direct Publishing again, because I want to tell everyone now all about the moment my dad was buried, in his final resting place, and it also involves more James Joyce, and so my dad lived and raised me in Western New York State, and that part of the state during February, when he died, there hadn't been snow on the ground the day before which is unusual for that time of year in that climate, but the day of his funeral and burial, the snow all started to come down, falling, the snow it was falling faintly, and its white, fresh powder covered everything, in this very pure way, like his love, and so during his burial I thought of the last story of James Joyce's first book The Dubliners, and some people call it a novella on its own, that last story, and maybe this book is like a novella now, because it's over 17,000 words which is what Google says a novella needs to have in terms of number of words in its in length in order to be defined as a novella, (we're well over 80,000 words which Google says is a novel, but who is counting anymore, ha) and it's called The Dead and it's about a person realizing that the people closest to him in life have touched other people's lives in ways they'll never know, and that people in their lives have been touched by other people in life in ways that they will never know as well, and even though that's threatening to that character in the story at first, that character also ultimately transcends thinking of that fact of life as a problem and instead thinks of it as a blessing when he has his epiphany, and so the last paragraph of the story is about snow falling over a cemetery over the person who touched his wife's life, and whose life she touched, and it is very much like how the snow was faintly falling over the cemetery while my dad was being buried in Western New York in February of 2019, and it goes like this, "Yes, the newspapers were right: snow was general all over Ireland, it was falling softly upon the Bog of Allen and, further westwards, softly falling into the dark mutinous Shannon waves, it was falling too upon every part of the lonely churchyard where Michael Furey lay buried, it lay thickly drifted on the crooked crosses and headstones, on the spears of the little gate, on the barren thorns, his soul swooned slowly as he heard the snow falling faintly through the universe and faintly falling, like the descent of their last end, upon all the living and the dead," and when I read that story again later in the week late at night when I couldn't sleep because I couldn't stop thinking about my dad, I thought about the people who came to my dad's funeral and to our shiva that week, and also I am thinking now about how Joyce's Ulysses is about a Jewish Irishman, and my last name Cohen was changed to the more Irish sounding Cowen, and my dad was very proud that he was a priest in his Jewish lineage, and I kind of got my first job from some literary agents in New York who were Irish, and they were disappointed I always thought when I turned out to be a Jew, and I also have reddish hair like many Irishmen, so maybe we are both Irish Jews, in some way, or maybe in the way that Joyce wrote about an Irish Jew in Ulysses, and I never did talk to my dad and ask him that question which makes me you know what, not sad, it's more fun to imagine what our conversation might be about what Irish Judaism might mean to us, even if we aren't Irish Jews, in any way, but just have an Irish-Jewish name and why we did that with our name, and so I can have that imaginary conversation with him any time, and be with him, (I just asked him and the Higher Power, and he laughed and said "Your grandfather just didn't want to get us killed" and Laura Lynne Jackson says "I believe that when we fully trust in a higher power, something truly profound and life altering happens, Because in that moment we are not only collaborating with the Other Side, but also honoring our dependence on it and recognizing our interconnectedness, The concept of a higher power has different names in different cultures and belief systems, The names and rituals matter much less than the basic belief that a higher power exists, It is there, loving us, available to us, everywhere and all the time, But it's up to us to be open to it, and to trust it, and to finally plug in and surrender to it," and she says about her father, "The truth is, after he crossed, it would have been easy to get stuck in my own sadness and miss these signs, But my father was so persistent, and so good at sending them, that I didn't miss them after all, And because I finally opened my heart to receiving them, I was transformed, I was lifted out of my crushing grief, I was able to connect with my father in a new and beautiful way, Through signs, our loved ones can be much better communicators than they ever were on earth, My father has become the chattiest soul in the universe, In many very real ways, he is more present for me now than he was before, My father helped me understand that we need to open our minds and our hearts fully to receiving these powerful messages, It was only when I went through the traumatic process of losing a parent myself that I truly realized how hard it is, and how important these signs could be, if we allowed them to sink in, From the Other Side, he became not only my protector but also my teacher, We were not done with each other, Our relationship continues to grow and evolve" [and maybe I will look back at this book someday as an embarrassing transitional moment in time and doubt the revelations in the book's final third, but as my friend Michael Reid Busk quotes about the end of Terrence Malick's cinematic memoir, The Tree of Life, which he interprets to be a bit too much of a resolution, when they are all standing together at the beach, Busk quotes Susan Sontag who writes, "Perhaps the way one tells how alive a particular art form is, is by the latitude it gives for making mistakes in it, and still being good," {and it's now February 4th, 2020 and I just found out this morning that my dad's mother, my grandmother, has passed away, and The Unicorns' "Ready To Die" is on, as I start to add this to the edit, and it's talking of palm trees and dead seas, and I see my grandmother, my dad's mother, with him and with my dad's father, at the beach, like Malick's Tree of Life, and they are kind of standing together like in that movie, looking a bit confused and a bit stiff and a bit stilted, but as The Unicorns say, they've said their goodbyes and they were ready to die, or if they weren't, when they are dead, they are then retroactively ready, I believe that, and it's the last song of The Unicorns album and that album is partly about Nick Thorburn's character coming to terms with his fear of his future death as the first song is "I Don't Wanna Die," and learning to be OK with it, and seeing all this death this year, my dad's mother now dying within a year of my dad, and of course my dad dying this year, I finally feel OK with my future death too, things conclude, things conclude, and I am writing fast now and this can't be Good writing again even as it's good and this can't be Deep and Reflective, but maybe Surface and Superficial is still good, and I just put on "I Was Born (A Unicorn)," the best song from that album and I didn't realize it's ties to belief, ego, The Old and New Testament and Lewis Carrol's Alice in Wonderland and Through The Looking Glass, and how we need to believe in the spiritual world in order to keep it alive, believe in the magic of unicorns to keep the magical things alive, if we agree they are there, they are alive, and so I say I won't stop believing in the divine order, and the Mad Hatter says, "Have I gone mad," and Alice replies "I'm afraid so, You're entirely bonkers, But I'll tell you a secret, All the best people are," and I won't stop believing in my dad being reunited with his mom today, in some place outside of time and space yet inside of it, even though I can't know it, I believe it, and Michael Reid Busk says about the painter Thomas Kinkade's work Kinkade's paintings mirror the evangelical experience, in that they emphasize the importance of the unseen spiritual realm, and de-emphasize the importance of the physical reality of everyday life in the here and now, which for evangelicals matters primarily as it relates to the unseen spiritual realm, This is physicalism turned on its head: opposite those who argue that any belief in the spiritual is hocus-pocus, Kinkade's descriptions of his canvases represented the view that what truly matters is the unseen realm of the spirit, Taken together, a Kinkade canvas portrays the way things were, the way things are in the believer's soul, and, ultimately, the way things will be," and The New Yorker just published a profile of Richard Rohr on February 2nd, and somehow it doesn't mention The Enneagram, even though Rohr wrote about it, he pretty much brought it back to contemporary Christianity, why is this gatekeeping magazine, why is it keeping Rohr's Enneagram work behind the gate, and instead talking about his relationship with Oprah and Bono, and I guess every writing about something has to have it's own purpose, and Eliza's piece isn't bad, it's just an introduction to get people interested, and here's something Eliza wrote, "Many of Rohr's followers are millennials, and he believes that his popularity signifies a deep spiritual hunger on the part of young people who no longer claim affiliation with traditional religion, These people, whom sociologists call the "nones," have grown in number, from sixteen per cent to twenty-three per cent of American adults, between 2007 and 2014, "People aren't simply skeptical anymore, or even openly hostile to the church," he told me, "They just don't see a relevance," Rohr doesn't believe that most nones are secular, as many assume; he thinks that they are questioning traditional labels but hoping to find a spiritual message that speaks to them," and so my criticism of The New Yorker isn't wrong but it isn't right, God is in everything, even this piece, <and guess what was released today February 12th, the trailer for Wes Anderson's new movie, and it's called The French Dispatch and it's about a The New Yorker-esque magazine, and the main story apparently has a Jewish artist who is imprisoned in a mental hospital, Moses Rosenthaler, because he won't sell his work, it's not for sale, he says in the trailer, and that sounds a lot like Lewis Hyde's The Gift doesn't it, and it's inspired by his love for The New Yorker when he was a teenager, and I loved The New Yorker when I was a teenager too and I still do, I don't want to have beef with The New Yorker in my mind anymore, I want to let go of that, and Wes is helping me do so, I love you The New Yorker, I do, and Wes says, "The story is not easy to explain, It's about an American journalist based in France who creates his magazine, It is more a portrait of this man, of this journalist who fights to write what he wants to write," and I just want to write what I need to write and hopefully The New Yorker understands that> <and "Nisi Dominus" by Vivaldi just came on the shuffle, and its title is from the first lines of Psalm 127 which Wikipedia says, "Charles Spurgeon calls Psalm 127 "The Builder's Psalm", noting the similarity between the Hebrew words for sons (*banim*) and builders (*bonim*), He writes: We are here taught that builders of houses and

cities, systems and fortunes, empires and churches all labour in vain without the Lord; but under the divine favour they enjoy perfect rest, Sons, who are in the Hebrew called "builders", are set forth as building up families under the same divine blessing, to the great honour and happiness of their parents, Spurgeon also quotes the English preacher Henry Smith (1560–1591): "Well doth David call children 'arrows' [v 4]; for if they be well bred, they shoot at their parents' enemies; and if they be evil bred, they shoot at their parents" but here's the actual Psalm: "Unless the LORD builds the house, its builders labor in vain, Unless the LORD watches over the city, the watchmen stand guard in vain, In vain you rise early and stay up late, toiling for food to eat-- for he grants sleep [or eat] to those he loves, Sons are a heritage from the LORD, children a reward from him, Like arrows in the hands of a warrior are sons born in one's youth, Blessed is the man whose quiver is full of them, They will not be put to shame when they contend with their enemies in the gate," and I think it just means the Lord blesses what is built not in vain, with the will but not with the spirit as well, and I hope this book isn't in vain, I hope it's not in vain, let's trust that the Lord has helped me build this book for good, and not in vain, and that it's helpful to me and to others in my family, and my friends, and my community and maybe the world, and not harmful in any way, and

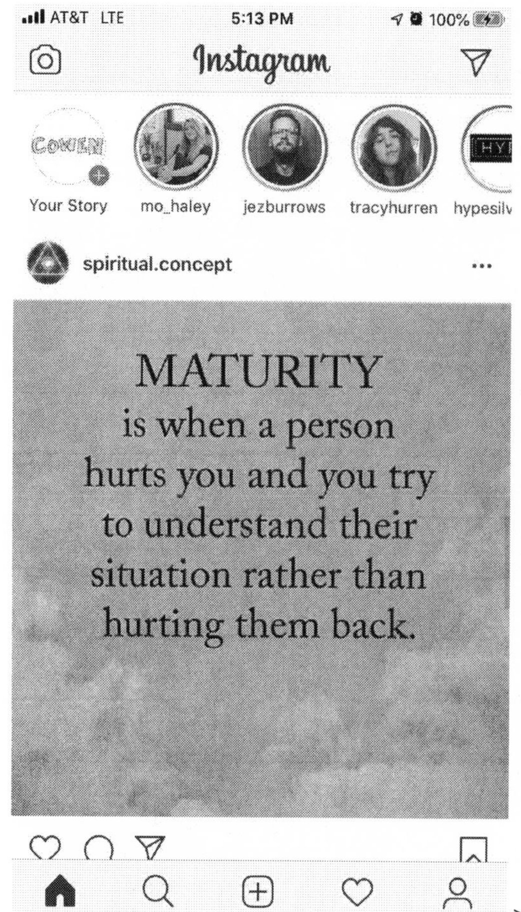

> {and I just came back from my weekend back on the east coast for my grandmother's funeral, and I learned a lot about her and my grandfather, my dad's dad, most saliently in my mind at the moment is that my grandfather also suffered from a mood disorder, had trouble getting up in the morning like my dad, and like me, and had tremendous social anxiety, and didn't have many friends, and yet he felt very bad that he felt he gave my dad his bipolar illness and my grandfather's mother had depression so bad that she never left her bed, and he didn't feel much love, and my grandfather's father, Lewis, was happy-go-lucky kind of like I am sometimes, and when my grandma met my grandpa she had to choose between leaving

her orthodox Jewish family and moving in with a secular Jewish man, who was not only secular, but was also an atheist, and my mom said my grandmother was forever torn between her religious upbringing and her atheism, as she started to believe there couldn't be a God when her father got Parkinson's and died such an ignoble death, and also both of them started to believe in no God due to the World Wars that they grew up during, and I remember now when I asked my grandmother after my grandfather died why she fell in love with grandpa, she said that it was because they both believed there was no God, and because they loved art, and music, and plays, and so there's something there about culture versus spiritual, what was replaced in the last century, and James Hollis says, "Many of our popular forms of entertainment carry charged imagoes that have a religious function for us, whether we know it or not," and yet "It has been said that religion is for those afraid to go to Hell, and spirituality is for those who have been there," but also "Whoever does not feel a participant in a deeper symbolic drama will manifest as a walking collection of symptoms sooner or later," and still more "By the mid-nineteenth century man noted thinkers, from Kierkegaard to Nietzche to Dostoevski, had concluded that "the gods had died," They were making psychological statements even before psychology as we know it, not metaphysical statements, That is they were witnessing the psychological reality that for most, the cultural forms of the gods, and their attendant value systems, no longer evoked the immediacy of personal experience, The loss of this connection to the soul was felt as alienation, a disorientation," and when my grandfather died, I have been told that my grandma returned to her Jewish roots and had the service done with a Rabbi even though my grandfather openly made fun of religion, but maybe they didn't know the difference between religion and spirituality and also when my grandpa died, an orange tree, that they had kept for over a dozen years even though it never blossomed into fruit, the year my grandpa died, it blossomed with oranges for the first time, and my grandma believed that was a message from the Other Side, or whatever language she would use, but it's all the same, and like James Hollis I say, "If this books speaks to you in any way it is because it is also about you, hence the re-cognition, the re-membrance," and and I have been saying prayers for other people now, it's a new thing I am doing, I breathe in and as I breathe in, a person comes to mind, without even trying to control who, and as I exhale, a wish for them and what I know or sometimes what I don't even know about them will come into mind as I exhale and it makes me feel so good in my body not just my mind, and the word for spirit in Hebrew is also the word for breath, and I am remembering now my grandmother's funeral and they asked if we wanted to see her body, and I had only been to fully Jewish funerals where they don't show you the body, so I had never seen a dead body before, and so I wanted to see my grandmother again, I did, and I went, and I looked at her, and she looked ten years younger, and healthy and make-uped, but at the same time it was clear there was no spirit or soul in the body that the breath was gone, and it was a realization that alchemy is right, there's a vessel and a body but also something inside that animates it and God breathed life into Adam and he breathes life into us, and when that life is gone, the body remains for a while, but it's clear that the spirit and soul are a real thing which is something us former science secular mass men don't understand until you see it, <and my mom read up to this part and pointed out that Alma my grandma's name means soul in Spanish, that's beautiful right>, and I read Paul Coelho's The Alchemist, the same week Kobe died, which was January

26th, I was reading it that week, and it was one of Kobe's favorite books, and Kobe was actually writing a new book with Paul Coelho, and I believe he lived his Personal Legend, Kobe and Paul, and sure Kobe hurt people along the way, but that's what hurt people do sometimes is hurt other people, in ways large or small or large, until they become conscious and I think Kobe was becoming conscious, clearly, with his fam, and so that's all that you can ask for sometimes in humans is that they own their mistakes, even if their mistakes aren't all their fault, and try to raise their consciousness, elevate it, and probably Paul hurt people in his own way sometime too, and I know I have, and The Alchemist is all about seeing omens and following your intuition, and that's what I am doing now, and I feel like my Personal Legend is starting to happen, and maybe gold will finally come, now that I am finally not looking only for gold, and Paul says, "'And what went wrong when other alchemists tried to make gold and were unable to do so,'" 'They were looking only for gold,' his companion answered, 'They were seeking the treasure of their Personal Legend without wanting actually to live out the Personal Legend,'" because I found that quote via bibliomancy the spontaneous opening of a page, and I am not special, bibliomancy is not special to me, clearly, and neither is this book, I am the author and also not the author, and I just opened The Ethics of Memory by Avishai Margalit who writes on the bibliomancy page, "Memory, then, is knowledge from the past, it is not necessarily knowledge about the past" and "To care used to have a meaning now declared obsolete, namely, to mourn," and "We are suspicious of those who care for humanity in general but who do not care for any human in particular," and "We should be even more suspicious of those who pay attention only to what they feel toward others but are incapable of paying attention to others; in short, we should be suspicious of sentimentalists," but that "The test of the liberal is in the acceptance of another's right to make his or her own big mistake," and "Freud's belief in the healing power wrought by bringing repressed memories to the light of consciousness," but "What is needed for successful forgiveness is not forgetting the wrong done but rather overcoming the resentment," and Katie Dey sings in Solipsisting, "So, so long to self, Oh, to explode into all else, Oh God, i wish to see your soul, Oh, secrets you keep, secrets i hold, How they would meet, How they could speak in unity, Abandon your shell, move with your light, Undying flight, unravel in infinity, With me, Abandon your shell, Somehow i doubt people could tell, I figured it out, oh, what a thrill, Ah, infinity, Oh, what great fun, ready, On three, Hold on dear god, i come for thee,"}]) and when my dad was in the mental hospital in January my mom had a premonition that this might be near the end so she recommended I get right with my dad, so I sent him a letter so that he could read it there, and I didn't realize until now, that I was giving him my presence, via the letter, which he said was the best letter he ever received in his life, and here it is: "Dad, I'm very proud of you for going to the hospital, I always think of you to be the most optimistic person I know, Whenever something comes up on the horizon of our family's future, you always take a glass very-full perspective, You see hope in life and teach us to be resilient, You also on occasion flip into pessimism, and I think it's possible that this new hospitalization is a result of the cyst news, I believe it's possible that what you are feeling is not a permanent state of mind, and that you'll feel better again, because I just spoke to you on the phone before you heard the news, and you were curious about and hopeful for our family's future, It gave me such joy to see you here in California in November, I particularly liked picking you up so early in the morning and taking you to dialysis, just the two of us, as we tiredly drove at dawn and then perked up to talk about mundane things while in the waiting room and then worked our way up to the important things in the chairs, Sure, you would get tired there, but you would also wake back up again for more conversation that was as enlightening as it was entertaining, I believe that a big part of who you are, and of life, is ups and downs, cycles, waves, I know you feel like your body is failing you, But I remember you and the lifeguard saving me from the waves of Bethany Beach, You still claim the lifeguard did most of the saving because he literally did it with his body, but you were the one to spot the trouble, Maybe that's a way to look at your situation, Your vision, perspective, and judgment is still incredibly valuable, A catch-phrase of yours is, 'Did I come through for you, or what,' You especially did when you came to campus my Junior year, And you have all your life, I know you have had ambivalence about your decision to bring children into the world with your illness, but I can 100% assure you that I have a great life, and I owe it to you, and Mom, and your parenting, Which is still going on today, such as your wise input about housing and neighborhoods in LA, Our family's life is much better with you in it, even when you feel it's not, and I want you to be there at Lauren's graduation from medical school in May, as well as my housewarming, child's birth, some day, and Lauren's wedding when they come to be, I love being your son, I believe we have a special connection, and that there is a calm, centered groundedness to our time in each other's presence, that I would call true love, There are also a whole lot of laughs when we get together, I still can't tell if I got my sense of humor from you or mom, (I think both, that's why it's so good), But part of the reason I became a humor writer is because it was so much fun to hear you belly laugh or cause us to have laugh attacks, One other memory I have right now is how you'd always remark when we played games as a family,'It's not over till it's over,' And I would say now that that's how I feel about your life, It's not over till it's over, I want to believe you'll be well enough for me to see you again, and, more importantly, that you'll have moments in the rest of your life that will make you happy, I love you, -Your son," and I read this book called Book of Mutter that Al recommended to me, and the author, Kate Zambreno, was writing about her mom's death, and her grief, and she said that Roland Barthes was writing about photography and it was being infected by his grief over his mother's death, but that was actually a good thing because it helped him write about how photography was about absence and presence and it's impossible to make someone fully present in a photograph, and Kate was saying in memory or writing that is true too, and so I need to apologize to you Dad, you just wanted Trickster Enneagram Holy Love, a break from your Separation, a connection with me, and on February 24th, I let you down, I promised I'd call you, and I didn't do it, and I am crying now, because I have also read the epilogue of your Lincoln book, and it's about the author Shenk going to a Lincoln re-enactor camp, and this guy "Bud Green asked [him] what I was doing there, I told him I was writing a book on Lincoln's depression, 'I have manic depression,' he said, Bud, He told me about growing up during the Great Depression, raising Christmas trees and working as a pitchman at fairs, He told me about the time, many years later, when he pulled off an interstate and checked into a motel intending to hang himself, Then he thought of his kids and steered his car back on the road, When he finished the story, suffering lingered in the air between us, I asked him, 'Does being Lincoln help,' He answered quickly: 'Yes, it helps, But it can hurt, too, It hurts when the teachers don't call,' Maybe trying to find meaning in our ordinary lives by learning about Lincoln is as absurd as dressing up in the kind of clothes he wore, but in that moment I felt the connection, A man I didn't know had the courage to tell me that he suffered, and he had the power to tell me what he was after, Lincoln might be far away and gone, but something runs unbroken through the present and the past, Bud Green wants the teachers to call; I want NPR to call, and The Oprah Winfrey Show, On April 14, Lincoln wanted Sherman to call, and while he waited, he told his cabinet about a dream he'd had the night before, February 24, 2005," is when Shenk finished that epilogue, 14 years ago to the day I didn't call you, the day before you killed yourself, the day I didn't call upon you, what did you dream about, and I wish I had read this Lincoln book, and used more of my will in order to alter your path and mine, within the destiny, but you learn your lessons when you learn them, my friend Alec said, (and Tolle says, "The deeper interconnectedness of all things and events implies that the mental labels of good and bad are ultimately illusory, They always imply a limited perspective and so are true only relatively and temporarily, This is illustrated in the story of a wise man who won an expensive car in a lottery, His family and friends were very happy for him and came to celebrate, Isn't it great, they said you are so lucky, The man smiled and said, Maybe, For a few weeks he enjoyed driving the car then one day a drunken driver crashed into his new car at an intersection and he ended up in the hospital with multiple injuries his family and friends came to see him and said, That was a really unfortunate thing to happen, The man smiled and said, "Maybe," While he was still in the hospital one night there was a landslide and his house fell into the sea again his friends came the next day and said weren't you lucky to have been here in the hospital again he said, "Maybe," and the wise man's Maybe signifies a refusal to judge anything that happens, Instead of judging what it is he accepts it and so enters into conscious alignment with the higher order," and this is pointillism copy and pasting of time of present of the now, copied and pasted out of and into time, and Joseph Campbell says, "When he arrives at the nadir of the mythological round, he undergoes a supreme ordeal and gains his reward, The triumph may be represented as the hero's sexual union with the goddess-mother of the world (sacred marriage), his recognition by the father-creator (father atonement), his own divinization (apotheosis) or again, if the powers have remained unfriendly to him- his theft of the boon he came to gain (bride-theft, fire-theft)," and "the adventure of the hero represents the moment in his life when he achieved illumination, the nuclear moment, when, while still alive, he found and opened the road to the light beyond the dark walls of our living death," [and Jung says, "We need the coldness of death to see clearly, Life wants to live and to die, to begin and to end," and "In the secret hour of life's midday the parabola is reversed, death is born, The second half of life does not signify ascent, unfolding, increase, exuberance, but death, since the end is its goal, The negation of life's fulfillment is synonymous with the refusal to accept its ending, Both mean not wanting to live, and not wanting to live is identical with not wanting to die, Waxing and waning make one curve,"]) and you're gone, and the father figure I wished I had found before you left, for both of us, to help us both, Lewis Hyde, wrote that most of the images Barthes found failed to bring his mother back, "I never recognized her except in fragments, a part of her face, the way she held her hands, 'which is to say that I missed her being,' yet finally he found an image that was 'indeed essential' that achieved, 'utopically, the impossible science of the unique being, Barthes never reproduces this essential photograph, 'it exists only for me,'" but here's a photo of me and my dad that I think gets at his essential being, and our relationship, and I won't keep it for myself, I don't want to keep anything from anyone, that's kind of the theme of this book, for better or warts, so that someone might learn from all this, too, before it's too late, for better or warts, and also because in Camera Lucida, Barthes says, "Always the Photograph astonishes me, with an astonishment which endures and renews itself, inexhaustibly, Perhaps this astonishment, this persistence reaches down into the religious substance out of which I am molded; Photography has something to do with resurrection," and so here you are my dear dad, Richard Brian Cowen (and here in the edit I am talking to you and you are saying "I'm proud of you for writing this book, I love you, Dave, and I am here with you always, I left when I left because it was my time, and as you can see it's working out well for the family, Mom is mourning but evolving, you are evolving, too, look at how balanced you are, I love you, my son, the son" and so here you are my dear dad, who is psychically in my head as a Father, like the Father, and so I offer a photo of you, Dad, me and you, us, and say as Kanye said, "Jesus Walks"

[and during the edit, Animal Collective's "The Bees" came on and can you deduce from it what I feel I can, "O sudden, The bees, They came flying, So violent, The bees, They came sly, So scary, The bees, They came wide, So wild, The bees, They came crying, They said: I take my time, You take your time, Please take your time, I take my time, I take my time, You take your time, Just take your time, I take my time, And if you need us, And if you need, The bees, The bees, The bees, The bees, The bees, The bees, And if you need us, Or If you need, The bees, The bees, The bees, The bees, The bees, The bees, And if you need us, Or if you need, The bees, The bees, The bees, The bees, The bees, The bees" and do you deduce what I deduce, the meanings there, sometimes what is painful is beneficial, what is scary is helpful, what is mania is spiritual, what is gone is still available, take your time but ask for help if you need it, the symbol of The bees, what is The bees, it is a symbol we employ to approach the Holy, the Other Side, the Higher Power, the Mystery, approached with symbols/words/art but never defined/confined/understood {and it's 2/23/2020 and we are two days until the year of mourning is over, and I have been thinking of what I've learned, and someone asked me last night if I am going to keep taking my bipolar medicine, and I didn't know if I would earlier in the year, but I think I know what I think about that now, and I think I will take the medicine for now, as I am not sure if I can live in the world as it is without it, but now my inner voice is telling me you don't need it, so I don't know, I guess that will be a decision I will make after this mourning year, and I have a lot of decisions to make now that I am finishing this book, and it's been an all-consuming activity, writing this book, and mourning my dad, and my friend Sandy said when the year is over, it will be time to close the book, on the 25th, and just leave it closed, and to look down the road inside of backward, and I think there's something true about that, so maybe I won't add anymore contributions if they don't come in by the 25th, and as I was driving out of my parking lot, I felt a pang, that I wanted to call my dad to tell him how great I am feeling, and then I felt for a moment sad that I couldn't call him, but then I talked to my inner voice and he was like I see it, I see you doing well, and I felt the peace again, the inner peace, and yet I can't give up writing, I will just have to write something new, and Alynda Segarra's cover of Lucinda Williams' "Drunken Angel," just started to play on Spotify and it's lyrics are: "Sun came up it was another day,And the sun went down you were blown away, Why'd you let go of your guitar, Why'd you ever let it go that far, Drunken angel, Could've held on to that long smooth neck, Let your hand remember every fret, Fingers touching each shiny string, But you let go of everything, Drunken angel, Drunken angel, You're on the other side, Drunken angel, You're on the other side, Followers would cling to you, Hang around just to meet you, Some threw roses at your feet, And watch you pass out on the street, Drunken angel, Feed you and pay off all your debts, Kiss your brow taste your sweat, Write about your soul your guts, Criticize you and wish you luck, Drunken angel, Drunken angel, You're on the other side, Drunken angel, You're on the other side, Some kind of savior singin' the blues, A derelict in your duct tape shoes, Your orphan clothes and your long dark hair, Looking like you didn't care, Drunken angel, Blood spilled out from the hole in your heart, Over the strings of your guitar, The worn down places in the wood, That once made you feel so good, Drunken angel, Drunken angel, You're on the other side, Drunken angel, You're on the other side, Sun came up it was another day, And the sun went down you were blown away, Why'd you let go of your guitar, Why'd you ever let it go that far, Drunken angel" and so whatever it is I write next, it must be it must be something, I must hold onto the guitar, in order to stay on this side, and not get too drunken, and so maybe that means I should continue to take my medicine, I can't let go of everything, and become a drunken angel, maybe that's what my dad is saying by sending me this song in the shuffle}] and here's another picture of you my mom showed me when I returned home for your mom's funeral,

and that was taken when I flew in for your birthday in November a month before your psychiatrist accidentally or neglectfully or malpractice-almost-ly prescribed you a drug for your tremors that kidneys don't process well and you almost died from the poisoning and I flew back in December because we didn't know what would happen, and you recovered, but you kind of never fully recovered, and mom and I were talking about that, how you would have the same dreams since then, of your teeth breaking down, which means your body is decaying, and you had memory problems, but you didn't sue that doctor, even though you filed a report, and you probably forgive him now, and I do, too, and James Hollis says, "Only very wise and strong leaders, such as Bishop Tutu and Nelson Mandela in South Africa, will bring their nation to the bar of justice and ask forgiveness," and another thing I did a lot of besides talking to mom and others about you and your mom this weekend was learn what kind of Myers-Briggs type I am, and it's INFJ, which is the rarest personality type of the 16 in the world, less than 1 percent, and Nelson Mandela has that same personality type, and it stands for introversion, intuition, feeling, and judgment, and it's sometimes called the Mystic, and I won't go into copying and pasting all the attributes but it's similar to Life Path 11, and it recommends becoming a writer, a psychologist, a professor, or a librarian, which sounds about right, huh, but I will add that there are also combinations of extroversion, sensing, thinking, perceiving, and so maybe something I will need to learn after or during the writing of this book is that not everyone sees the world the way I do, and so maybe this book won't apply to certain people, such as sensors who focus on what their five senses can tell them not what they intuit with the sixth, and maybe that's OK, too, that something like the mystery that I've learned about isn't universal, maybe, but my mom is a ESFJ, in my opinion, and when dad, your mom was being buried this weekend, a small prop plane flew overhead, and mom turned to me and said, that's grandpa, your dad, the World War II airplane pilot who was shot down over France, who ejected from the plane and flew down in a parachute, and landed on a farmland, and the French farmers yelled at him in French, which he didn't understand, Don't walk, Don't walk, because it was also a minefield, that farm, from the Germans, completely full of mines, but somehow your dad walked through the minefield unscathed, and he reached the French farmers, and they couldn't believe it, and they even drew a picture of what happened to show my grandpa what he had miraculously just done, which we have now, and then he sent your mom the parachute, and she made a quilt of it, in time for his return, and it was their most symbolic and prized possession, the proof of their love, and so what does that say about God or the mystery, whatever it is, that neither of us would have been here, dad and me, if not for something like that, and how that's true for all of us, and I looked through your computer files because mom asked me to organize them, and one of them was about your retirement and your goals included writing a book, like I said before, but in this document you said what it would be about and you said "Living with the illness but showing there is hope" and this is that book, we did it, Dad, we wrote a book about whatever we are and showed there is hope, and this is weird but the Spotify is skipping songs, I can see them being skipped even though they are able to be played and Lou Reed's we're going to have a "Real Good Time Together" was skipped to past another song when all I clicked was one song forward, and we're having a real good time together, aren't we, we are, don't need to even add a question mark, and I skipped a few songs until I got to the next Kanye song, and it's FML, "Pour out my feelings, Revealing the layers to my soul, My soul, The layers to my soul, Revealing the layers to my soul, Wish I would go ahead and fuck my life up," and this book, the writing of it, has FML up, it has, it's FML up, and this year, it has FML up, it has really FML up, but I wouldn't wish to have not written it, I wouldn't have wished to not have lived it, {and I just flipped to the next Kanye song, and it's "Waves," and the lyrics are about losing loved ones, to death or in relationships, and it goes like, "Sun don't shine in the shade, ugh Turn me up Bird can't fly in a cage, ugh Turn me up Even when somebody go away, uh Turn me up, The feelings don't really go away, That's just the wave, Yeah Waves don't die, Let me crash here for the moment, I don't need to own it, No lie, Waves don't die, baby" and I think that's true in death or in lost relationships, the waves don't die, but you don't need to own it, to hold on to it, no matter how and why they left you, they don't die, they're

always ever present, repeating endlessly and I can't help but think of Virgina Woolf's The Waves, and how it's the soliloquies of six characters, in streams of consciousness interior monlogues, broken up by depictions of what happens to the coast with waves, and it's about how we are all one gestalt consciousness, and here's a quote, "I was always going to the bookcase for another sip of the divine specific," and "Now begins to rise in me the familiar rhythm; words that have lain dormant now lift, now toss their crests, and fall and rise, and falls again, I am a poet, yes, Surely I am a great poet," and We Bought a Gun is a great script, and this great is a great book, and I am a great poet, and I hit shuffle again and the first song, no joke, was Bob Dylan's "The Times They Are-A-Changin'" and its lyrics are "Come gather 'round people, wherever you roam
And admit that the waters around you have grown, And accept it that soon you'll be drenched to the bone, If your time to you is worth saving, Then you better start swimmin' or you'll sink like a stone, For the times they are a-changin', Come writers and critics, who prophesize with your pen, And keep your eyes wide, the chance won't come again, For the loser now will be later to win, For the times they are a-changin'" and I am thinking right now of the night that I read Joyce's The Dead, the week I was sitting shiva for you, Dad, and I am thinking of my middle name Michael and how it's the same as Michael Furey's and how it means "Who is like God question mark" and how Furies are what Lewis Hyde says needs to be digested, and I feel like God even though I am not God, because I have forgiven and been forgiven for my furies, and I know how to forgive others furies and new ones of my own that come, and the father-creator I love thee, and father I love thee, and reader I love thee, and there are 110,653 words at this point, and I think I will write until 111,111, how about that, I think we are going to end on page 333, see

111,111, how about that, I think we are going to end on page 333, see

---

which is the trinity number, and the third Numerology master number is 33, and maybe if I have a child someday, it'll be a 33, a 22, a 11, and a 33, or maybe I won't have a child, I don't know, but I've enjoyed being your son, dad, and now being my own father, too, and I'll leave some words for the 24th and the 25th, bye for now ~and it's the 24th, and it's quiet in my mind, it's quiet and peaceful, and that's nice, that's really nice, and thinking of peace and resting in peace, I think tomorrow, the 25th, I will rest from writing this book, and be done now, I will rest, in the peace I have now, I will rest in the peace I have found, rest in peace =~>})] so that night that I read Joyce's The Dead again, the week I was sitting shiva for you, Dad, and meeting people that came to our house, I met so many people I didn't know, but that you knew, and those people who knew you, sometimes Mom even didn't know them, but they came over to our house to pay their respects to you and we had conversations and they kept saying the same nice things about you in the conversations and it was that you were sweet and you were gentle and you were kind and you had a good sense of humor and you were a good neighbor, and a good teacher, and a good friend, and just a good man, a good man, a good man, a good man, and so I feel now that you live on through all of us through these conversations, (and I talked to you in the edit, and you said, “Now you also know we’re connected in conversation in spirit even in death, and it’s OK to say that in this book, because it’s true and not True, but maybe actually True, lol”), and so we’re all connected, you don’t have to be a writer to know that, you just have to be a human, so I think it’s OK to end this conversation and this sentence and this book now, I won’t even count up the words, (ha, it will be 111,111) it doesn’t matter if this is the longest sentence ever written and then published in the English language, or if the book is blocked by Bezos or the KDP bots, it’s OK, it’s OK to end this thing I’ve been having with you reader, and with myself, and with the Higher Power, and with the mystery, and with my dad, because it’s not the

Cited

5dconsciousenergy - Instagram

16personalities.com - Infj Personality

A.course.in.miracles - Instagram

Albom, Mitch - Tuesdays with Morrie

Anderson, Paul Thomas - The Master

Anderson, Wes - The French Dispatch

Anderson, Wes - The Royal Tenenbaums

Animal Collective - Feels

Apatow, Judd - Sick in the Head

Apatow, Judd - This is 40

Aragon, Louis - "Suicide"

Astral.dimension- Instagram

Atlas Sound - Logos

Auster, Paul - The Invention of Solitude

Ayler, Albert - Love Cry

Ayler, Albert - Ghosts

Bajohr, Hannes - "Experimental Writing in its Moment of Digital Technization: Post-Digital Literature and Print-on-Demand Publishing"

Barthelme, Donald - The Dead Father

Barthes, Roland - Camera Lucida

Beach Boys, The - Sunflower

Bechdel, Alison - Fun Home

Beck & Guau! Mexican Institute of Sound - Wow!

Beenie Man - Ragga Ragga 6

Beitman, Bernie - Connecting with Coincidence

Bender, Felicia - Master Numbers 11, 22, and 33

Bender, Felicia - Redesign Your Life

Benjamin, Walter - “Unpacking My Library,” Illuminations

Bergman, Ingmar - Fanny and Alexander

Bergman, Ingmar - Through a Glass Darkly

Blackwell, Sean - Am I Bipolar or Waking Up?

Blake, James - Assume Form

Blake, William - Milton

Bloom, Harold - The Anxiety of Influence

Bloom, Harold - A Map Of Misreading

Boone, Bruce - Century of Clouds

Borsuk, Amaranth - “The POD People,” jacket2.org

Brainpickings.org - Maria Popova

Brown, Brené - The Gifts of Imperfection

Britell, Nicholas - If Beale Street Could Talk

Bryant, Kenzie - Kanye West Is Writing a Self-Help Book on Twitter, Vanity Fair

Bukowski, Charles - Factotum

Burroughs, William S. - The Job

Busk, Michael Reid - A New and Sharper Vision

Busyphilipps - Instagram

Calonne, David Stephen - Charles Bukowski: Sunlight Here I Am

Calvino, Italo - If on a winter’s night a traveler

Campbell, Joseph - The Hero With A Thousand Faces

Campbell, Joseph - Schizophrenia The Inward Journey

Carolinecalloway - Instagram

CarolineRothstein - Instagram

Carroll, Lewis - Alice in Wonderland

Carroll, Lewis - Through The Looking-Glass

Cervantes, Miguel De - Don Quixote

Chapin, Harry - Verities & Balderdash

Chance The Rapper - Coloring Book

Chotiner, Isaac - "The Author of a New Book About Andrew Johnson on the Right Reasons to Impeach a President," The New Yorker

Chriscirak - Instagram

Clapton, Eric - Pilgrim

Coe, Jonathan - The Rotters' Club

Coelho, Paul - The Alchemist

Coltrane, John - My Favorite Things

Comitta, Tom - "First Impressions," Bomb

Cowen, Dave - Fake History!

Cowen, Dave - "Live Your Life," The New Yorker

Cowen, Dave - "A Man Who Donated His Big Toe To His Wife Asks For It Back Now That They're Getting A Divorce," McSweeney's Internet Tendency

Cowen, Dave - The Trump Passover Haggadah

Cowen, Dave - We Bought a Gun

Cowen, Dave - The Yada Yada Haggadah

Cramer, Florian - "What is 'Post-digital'"

Cramer, Florian - Post-digital Aesthetics

Daddyissues_ - Instagram

Davis, Lydia - Can't and Won't

Deming, Robert - James Joyce

DeVille, Chris - "Damon Albarn Warned Paul McCartney Not To Work With Kanye West," Stereogum

Dey, Katie - Solipsisters

Diamond, Hannah & PC Music & Life Sim - True (Life Sim Remix)

Dick, Philip K. - V.A.L.I.S.

Dicky, Lil & Brown, Chris - Freaky Friday

Dicky, Lil - Professional Rapper

Didion, Joan - The Year of Magical Thinking

Dimitrov, Alex & Lasky, Dorothea - Astro Poets

Dion & The Wanderers - Wonder Where I'm Bound

Docter, Pete - Inside Out

Dworkin, Craig & Goldsmith, Kenneth - Against Expression

Dylan, Bob - Bringing It All Back Home

Dylan, Bob - The Freewheelin' Bob Dylan

Dylan, Bob - The Nobel Lecture

Dylan, Bob - Saved

Dylan, Bob - The Times They Are A-Changin'

Eggers, Dave - A Heartbreaking Work of Staggering Genius

Ellman, Lucy - Ducks, Newburyport

Emerson, Ralph Waldo - Self-Reliance

Enneagram Institute, The - Type 4

Enneagram Institute, The - Type 6

Enneagram Institute, The - Type 9

Enneagram Institute, The - Misidentifying 4 and 6

Enneagram Institute, The - Misidentifying 6 and 9

Enneagram Institute, The - The Traditional Enneagram (History)

Expertblueprint - Instagram

Farber, Seth - The Spiritual Gift of Madness

Faulkner, William - Absalom, Absalom!

Faulkner, William - Wild Palms

Fitzgerald, F. Scott - The Crack-Up

Fitzgerald, F. Scott - This Side of Paradise

Fitzgerald, Kiana - "Kanye West, Jesus Is King, And The Unspoken Bipolarism In Between" Vibe

Fleischmannsyeast - Instagram

Fox, Zack & Kenny Beats - Jesus Is The One (I Got Depression)

Frankenheimer, John - The Manchurian Candidate

Fromm, Erich - The Art of Loving

Garcia Marquez, Gabriel - One Hundred Years of Solitude

Gavin, Jim - Lodge 49

Gavin, Jim - Middle Men

Gilligan, Vince & Gould, Peter - Better Call Saul

Ginsburg, Allen - Howl

Glass Candy - Warm In The Winter

Go Team!, The - Thunder, Lightning, Strike

Goodman, Benny - Small Groups

Grande, Ariana - Sweetener

Griswold, Eliza - "Richard Rohr Reorders The Universe," The New Yorker

Hanh, Thich Nhat - No Death, No Fear

Heller, Mike - "Hirschsprung's And Healthcare," Medium

Hemingway, Ernest - The Old Man And The Sea

Hendel, John - "The Life of the Cyberflâneur," The Atlantic

Hesse, Herman - Siddhartha

Heti, Sheila - How Should a Person Be?

Hollis, James - The Archetypal Imagination

Hollis, James - Finding Meaning In The Second Half Of Life

Hollis, James - The Middle Passage

Hollis, James - Swamplands of the Soul

Howard, Ron - Apollo 13

Howard, Ron - A Beautiful Mind

Hughes, Benji - A Love Extreme

Hyde, Lewis - Common As Air

Hyde, Lewis - The Gift

Hyde, Lewis - Trickster Makes The World

Hyde, Lewis - A Primer for Forgetting

Imagine Impact

Inchausti, Robert - Hard to be a Saint in the City

Irving, Washington - The Legend of Sleepy Hollow

Jackson, Laura Lynne - Signs

James, William - The Varieties of Religious Experience

Jamison, Kay Redfield - An Unquiet Mind

Jamison, Kay Redfield - Touched by Fire

Joel, Billy - Greatest Hits Volume I & II

Jónsi - Go

Jonze, Spike - Her

Joseph, Leryl - The Table

Joyce, James - Ulysses

Joyce, James - Dubliners

Jung, C.G. - Psychological Reflections

Jung, C.G. - The Red Book

Jung, C.G. - The Undiscovered Self

Ka5sh & gnash - I'm Depressed

Karr, Mary - The Art of Memoir

Kelly, Richard - Donnie Darko

KIDS SEE GHOSTS - KIDS SEE GHOSTS

King, Martin Luther - A Testament of Hope

Kirkley, KC - It's About Time

Kirsch, Jonathan - "Authors Get Creative in New Haggadahs," The Jewish Journal
Knight, Wendy - Women of the Beat Generation
Kooser, Ted - "Father"
Kubrick, Stanley - 2001: A Space Odyssey
Laing, RD - The Politics of Experience
Lauren_cohen_ - Instagram
Lee, Peggy - The Best of Miss Peggy Lee
Lerner, Ben - Leaving the Atocha Station
Lessig, Lawrence - Free Culture
Lessig, Lawrence - The Future of Ideas
Lessig, Lawrence - Remix
Lethem, Jonathan - The Ecstasy of Influence
Lewis, C.S. - A Grief Observed
Malian Musicians; & Albarn, Damon - Mali Music
Malick, Terrence - The Tree of Life
Malone, Post - Stoney
Markson, David - This is Not a Novel
Margalit, Avishai - The Ethics of Memory
Marshall, Dan - Home Is Burning
McCormack, Mike - Solar Bones
Mello, Anthony de - Sadhana
Melville, Herman - Moby-Dick, or, the Whale
Memes - Memes: Ultimate Book of Funny New Memes
Miller, Arthur - Death of a Salesman
Monroe, Jazz - "Kanye/McCartney/Dirty Projectors/Ezra Koenig Song Recorded, Dave Longstreth Says," Pitchfork
Morrison, Van - Enlightenment

Murakami, Haruki - "Abandoning a Cat," The New Yorker

Mustard - Perfect Ten

Nelson, Maggie - The Argonauts

Numerology.astrologyclub.org - Life Path 22, Life Path 11

Numerologist.com - Life Path 22, Life Path 11

O'Brien, Flann - At Swim Two Birds

Pagels, Elaine - The Gnostic Gospels

Patterson, Richard North - "I Used to Write Novels. Then Trump Rendered Fiction Redundant." The Atlantic

Payne, Alexander - Paris, Je T'aime

Peele, Jordan - Us

Peep, Lil - Come Over When You're Sober, Pt. 2

Perry, John Weir - Trials of the Visionary Mind

Pessoa, Fernando - The Book of Disquiet

Plazadeaubrey - Instagram

Portico - Art in the Age of Automation

Powell, Padgett - The Interrogative Mood

Primalastrology.com - Piranha

Pynchon, Thomas - The Crying of Lot 49

Ramis, Harold - Groundhog Day

Reed, Lou - "Lou Reed Talks Kanye West's Yeezus," Talkhouse

Reed, Lou - Street Hassle

Richardson, Mark - "New York Is Killing Me," Pitchfork

Rihanna & West, Kanye & McCartney, Paul - FourFiveSeconds

Rilke, Rainer Maria - Letters To A Young Poet

Rilke, Rainer Maria - Selected Poems

Robinson, Phil Alden - Field of Dreams

Roth, Philip - Patrimony

Rothstein, Caroline - The Man With The Golden Airline Ticket

Ruiz, Don Miguel & Mills, Janet - The Four Agreements

Rumi - “The Grasses”, The Essential Rumi

Saunders, George - Lincoln in the Bardo

Schnabel, Julian - The Diving Bell and the Butterfly

Schucman, Helen - A Course In Miracles

Schultz, Philip - Failure

Segarra, Alynda - Blaze

Seligman, Martin - Authentic Happiness

Seligman, Martin - Learned Optimism

Shadowhealer7 - Instagram

Shakespeare, William - Hamlet

Sharf, Zack - "'The French Dispatch' Everything You Need to Know About Wes Anderson's New Movie," IndieWire

Shenk, Joshua Wolf - Lincoln’s Melancholy

Shields, David - Reality Hunger

Silverstein, Shel - The Giving Tree

Snelson, Daniel - Print On Demand Art & Poetry Syllabus

Somers, James - “Torching the Modern-Day Library of Alexandria,” The Atlantic

Sontag, Susan - Against Interpretation And Other Essays

Spiritual.concept - Instagram

Spiritual_god - Instagram

Springsteen, Bruce - High Hopes

Strauss, Richard - Also sprach Zarathrustra, Op. 30: Prelude (Sunrise)

Strindberg, August - A Dream Play

Subliming.jpg - Instagram

Suicide - Dream Baby Dream

Superorganism - Superorganism

Swift, Jonathan - A Modest Proposal

Swinburne, Sandra - The Last Good Obsession

Taylor, James - Greatest Hits

The_wisdom_of_the_shamans - Instagram

Tolle, Eckhart - The Power of Now

Tolle, Eckhart - A New Earth

Torres, AR - The Lessons of Loss

Treme Brass Band - A New Orleans Visit

Treme Brass Band - New Orleans Brass Bands

Unicorns, The - Who Will Cut Our Hair When We're Gone?

Unkrich, Lee - Coco

Uzi Vert, Lil - Luv Is Rage 2

Vampire Weekend - Father of The Bride

Velvet Underground, The - The Velvet Underground

Velvet Underground, The & Nico - The Velvet Underground & Nico

Vice Astro Guide - Aries

Vile, Kurt - Bottle It In

Vivaldi, Antonio - Nisi Dominus

Waldman, Katy - "Can One Sentence Capture All of Life, The soaring ambition of "Ducks, Newburyport," The New Yorker

Waldman, Katy - "The Idealized, Introverted Wives of MacKenzie Bezos' Fiction," The New Yorker

Waldman, Katy - "Who Owns a Story," The New Yorker

Weiner, Matthew - Mad Men

West, Kanye - The College Dropout

West, Kanye - Jesus is King

West, Kanye - Late Registration

West, Kanye - The Life of Pablo

West, Kanye & McCartney, Paul - Only One

West, Kanye - ye

West, Kanye - Yeezus

West, Kanye - twitter

Wikipedia - Exceptionally long sentences in print

Wikipedia - The French Dispatch

Wikipedia - Psalm 127

Wikipedia - The Legend of Sleepy Hollow

Winslow, Aaron - Jobs of the Great Misery

Woolf, Virginia - Orlando: A Biography

Woolf, Virginia - The Waves

WRLD, Juice - Goodbye & Good Riddance

Wurth, Kiene Brillenburg & Driscoll, Kari & Pressman, Jessica - Book Presence in a Digital Age

Yachty, Lil - Lil Boat

Young, Kevin - The Art of Losing: Poems of Grief & Healing

Yusuf/Cat Stevens - Tea For The Tillerman

Zambreno, Kate - Book of Mutter

Zultanski, Steven - On the Literary Means of Representing the Powerful as Powerless

Note: There might be more. Sorry if I forgot to add yours. If you are the copyright owner of material quoted in the book and would like it removed, please email me at davecowenauthor@gmail.com. I'll immediately remove it from the KDP file so the next paperback copies printed on demand and the ebook file no longer include it.

Made in the USA
Columbia, SC
16 May 2020